W9-AFG-826

Strategic Planning
in Social Service
Organizations

Strategic Planning in Social Service Organizations

A Practical Guide

Gayla Rogers, PhD
Donna S. Finley, MBA
John R. Galloway, MBA

Canadian Scholars' Press Inc.   Toronto   2001

Strategic Planning in Social Services Organizations: A Practical Guide
by Gayla Rogers, Donna S. Finley, and John R. Galloway

First published in 2001 by
Canadian Scholars' Press Inc.
180 Bloor Street West, Suite 1202
Toronto, Ontario
M5S 2V6

www.cspi.org

CSPI acknowledges the financial support of the Government of Canada through the Book Publishing Industry Development Programme for our publishing activities.

Canadian Cataloguing in Publication Data

National Library of Canada Cataloguing in Publication Data

Rogers, Gayla
        Strategic planning in social service organizations : a practical guide

Includes bibliographic references and index.
ISBN 1-55130-196-2

1. Strategic planning. 2. Nonprofit organizations. I. Finley, Donna S. (Donna Shirley), 1958-   . II. Galloway, John R. (John Robert), 1958-   . III. Title.

HD30.28.R635 2001   658.4'012   C2001-930679-2

Managing Editor: Ruth Bradley-St-Cyr
Production Editor: Jo Roberts
Marketing Manager: Linda Palmer
Marketing Assistant: Renée Knapp
Page layout: Brad Horning
Cover Design: Jean Louie

01   02   03   04   05   06   07   7   6   5   4   3   2   1

Printed and bound in Canada by AGMV Marquis

This book has been inspired by the leadership and life philosophy of Donald G. Gow and the many professional social workers and volunteer Calgarians who help people in need in our community, particularly those at United Way of Calgary and Area who are continuously striving to make a difference.

Lloyd, Robin and Brian — you can expect us home for dinner tonight!

Table of Contents

SECTION 1
Context and Planning Framework

Chapter 1
Strategic Planning in Social Service Organizations

Chapter 2
The Strategic Planning Model

Chapter 3
The Strategic Planning Process

SECTION 2
Establishing and Maintaining
the Environment for Successful Planning

Chapter 4
Getting Started

Chapter 5
Defining Roles

Chapter 6
Engaging Stakeholders

Chapter 7
Facilitating the Process

SECTION 3
The Steps Leading to a Practical Strategic Plan

Chapter 8
Situation Assessment

Chapter 9
Strategy Definition

Chapter 10
Agree on Action

Foreword

A strong community is defined by the strengths and healthy functioning of individuals and, in turn, individuals are shaped and strengthened by the presence of strong community supports. Reflecting the societal trend away from governmental intervention toward the role of the community in developing solutions, social service organizations are increasingly called upon to be part of the strategy for building a strong, connected and healthy community. United Way of Calgary and Area represents the broad spectrum of community like no other organization. Our strategic planning work is typical of many social service organizations — there are many similarities along with some unique characteristics that do not lend themselves to a cookie cutter approach offered in most texts on the subject. This book offers a guide that will enable an organization to custom-fit a process and evolve a strategic plan to suit the organization.

History of United Way of Calgary and Area

Historically, the role of United Way of Calgary and Area had been primarily financial — raising money and providing much-needed funding to vital community services. Financial solutions served the needs of the community well. In recent years, however, shifting demographics, changing needs and shrinking government support have had profound effects on the community and United Way. Like many other businesses and organizations, United Way has had to rethink its approach and shape a new vision for the future of a renewed organization. We wanted to build on our record of excellence and work with others to ensure that our services were responsible, relevant, and effective in meeting the diverse needs of our rapidly changing community. We wanted to work differently in the community. To achieve this, United Way embarked on a full-scale strategic planning process to chart its course and effectively deliver results to and for the community. Through this planning effort, we learned much about our organization, our community and our aspirations for the future. We also learned much about the importance of strategic planning as a process and an outcome.

Defining a New Strategic Direction

In 1994, United Way began a process of planning and community consultation that led to the development of a new strategic direction. In November 1995, we talked to nearly 100 Calgary community members from diverse sectors and areas of interest during a series of public consultations. Our intent was to enlist their help in clarifying and forming United Way's primary mandate and priorities for the future.

What emerged from the round of consultations was a clear and new direction for United Way of Calgary and Area. Most importantly, community members agreed that United Way needs to show what impact the programs which receive United Way funding have on our community and be accountable to all the people it serves, whether they be donors, partnering agencies or other members of the community.

The strategic direction built from community consultation represents a fundamental shift in emphasis for United Way. We are moving away from measuring our impact through "money raised and agencies funded" to a focus on results and measuring our contributions by "difference and changes made and the value of services provided." This shift is a direct result of the approach we took to strategic planning — an approach we are pleased to share as an example throughout this book.

Continually Challenge Ourselves and Others

The success of an organization depends on it evolving over time by engaging in a cycle of critical inquiry through strategic planning. If United Way is to grow and achieve its new vision into the future, it must continually challenge its own approaches, strategies and decision-making processes. This means asking ourselves some tough questions about how we work. As we stand on the threshold of the 21st century, United Way shares a vision of a brighter future with our community.

The discipline of planning and review is critical to helping an organization focus on and achieve its goals. The stronger the process used, the better will be the results. For us, the journey has not always been easy nor the path forward clear. A book like this one would have been invaluable for us. That is why we are pleased to share aspects of our journey with you.

Ruth Ramsden-Wood,
President, United Way of Calgary and Area
April 2001

Preface

This book is a product of a unique collaboration between two MBA planning consultants and a social work professor. We first came together as part of a multi-disciplinary planning team working on a strategic planning initiative at the University of Calgary. We discovered that we had similar frameworks, complimentary approaches with different ways of articulating the consulting work we had each done over many years with social service organizations. We also discovered that many of the tools and tips we had found to be effective across a range of organizations did not appear in any of the textbooks on the subject of strategic planning. Combining the best of techniques from business and corporate planning with up-to-date knowledge and skill of social service management, our unique partnership blends processes and adapts models to provide a useful guide to strategic planning for social service organizations of various sizes and degrees of complexity.

This book is not about measuring program outcomes or program evaluation. These topics are well covered by other texts and manuals as a discrete activity important to social service organizations. The focus of strategic planning on the other hand is about a way to envision and define a future and the steps required to achieve that future. Therefore, strategic planning comes before specific programs and measurable objectives are articulated.

Introduction to This Text

This book consists of 17 chapters, divided into four sections.

Section 1: Context and Planning Framework defines strategic planning and describes why strategic planning is important within the social service sector. A strategic planning framework, consisting of a basic planning model and an effective planning process, is introduced.

Section 2: Establishing and Maintaining the Environment for Successful Planning describes, in four chapters, the key ingredients required to establish and maintain an environment for successful planning: assessing whether the organization is ready to initiate and sustain a strategic planning effort; defining the roles of the various stakeholders; engaging stakeholders through an effective communication strategy; and determining how to facilitate the planning process effectively.

Section 3: The Steps Leading to a Practical Strategic Plan details the four major steps of the strategic planning process, beginning with understanding the organization's internal and external environments and identifying the critical issues. The second step, defining the organization's strategy, involves identifying the organization's unique purpose and position in the sector. Step three addresses how to turn the strategy into implementable action. The fourth step discusses how to implement the strategy and action and how to gauge progress and performance.

Section 4: Beyond the Basics: Tools and Techniques for Advancing Strategic Thinking and Planning presents a collection of advanced tools and techniques suitable for the more experienced planner. Planning frameworks are provided for developing a vision, using market research for strategic planning purposes, understanding and conducting segmentation, marketing and communications planning, fundraising planning and technology planning.

This book presents a basic but practical approach to strategic planning, appropriate for first-time and experienced planners. Experienced planners may be able to move quickly through (or past) Sections 1 and 3, but will find the second and fourth sections more informative. Each chapter is augmented by worksheets as well as examples from United Way of Calgary and Area — an organization prominent in the social service sector that has lived through the initiation and development of a strategic plan over several years.

Gayla Rogers, Professor and Dean, Faculty of Social Work, University of Calgary
Donna S. Finley, President, FRAMEWORK Partners in Planning Inc.
John R. Galloway, Vice President, FRAMEWORK Partners in Planning Inc.

Authors and Contributors

Authors

Gayla Rogers

Gayla Rogers received her education both in Alberta and England: BA (University of Alberta), BSW (University of Calgary), MSW (University of Calgary), PhD (University of Newcastle upon Tyne, UK), and is a Registered Social Worker in the Province of Alberta. Dr. Rogers joined the University of Calgary, Faculty of Social Work in 1978 as a sessional instructor, and then as Assistant Professor and the Faculty's first Director of Field Education in 1987. She is now a full professor and the Dean of the Faculty of Social Work.

As the Field Director, Gayla worked with numerous social service agencies to help them create effective learning environments for social work students. This work enabled many social service organizations in Calgary to become "learning organizations" and led to additional consulting work related to program planning and evaluation. In 1996 Gayla stepped down from Field Director to spend 15 months on special assignment with the University working on an institutional strategic planning task force. For eight of those months she led a team that developed a strategic marketing and institutional positioning plan.

As a scholar, Gayla has garnered an international reputation in social work field education – the intersection of theory as taught in the University and practice as social work in a social service setting. She has developed and taught courses and workshops, and has provided consultation to social work programs, social service organizations and field instructors in Canada, the United States, Britain, Australia, and New Zealand. Gayla has presented and published papers on field education and has been a Master Teacher for the American Council of Social Work Education. Her recent books include *Social work field education: Views and visions* (Kendall/Hunt, 1995) and *The social work practicum: An access guide* (Peacock, 1996).

Donna S. Finley

Donna Finley holds a BA and BEd from Queen's University and an MBA from IMD, University of Lausanne, Switzerland. Organizations finding themselves in emerging competitive markets benefit from Donna's experience and leadership. Her diverse experience across many industries, disciplines and through many different situations, contributes to her skill in assisting senior managers and Boards in dealing with the challenge of strategic planning and change initiatives. She coaches organizations to look at their businesses objectively, addressing customer needs and competitive pressures. Then focusing on core competencies, she encourages leaders to move beyond conventional thinking to uncover new opportunities for growth.

Donna has led major strategic transformation and planning initiatives for large corporations, the public sector and not-for-profit organizations. Her strength lies in analyzing organizations and coaching leaders on articulating and implementing market-based principles and strategies into organizations not familiar or comfortable with these concepts. Donna has managed large-scale market assessments, strategy development and product introductions for natural gas transmission, telecommunications, post-secondary education, not-for-profit, petro-chemical, agri-food and software industries, both nationally and internationally. She has also led single consultant initiatives for these same organizations.

Donna began her career in medical research and later worked within the marketing function of Novacor Chemicals and Hewlett-Packard before starting her own management consulting company. She has authored several publications pertaining to her work.

Donna's flexibility and broad-minded thinking style are due, in part, to her extensive international exposure having lived, worked and studied in Switzerland, Scandinavia, Kenya, Japan, the United States and Canada.

John R. Galloway

John Galloway holds a Bachelor of Engineering Science and an MBA from the University of Western Ontario and is a registered professional engineer. John brings a wealth of experience and a broad perspective to his work. He has held a wide variety of positions with front-line responsibility including; marketing and sales management, project management and project engineering. His industry experience ranges from those that are technically based - industrial-automation, natural gas transportation, electric utilities, telecommunications, and software to the more people-oriented service sectors of post-secondary education, and not-for-profit. Internationally, John has managed projects in the former Soviet Union, Malaysia, Pakistan and the United States.

John has assisted companies in regulated industries through the process of adapting to rapidly changing environments and planning for the emergence of competition. Under his guidance these companies have broken away from thinking about their business in a traditional sense and adopted, for the first time, a market driven approach, using market research to guide the restructuring of products, services and pricing to meet customer needs. John is able to provide a link from the technical issues to a framework through which companies are better able to view their business more strategically.

John has led large national and international organizations through corporate strategy development sessions, serving as an advisor and facilitator to senior executives and Boards. He has helped companies to establish processes to analyze and assess their environment, define a vision and mission, then set strategies and action plans to realize their goals.

Contributors

Gord Allan, B.Sc. University of Alberta, MBA, University of Toronto

Gord's 15-year career has included work with the Canadian Imperial Bank of Commerce, Revenue Canada and management consulting with FRAMEWORK Partners in Planning Inc. He has led or contributed to several large, complex strategic and business planning and change initiatives in the public, private and not-for-profit sectors, always providing his financial perspectives. He is a highly effective team leader particularly where integrating the needs of a diverse group is required.

Gord helped draft sections of chapters, assemble figures and worksheets based on FRAMEWORK Inc.'s source materials and contribute to the index and chapter summaries.

Joy Claypool, B.Com., University of Saskatchewan

Joy has been engaged in strategic market planning efforts in the increasingly competitive telecommunications, power and post-secondary education sectors in Canada. She brings an operational perspective to the planning process in order to translate strategy into action plans. Throughout her career, Joy has been actively involved in directing market research projects and utilizing data for making business decisions. She has extensive experience in developing and implementing the detailed tactics of comprehensive marketing and communications plans. Joy consults with FRAMEWORK Partners in Planning Inc.

Joy contributed to **Chapter 13**, *Using Market Research for Strategic Planning Purposes*, and **Chapter 15**, *Marketing and Communications Planning Framework*.

Janet Gavinchuk, B.Com., MBA, University of British Columbia

Janet's 25 year career spans several industries, in particular those undergoing significant change driven by government cutbacks, deregulation or emerging competition: electric utilities, post-secondary education, not-for-profit organizations and municipal governments. From the United Nations to the United Way, her involvement has ranged from high level strategic and marketing planning through to implementation. She has an extensive background in process and market research management, program implementation, and communications planning and execution. Janet's specialty is conducting detailed market segmentation research and analysis. She consults with FRAMEWORK Partners in Planning Inc.

Janet contributed to **Chapter 4**, *Getting Started*, and **Chapter 14**, *The Art and Science of Segmentation*.

Jody L. Germaine, B.Sc., University of Idaho

Jody has close to 15 years experience in the software industry, including nine years working at Microsoft Corporation, where she served in various capacities from software testing to program manager for Internet Explorer, Windows 95 Networking Team, and Windows for Workgroups 3.11 Escalations. She has been involved in a number of successful start-up software companies, providing assistance with launching quality products and services that meet market needs. Currently, Jody holds a Certified Financial Planner designation and is president of a firm that provides consulting services to software and internet service companies.

Jody contributed to **Chapter 17**, *Technology Planning Framework*.

Katie McCunn, B.A. Queen's University

Katie has an extensive background in public policy development and implementation. Fluently bilingual, she has worked in both the private and public sectors where she has gained a wide range of experience dealing with all levels of government and non-governmental organizations. Throughout her career, she has worked in various capacities with the Department of Justice, the Canadian Centre on Substance Abuse and the University of Ottawa. Katie has worked as a Special Assistant to the Ministers of National Defence and Health and Welfare, providing policy advice and recommendations. She spearheaded the National AIDS Strategy and was involved in Canada's White Paper on National Defence, the National Drug Strategy, and the Family Violence Initiative.

Katie reviewed each chapter as it was written and provided critical feedback and commentary to the authors.

Andrea McManus, CFRE

Andrea McManus is a managing partner with The Development Group, a full service strategic philanthropic consulting firm. She holds the international accreditation of Certified Fund Raising Executive. Andrea has over 16 years experience in fund development, communications, media, public relations and marketing and has worked with a wide variety of non-profit and for-profit, local and national, organizations in the health, social services, arts and education sectors. Andrea is a dedicated fund-raiser committed to the professional development of the industry and its practitioners and to the establishment and education on Standards of Practice and fulfillment of the National Society of Fund Raising Executives (NSFRE) Code of Ethics. She has held a variety of local, national and international positions with NSFRE and is a part-time instructor at the Mount Royal College School for Business and Entrepreneurial Studies teaching a Fund Development and Corporate Philanthropy course to graduating students in the Applied Communications Degree (Bachelor's level) program.

Andrea contributed to **Chapter 16**, *Fundraising in the Social Service Agency*.

Elaine Proulx, CFRE

Elaine Proulx is a managing partner with The Development Group, a full service strategic philanthropic consulting firm. She holds a National Certificate in Voluntary and Non-Profit Sector Management as well as the international accreditation of Certified Fund Raising Executive. Elaine has been professionally associated with community development work in Toronto and Calgary for more than twenty-five years and retired from Shell Canada in 1993 as Manager, Community Affairs after nearly twenty-five years of service. Since that time she has focused her professional work in the non-profit sector and has significant experience in the direct development of strategy and creation and management of fund-raising campaigns.

Elaine contributed to **Chapter 16**, *Fundraising in the Social Service Agency*.

Marva Quist, B.Sc., Brigham Young University

Marva has close to 20 years experience as a leader, facilitator and planner whose specialty is working with diverse teams to achieve consensus decision-making and implement long-term direction into practical action. She has worked extensively within deregulating environments where new approaches, tools and skills are required by teams to be successful. Marva is a strong project manager, coach and pragmatist. She currently is a consultant with FRAMEWORK Partners in Planning Inc.

Marva reviewed the chapters within **Section 2**, *Establishing and Maintaining the Environment for Successful Planning,* and **Section 3**, *The Steps Leading to a Practical Strategic Plan*, providing the authors with critical feedback regarding content and offering suggestions for '*Process Tips*'.

Jay Spark, B.Sc., MBA (Organizational Behaviour and Labour Relations), University of Alberta

Jay Spark has over 20 years experience as a mediator, facilitator and trainer specializing in dispute resolution, collaborative workplace relationships, leadership development, and the management of strategic change. He has designed and delivered training in negotiation, consensus problem solving, alternative dispute resolution, leadership, and the management of change. In addition, he has extensive experience in facilitating collective bargaining, mediating workplace disputes, and management coaching. Jay is Principal Consultant of Spark Consulting Services.

Jay contributed to **Chapter 7**, *Facilitating the Process*.

Shirley Walker

For 30 years Shirley has worked as a text graphic production specialist responsible for template design and production, database development and document management. She has experience preparing computer-animated presentations, complex document layout and templates, and web-page design and layout. Shirley currently works as a consultant for FRAMEWORK Partners in Planning Inc.

Shirley produced all the figures, tables and worksheets as well as the original manuscript for this book.

Section 1

Context and Planning Framework

Context and Planning Framework describes, in three chapters, the different types of planning; the importance of strategic planning in the social service context; introduces the strategic planning model, and describes the strategic planning process.

CHAPTER 1

Strategic Planning in Social Service Organizations

What is it and why do it?

Strategic planning offers many benefits to social service organizations operating within an environment of funding cutbacks and emerging competition. This chapter defines strategic planning, contrasts it to other familiar types of planning, and describes why strategic planning is important for social service organizations.

Challenges Currently Faced by the Social Service Sector

The social service sector represents a significant component of the not-for-profit sector. The past decade has been difficult for most social service organizations, as funding from government sources has declined. At the same time that governments are scaling back the services they provide private service providers are beginning to enter the market to fill the gap left by governments. As a result, social service organizations find themselves in an era of increasing demand for their services with less public funding and increasing competition.

> *These are challenging times for the nonprofit sector. While voluntary organizations struggle with the immediate challenge posed by government funding restraints and rising demands for their services, the nonprofit sector as a whole is facing increased pressures to establish its identity and carve out its longer term role in relation to governments and for-profit providers of services.*[1]

In the current environment, there is also pressure to become ever more responsive to client and donor needs, maintain focus and relevance, and create unique services and programs that reduce overlap with other service providers.

In 1999, the Canada West Foundation surveyed 72 non-profit social service agency executive directors in the areas of counseling, crisis and emergency shelter services for women, and services for children and youth in western Canada. Anecdotal evidence

---

1 Hirshhorn, R. (June 1999). "Great Expectations: The Ideal Characteristics of Non-Profits." Alternative Service Delivery Project Research Bulletin, Canada West Foundation, Number 3, p. 7.

obtained in the survey allowed Canada West to create a list of organizational traits displayed by the most effective social service agencies. They are listed in alphabetical order:

- accountability (to clients, the community, governments, and supporters),
- adequate and stable funding,
- clear mandate,
- community integration (partnerships with other service providers and businesses),
- community support and involvement (volunteers, donations, grassroots support),
- creative and resourceful,
- good governance (effective board),
- good reputation in the community (respect, high profile),
- high service delivery and outcome evaluation standards,
- service-focused,
- sound fiscal management,
- strong values (commitment).

Many of these traits are enhanced with effective strategic planning. Others are outcomes of the strategic planning process.

What is Strategic Planning?

Strategic planning is an iterative activity focused on discussion and consensus building that clarifies and builds commitment to the organization's future direction and priorities, within a changing environment. The result of the *process*, or activity of strategic planning is a document — the Strategic Plan. However, virtually all veterans of strategic planning efforts will agree that the importance of the planning process overshadows the importance of the final document. Planning alone does not produce results; however, well-developed plans increase the likelihood that the day-to-day efforts of the organization will be coordinated, integrated and lead toward the desired results.

Strategic Planning versus Operational or Business Planning

As a future-oriented activity, strategic planning involves making decisions that are fundamental and directional in nature and have long-term implications for the organization. Business planning is used to describe a variety of processes. In the social service context, business planning is often used interchangeably with operational planning. Operational/ business planning, in contrast to strategic planning, tends to focus on short-term implementation choices that typically have immediate implications for the organization. Strategic planning defines the action priorities to be addressed over several years while operational/business planning defines the actions to be taken within the current year to work towards the strategic direction and priorities.

Strategic planning defines a framework for operational/business planning activities. The priorities defined by the strategic plan are converted into specific tasks in operational/ business plans and these specific tasks are translated into resource requirements in the annual budget.

Strategic planning forces critical issues to the surface, and charges managers and directors with making choices based on the best-available information, in a systematic way. Some of the most difficult choices in strategic planning often centre on what the organization will not do, or will stop doing as the organization refocuses its sights on the future direction.

In many organizations, strategic plans and operational/business plans are separate documents. The approach to strategic planning presented in this book combines the development of direction and strategy, and the translation of that direction and strategy into tangible action priorities into one planning document. This approach is well suited to social service organizations.

Strategic Planning versus Long-Range Planning

Long-range planning and strategic planning are terms that are often used interchangeably but in truth are different concepts. Long-range planning assumes that the current environment is reliable and predictable, with current trends continuing into the foreseeable future. Consequently, long-range plans tend to be extrapolations or forecasts, focused on assuming the most likely future and working backward to identify year-by-year action steps to be undertaken. According to Florence Green[2] this type of planning is characterized by asking the questions *"What business are we in?"* and *"Are we doing things right?"*

Strategic planning, on the other hand, focuses on decisions that help position the organization to respond successfully to an ever-changing environment and unpredictable future. This type of planning expects new trends to develop and changes to occur, sometimes at lightning speed. An organization engaged in strategic planning anticipates a range of possible futures and develops strategies based on an assessment of the current environment. According to Green, this type of planning is characterized by asking the questions *"What business should we be in?"* and *"Are we doing the right thing?"*

In addition, the process of strategic planning is ongoing. Through iteration, results improve with experience and time as the strategic plan continues to get reviewed and renewed and the organization learns to think more strategically and act more purposefully. Strategic planning becomes one of the most effective tools available to senior management and the board as the value of the process becomes apparent to the organization and its stakeholders.

Why is Strategic Planning Important?

Strategic planning allows an organization to clarify its unique purpose and positioning in a sector. The strategic planning process and the strategic plan foster understanding and commitment to organizational priorities, and if conducted within the right kind of environment can improve the way people work together as they identify and pursue these priorities. In the context of limited resources, strategic planning assists an organization to make choices among competing alternatives.

A strong strategic plan will:

- clearly state the organization's desired future direction and the action priorities required to move toward that direction,
- provide a clear blueprint for action that guides all decision-making,
- include performance indicators and milestones to measure progress,

---

2   Green, Florence (Feb. 1994). "Strategic Planning: Blueprints for Success," California Association of Nonprofits.

- include information that can be used to market the organization to the public and potential donors and funders.

A successful planning process will:

- broaden the perspective of the board and staff and help them understand the needs of clients better and determine how best to address those needs,
- focus the organization on what is really important, creating opportunities to eliminate unnecessary work and providing a focus for managing change,
- strengthen the team by improving communications, establishing common goals, increasing cooperation and coordination, prioritizing workload and enhancing bottom-up participation,
- link strategy to operating plans and improve consistency, conformity and continuity,
- develop commitment to and buy-in for the strategic direction and values.

Strategic Planning in the Context of the Social Service Organization

A strategic plan will differ greatly between a for-profit corporation and a not-for-profit social service organization. The planning process, however, is remarkably similar. Strategic planning was a widespread corporate tool by the 1970s, and has been adapted over time by governments and the non-profit sector. The material in this book has been tailored for the unique qualities and challenges of not-for-profit social service organizations although much of what is presented and discussed will appear very familiar to a corporate planner.

A few of the differences evident between social service organizations and for-profit corporations that may affect the approach to strategic planning are:

Make-up and role of the board — In a social service organization the board does not represent the owners of the organization as it does in a corporation. Therefore the social service board has traditionally taken on a different, more hands-off role, only recently changing to a body more actively concerned with strategy.

Customers — The concept of the customer is straightforward in a for-profit enterprise; it is the individual who purchases a company's product or service. Defining the customer in social service organizations is often less clear and can include the recipient of the services, volunteers, donors, and funders. For clarity and simplicity, the term "client" is used here rather than "customer" to define the recipient of the service provided by the social service organization. Clients are one group of stakeholders whose input is critical to the strategic planning process.

Stakeholders — In a for-profit corporation, the concept of stakeholder is relatively straightforward and usually includes customers/clients, shareholders, employees, and the community. A social service organization, on the other hand, has many stakeholders due to the complex political environment in which it exists. A stakeholder is defined as anyone internal or external to the organization who has an interest, or "stake," in the organization and its future, including those responsible for creating, approving, communicating and implementing its strategic direction. Individuals and groups affected by the strategic direction or those who could impact its successful implementation are also considered stakeholders. Consequently, clients, donors, staff, board members, funders, special interest groups, other agencies, private service providers, the community-at-large, and government are a few of the groups that need to be integrated into the planning process in differing ways and to differing degrees.

Use of volunteers — Volunteers are critical to the success of most social service providers, particularly in the current environment of strained resources. The issues of recruiting and retaining volunteers are quite different from those of managing paid employees. Volunteers play virtually no role in for-profit organizations. "Donor" is used to identify an individual who provides time, money and/or talent directly or indirectly to the organization. Consequently, "donor" encompasses those who volunteer or are funders to the organization. Donors are one of the stakeholders whose views need to be sought.

Competition — In business sectors, competitive analysis allows management to gain a better understanding of the dynamics of an industry and the opportunities and threats that exist or may exist for their company based on the activity of competitors. In a social service context, competitive analysis has varying degrees of relevance. While there is typically not profit-motivated competition for social services, there are often alternate sources of service that constitute increasing competition. In recent years the downloading of government services has necessitated a closer examination of who provides what services to whom and who funds those services. In addition, private for-profit service providers have emerged. From this perspective, analyzing alternative service providers and their funders, that is, "competitive analysis" is an important tool for planners in the social service sector.

How Much Time is Needed for Strategic Planning?

Several factors will impact the amount of time and resources required to successfully undertake a strategic planning initiative.

Strategic planning experience of leaders and the degree of planning sophistication within the organization — If the board chair and executive director have little experience in strategic planning, the process will require more time and in all likelihood require the assistance of outside strategic planning process expertise. If, on the other hand, the organization has a well-established planning cycle that is supported by up-to-date information and an informed board and senior management team, the strategic planning process can be designed to take advantage of these assets.

Size of organization — If the organization is large, complex, offers multiple services and programs and has multiple stakeholders then the strategic planning process will probably take longer and require more internal (and possibly external) resources to design and manage.

Management style — If the management style of the organization is one of inclusiveness and consensus decision-making (rather than command and control), the planning process will likely be more complex and take longer in order to engage as many of the key stakeholders as possible and to reach full consensus on all decisions.

Amount of up-to-date information available — The extent to which the organization needs to undertake primary market research related to environmental trends, competitive analysis and client/donor needs as the basis for informed decision making will greatly impact the overall schedule of the planning effort. In addition, the schedule and cost of the overall planning effort will be further impacted depending upon the decision to collect this information using internal resources or delegating the effort to an external organization.

Degree of alignment regarding the current values, mission and priorities — If there is strong agreement and consensus between the board and staff on the values, mission and priorities of the organization, the time and effort spent on these fundamental aspects of the planning model can be shortened. In particular, alignment around the values can greatly benefit the planning process by being a touchstone for any conflict or differences of perspectives that will undoubtedly arise.

Now that strategic planning is defined and described, a practical planning framework is presented in **Chapter 2**, *The Strategic Planning Model*.

Summary

The strategic planning process offers many benefits particularly in addressing the challenges facing the social service sector. Strategic planning is an activity where both the process and the outcomes are vitally important to its success. Strategic planning is differentiated from operational/business planning and long-range planning. Effective strategic planning enables clarification of purpose and assists an organization in describing its unique position in the sector. There are some similarities and differences in strategic planning in the corporate sector but interestingly both sectors can learn from each other. The amount of time required for strategic planning is dependent upon a number of factors such as readiness of the organization to plan, management style and prior planning experience.

CHAPTER 2

The Strategic Planning Model

What's all this mission/vision stuff?

Effective planning begins with a clear understanding of the model and process. This chapter describes a simple, practical model used successfully by social service organizations. While many planning models exist using fancy jargon and multi-layered procedures, the underlying concepts behind these models tend not to be substantially different from one another. The added complexity introduced by some of these models does not justify the additional effort required to understand and implement them. Choose a simple model and stick with it! The issues, and how your organization should respond, are difficult enough to manage without getting mired in an unproductive discussion about the latest jargon. Help your organization deal with the substantive issues from the very beginning.

The Value of a Strategic Planning Model

A common problem in social service organizations, is the introduction of different models over time by well-meaning volunteers, staff and/or consultants. Volunteers from a variety of backgrounds bring their previous planning experiences and tools to the organization. While this contribution is valuable and also encouraged in the budget-constrained social service sector, an organization can be quickly overwhelmed by the complexity this introduces. Similarly, a staff member learning new techniques or the introduction of a new consultant with a different "toolkit" can be detrimental to the advantages of a consistent planning model. Be very cautious about changing your planning model! Introduce new processes and techniques that complement your model and keep it fresh, but think twice about the benefits and impact of introducing changes to the model.

While this chapter introduces and describes the elements of the strategic planning model, suggested methods and approaches for developing each of these components within the context of your own organization are described in **Chapter 9,** *Strategy Definition.*

The Strategic Planning Model

Figure 2-1, *The Strategic Planning Model,* illustrates a simple planning model used successfully in the social service sector. This planning model focuses on identifying areas for fundamental change and/or significant performance improvement. Ongoing effort directed at day-to-day operations is not addressed by this planning model.

The model is depicted as a pyramid to reflect the relationship of the central purpose of the organization (that is, the mission or apex of the pyramid) to the broad base of action required to implement the mission (that is, the action priorities or the base of the pyramid). The values, mission, key success factors, goals and performance indicators are relatively stable over the longer term, while the action priorities and performance targets are dynamic in the shorter term, changing or updating one year to the next.

Each element of the strategic planning model is described in more detail in the remainder of this chapter.

FIGURE 2-1
Planning Model

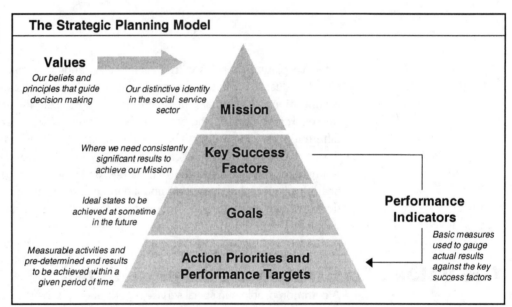

Values

Values are fundamental principles and beliefs that serve as implicit criteria guiding all actions and decision making. Explicitly stating the values helps the organization avoid decisions that are inconsistent with the organization's beliefs.

More than any other element of the planning model, values are slow to change. The frequent problems associated with organizational mergers are more often related to inconsistent values than inconsistent business strategies. Strategies can be readily changed while organizational values take years to evolve.

Figures 2-2A and **2-2B,** *Examples of Values,* illustrate how two organizations articulate their values.

Mission

The mission communicates the distinctive identity or purpose, which the organization seeks within the social service sector. It clearly, concisely and simply states what value

FIGURE 2-2A
Example of Values

Values
These are the beliefs and fundamental principles that have guided United Way of Calgary's actions and decision-making since 1993: • Be ethical, open and trustworthy • Value the contribution of volunteers and promote volunteerism • Be accountable to our donors and the general public • Engage and listen to the community to better understand community issues • Work collaboratively with all constituencies in the community • Ensure that our communication is clear, comprehensive and truthful *Source: United Way of Calgary and Area, 1993*

FIGURE 2-2B
Example of Values

Values
• We believe that people should focus on ability, not disability • We believe that there is value in including and integrating members with varied disabilities • Our programs are member-driven and member-oriented • We strive to provide a fun and challenging environment for our staff and our members • We believe that we must be fiscally responsible and accountable for our actions *Source: Calgary Between Friends Club, 1998*

the organization provides. Ideally, the mission should be one sentence, free of jargon, understandable, inspirational and memorable. The details of quantity, quality, cost and time should not be included except to the extent that they are the basis of the organization's distinctive identity.

The mission is future-oriented because it describes what the organization wants to become rather than what it may be today. This statement should only change as a result of a fundamental shift in the external environment or due to a change in the organization's strategic direction.

Ideally, the mission can serve as a rallying cry for staff and volunteers.

Figures 2-3A, 2-3B, 2-3C and **2-3D**, *Examples of Mission,* illustrate the mission statements of several social service organizations.

Vision Versus Mission

While it is true that 'vision' and 'mission' represent different concepts, the value of adding an additional concept does not outweigh the added complexity for novice planners. For basic planning, we treat these two concepts as one. For those organizations ready to increase the sophistication of their planning efforts, refer to **Chapter 12,** *Developing a Vision*, for guidance on how this step may be incorporated into your planning. The bottom line is whether your organization elects to express its direction and focus using a vision, mission or a combination of both does not matter, provided the intended direction is clear.

FIGURE 2-3A
Example of Mission

Mission
Build extraordinary communities, by linking people and resources, encouraging partnerships and cultivating giving.
Source: United Way of Calgary and Area, 1996

FIGURE 2-3B
Example of Mission

Mission
To provide services and resources to help blind, deafblind and visually impaired people achieve their goals.
Source: CNIB Alberta, NWT and Nunavut Division, 2000

FIGURE 2-3C
Example of Mission

Mission
Providing quality social and recreational opportunities in an accepting environment, focusing on children and young adults with disabilities.
Source: Calgary Between Friends Club, 1998

FIGURE 2-3D
Example of Mission

Mission
To build a city which is known worldwide for its respect of children and its encouragement of their participation as citizens in their community.
Source: Child Friendly Calgary, 1994

Key Success Factors (KSF)

Key success factors are the five or six characteristics, conditions or variables that when properly sustained, maintained or managed can a significant impact on the success of an organization competing in a particular sector. They are specific to an organization's selected strategic direction and the sector or market in which the organization operates. They help management and staff direct limited resources of time, money and people to where key results are required.

Key success factors state:

- results, not activities
- what, not how
- ends, not means
- outputs, rather than inputs

Like the mission, key success factors are stable over several years, changing only in response to fundamental shifts in the external environment or change in the mission. Key success factors are likely similar for organizations providing similar services.

Figures 2-4A and **2-4B,** *Examples of Key Success Factors,* list the key success factors of two organizations.

Goals

Goals articulate the longer-term areas targeted by the organization for emphasis. They provide direction for fundamental change and their time horizon typically extends beyond the annual budget cycle.

Effective goals are short statements — to the point; they leave mention of time and measurable results to the action priorities. Goals are related back to each separate idea or concept in the mission statement. As a rule, five or six goals should sufficiently articulate the salient aspects of the strategy.

Figures 2-5A, 2-5B and **2-5C**, *Examples of Goals*, present the goal statements developed by three different social service organizations.

FIGURE 2-4A
Example of Key
Success Factors

Key Success Factors (early draft)
• Positive impact on needs • Competitive growth in fundraising revenue • Motivated, skilled team • Advocacy • Community confidence *Source: United Way of Calgary and Area, 1994*

FIGURE 2-4B
Example of Key
Success Factors

Key Success Factors
• Clearly communicated need • Client responsiveness • Donor recognition • Demonstrated results • Individual identity realization • Availability of technical resources *Source: CNIB Alberta, NWT and Nunavut Division, 2000*

FIGURE 2-5A
Example of Goals

Goals
• **Community Action:** Impact social issues through collaborative community action. • **Spirit of Philanthropy:** Increase charitable giving and citizen involvement. • **People Care:** Improve quality of life for people served. • **Leadership:** Anticipate and respond to the evolving needs of the community. *Source: United Way of Calgary and Area, 1999*

FIGURE 2-5B
Example of Goals

Goals
• Motivate the public, private and non-profit sectors as well as private individuals to promote and deliver a better quality of life for children in Calgary. • Raise the self-esteem of children in Calgary by encouraging them to believe they have an infinite capacity for growth and achievement. • Help children understand their rights and responsibilities as citizens of a larger community. • Create opportunities for children to participate in their community. • Make Calgary a unique destination to visit. *Source: Child Friendly Calgary, 1998*

FIGURE 2-5C
Example of Goals

Goals
• Revitalize our fundraising strategies to reflect current and emerging trends and to respond to the needs of current and potential donors. • Significantly increase the resources available to clients and enhance the organization's ability to deliver services by realizing win-win partnerships with selected organizations. • Deliver services, in the context of resource constraints, that meet the needs of target clients. • Increase public profile of and recognition of the needs of the visually impaired and the CNIB's role. • Achieve a significant increase in volunteer commitment and support made possible by changing demographics. • Evolve the organization's mindset and establish organizational processes and structures locally and nationally to better reflect the opportunities, challenges and dynamics of our changing economy and society. *Source: CNIB Alberta, NWT and Nunavut Division, 2000*

Action Priorities

Action priorities are the specific steps, or tasks, needed to implement the goals. These steps are tangible in their description of what is to be accomplished, in what timeframe and by whom. This is where strategy integrates with organizational operations. Characteristics of action priorities include:

- realistic to the planning period under consideration
- specific with respect to quantity, quality, time and resources
- related to strategic change, not ongoing activities

Action priorities consist of two elements, objectives and action plans.

- **Objectives** — are concise statements of what is to be accomplished or the outcome to be achieved. For example: *Achieve a 20% increase in service coverage by year-end.*

- **Action Plans** — outline what tasks will be performed in order to achieve the objective. For example: *(1) Hire and train additional service staff; (2) Open two new service delivery locations; and (3) Develop and implement promotional campaign to increase awareness of service availability.*

The number of action priorities should be kept to a manageable number. More than five or six can unduly stretch the resources of the organization to implement effectively.

Figure 2-6A, *Example of Strategic Action Priority,* and **Figure 2-6B,** *Example of Operational Action Priority,* illustrate strategic and operationally focused objectives and action plans.

Performance Indicators (PI)

Performance indicators are the measures used to gauge actual results against the key success factors. For each key success factor, one or more performance indicators are typically defined. Usually, each indicator is applicable to more than one key success factor.

Characteristics of performance indicators are:

- simple,
- quantifiable,
- enduring,
- focused on areas the organization can control or influence,
- reflect routine activities and change objectives.

In addition, it is helpful to view performance indicators in two categories: leading indicators and lagging indicators. Leading indicators gauge where an organization is going and its likelihood of success. Lagging indicators measure how well the organization met its objectives after the fact. The frequency of reporting results for each indicator may be monthly, quarterly or annually depending upon the specific indicator.

Figure 2-7, *Example of Performance Indicators,* illustrates the leading and lagging performance indicators of the Resource Development group of United Way of Calgary.

Performance Targets

The organization defines the end result it desires to achieve for each performance indicator within a specified period of time. These desired end-results are called performance targets. Effective targets are demanding on the organization but attainable. Results that exceed or fall short of a target should cause management to re-examine resource allocation relative to established priorities. Consequently, performance targets can be more dynamic than other elements of the planning model, changing in response to either management discretion or circumstances. Successful performance targets are:

- constantly readjusted to drive continuous improvement,
- demanding but realistic,
- changed or adjusted over time to reflect new standards of success,
- specific and quantifiable,
- used to alert management when deviation from desired values are observed.

FIGURE 2-6A: Example of Strategic Action Priority

Example of a Strategic Action Plan

Objective 1: *Complete the implementation of the strategic planning framework.*

Action	Accountability	Target Completion Date	Comments
1.1 Consolidate strategic planning conclusions and framework	Strategic Planning Task Force Committee	Sept. 18, 95 Board meeting for approval	Leverage the work performed by the Board and Management teams in order to present a more comprehensive picture of the current environment, initiatives and priorities; provide people with the opportunity of recognizing the importance of their contributions; and provide a record of the current thinking which is consistent/ complete and can be used for multiple communication sessions with stakeholders.
1.2 Design and launch a Community Consultation Process focused on the new strategic direction 1.2.1 Consolidate and streamline the list of target audiences 1.2.2 Identify what information needs to be communicated to each target group 1.2.3 Identify when, how and by whom consultation will occur	Strategic Planning Task Force Committee	Sept. 18, 95 Board meeting for information, and Dec. 11, 95 Board meeting for approval	Build on the work initiated in November 1994.
1.3 Identify key success factors and performance indicators at the Board and Management team levels 1.3.1 Identify 5 to 8 key success factors, each with a supporting performance indicator and stretch target 1.3.2 Identify performance indicators and targets that support the organization's indicators for each of Management's respective areas.	Strategic Planning Task Force Committee	Dec. 11, 95 Board meeting for approval	This effort would include developing a process to incorporate input from Board and Management team members, and may include competitive benchmarking to assist the Committee in establishing realistic targets.
1.4 Identify and prioritize a list of "visible signals" that "things are different" at the United Way as a result of the new strategic direction	Strategic Planning Task Force Committee	Dec. 11, 95 Board meeting for approval	This signal could take one of several forms, for example: • Identify and prioritize Board restructuring opportunities to streamline operations and promote integration between various Committee efforts. • Identify and prioritize 3 to 4 cross-functional processes that require redesign. • Stop one major initiative that may no longer be relevant within the new direction.
1.5 Develop a process for continually reviewing and renewing strategic action priorities	Strategic Planning Task Force Committee	Jan. 96 Board meeting for information	Consider how this process links to the budgeting process, Board orientation and other current initiatives, as well as who is accountable/responsible for the renewal process.

Source: United Way of Calgary and Area, 1995

FIGURE 2-6B
Example of
Operational
Action Priority

Operational Action Priority		
Objective 1: *Ensure communications plan is strategic, clear and linked to organizational communication efforts.*		
Action Plans	**Accountability**	**Target Completion Date**
1.1 Perform an audit of current communication processes, vehicles and materials; identify a limited set of areas for improvement	Communications Director	Mar 2002
1.2 Provide feedback on current communication tools and suggestions for new tools	Communications Director	Mar 2002
1.3 Revise communication strategy plan based on input from 1.1 and 1.2 above.	Communications Specialist	May 2002
1.4 Identify key messages to communicate progress on performance	Communications Specialist	June 2002
1.5 Assess current verbal and presentation skill sets and develop standards to be achieved	Communications Specialist	Aug. 2002
1.6 Streamline the media relations process to significantly improve the coordination and quality of information	Communications Specialist	May 2002

Linking to Unit and Individual Plans and Budgets

The planning process links goals and action priorities across the organization. These priorities ultimately provide direction to each individual and provide input to the budget. Experience has shown that in larger social service organizations planning at both the

FIGURE 2-7
Example of
Performance
Indicators

Performance Indicators	
Leading Indicators	**Lagging Indicators**
1. Volunteer Satisfaction Index 2. Number of Donors 3. Number of Donors Retained 4. Consistency of Giving History (year/year) 5. "WOW" Factor 6. Number of Volunteers 7. Percent Increase in Average Gift 8. Employee Satisfaction Index	9. Donor Satisfaction Index 10. Dollars Raised 11. Dollar per Donor Raised (average gift)
Source: United Way of Calgary and Area; Resource Development Plan 2000	

organizational and unit levels are required to translate the mission successfully into manageable, concise action steps. In smaller organizations, the strategic plan can be directly linked to individuals and the budget.

Figure 2-8, *Levels of Plans*, is an inverted pyramid illustrating these two levels of planning and their linkage to individuals and budgets. The strategic plan, the top of the pyramid, provides the broader scope and direction for the more operationally focused unit plans. In turn, these unit plans provide specific input to individual priorities and resource requirements for the annual budget.

FIGURE 2-8
Levels of Plans

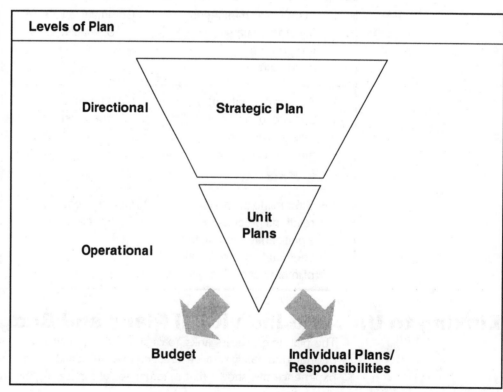

Levels of Plan

Directional   Strategic Plan

Operational   Unit Plans

Budget   Individual Plans/ Responsibilities

Unit plans are developed for key functions, or processes that span the organization (for example, Information Technology Plan). These plans contain the same components as the strategic plan but are specific to the issues of a particular unit.

The budget is derived from the strategic plan, rather than driving the strategic plan. Budgets are predominately a control mechanism. They should be a result of strategic decisions on funding and resource allocation — not the starting point.

Unfortunately, some organizations view budgeting as their only planning effort. Rather than spending some time thinking about longer-term direction and priorities, they exhaust their planning resources developing a budget. Without the discipline to consider a broader view, planning becomes an extrapolation of the current environment. This approach typically produces organizations that are reactive and shortsighted.

Every level of plan includes some element of longer-term strategy as well as shorter-term tactics. Plans rely on judgment, and in some cases best guesses, in the absence of complete or conclusive information. The strategic plan tends to require more judgement than the more operational unit plans.

With the model in hand, it is time to discuss the process needed to develop a plan. **Chapter 3,** *The Strategic Planning Process,* introduces the process that utilizes the model in developing an effective strategic plan.

Summary

For most social service organizations, indeed for almost all organizations of any kind, it is critical to choose a simple planning model and stick with it. The temptation to modify or enhance the model is a decision not to be taken lightly. Complexity can easily discount the effectiveness of the strategic planning model as a management tool. The planning model introduced and described in this chapter has been successfully utilized by various not-for-profit and social service organizations over the years. The planning pyramid has as its apex the strategic elements of mission and key success factors (influenced by values and leading to goals). The base of the pyramid represents the tactical elements of action priorities and performance targets.

In a small organization, one level of planning will be sufficient while larger organizations will require unit plans to properly link the strategic plan to individuals and annual budgets.

The plan will derive the operating budget. A strong plan will combine elements of longer-term strategy and shorter-term tactics, and will rely on judgement where complete information is not available.

CHAPTER 3

The Strategic Planning Process

*How do you develop
a strategic plan you can use?*

The *process* of defining an organization's future is a critical component of its success, recognized and managed by top-performing organizations. However, without an explicit planning process that engages staff and volunteers, few social service organizations (in our experience, none!) are able to achieve this top-level of performance or the desired impact on the communities they strive to serve.

A well thought out strategic planning process encompasses two key aspects:

- the process involved in establishing and maintaining an environment that engages stakeholders in meaningful ways and promotes consensus building; and
- the sequential steps leading to a strategic plan.

The equal importance of both aspects cannot be overstated. Both must be planned for and implemented in parallel; however, many organizations tend to focus on the sequential steps in the process without adequately establishing the environment that will ultimately lead to implementation success. Although presented as discrete aspects, they are highly interdependent and must be integrated, coordinated and customized to meet the unique needs of individual organizations.

This chapter introduces a high-level overview of the planning process used by social service organizations for establishing strategic priorities. For more detail, **Section 2**: *Establishing and Maintaining the Environment for Successful Planning* introduces concepts for creating and sustaining the environment required to optimize participants' input, understanding and buy-in, and commitment to implementation. **Section 3**: *The Steps Leading to a Practical Strategic Plan*, further describes how to research, analyze and develop the components of a strategic plan through a sequence of steps.

The Iterative Art of the Strategic Planning Process

The planning process is the ongoing responsibility of management, not a one-time project to be completed. It is an iterative activity focused on discussion and consensus building, resulting in well-defined action. The most visible and tangible deliverable of the process is a document commonly referred to as "the plan" (the elements of which are described in **Chapter 2,** *The Strategic Planning Model*). The less tangible outcomes that are at least as important are also the focus of this chapter. They include:

- Organizational alignment through a common understanding of the situation in which the organization is operating and the critical issues to be addressed;
- Commitment to the organization's mission and long-term goals; and
- Organizational and individual buy-in to action priorities and commitment to their implementation.

Staff, volunteer and key stakeholder alignment around what is important and what is to be done is far more significant and difficult to achieve than writing a plan. Watch out for leaders who are driven to produce a document so they can check it off their "to do list," without any real commitment to engaging key stakeholders in the process. This approach inevitably fails. These plans become dust collectors.

The process of planning is not an exact science. Like all processes, the planning process can be improved with practice and concerted effort. Similarly, planning skills can also be improved over time. Through an iterative approach, the organization gains experience and expertise enabling it to continually increase its focus and effectiveness. Like the continuously improving nature of the process, the plan becomes more strategic and focused over time.

> *Process Tips: The act of discussing and building consensus in order to clarify and increase commitment to the organization's future direction and priorities within a changing environment is more important than the final document (or plan) produced.*

Objectives of the Strategic Planning Process

A creative and flexible strategic planning process enables stakeholders to reach a common understanding of the organization's environment and its strategy, unique position in the social service sector, and action priorities. The objectives of the planning process may include:

- increasing participants' understanding of the marketplace and competitive environment, including specific opportunities and threats,
- assessing the organization's strengths and weaknesses relative to other players in the sector,
- identifying the key issues facing the organization,
- exploring selected areas of strategy in greater depth,
- articulating a clear mission for the organization,
- defining what results must be achieved to be successful,
- developing action priorities to achieve the mission,
- developing measures to gauge progress.

Process Key Success Factors

The planning process should be designed to be fast-paced with the following characteristics:

Planning Champion — a strong, involved senior leader driving the effort; a facilitator will not achieve lasting results on his/her own.

Quick and simple — requiring a minimal amount of time using straightforward methods.

Fact-based — replacing personal conjecture and opinion with facts about the external and internal environment.

Action oriented — focusing on conclusions about the action required to implement the chosen direction.

Commitment and support — those responsible for implementation must be involved in developing the plan in order to obtain their understanding, commitment and support.

Flexible — responding to the needs of the participants, the information available, the learning acquired during the process, and the outcomes to be achieved.

Inclusive — it is best to make strategic planning as "inclusive" as possible by including representation of staff and volunteers from each of the key functional units within the organization. In addition, including board and board committee volunteers in the process will guarantee an enriched, diversified, objective and often "fresh" perspective.

Iterative — reviewing and revisiting concepts and conclusions reached in previous steps, allowing the opportunity for "soak time" and objective review.

Evolutionary — viewing each phase of the process as one step closer to the developing and evolving strategy. By continuing to evolve the strategy, it becomes clearer, more comprehensive and focused.

> *Process Tips: Be careful! The planning process will take as long as you give it. Establish the scope, schedule and outcomes at the outset. Resource the effort appropriately.*

Establishing and Maintaining a Successful Planning Environment

Four key components will ensure the planning environment is properly established and effectively maintained: 1) getting the organization and its key stakeholders ready to launch a strategic planning effort; 2) defining the roles of those involved in the planning process and those whose input is important to the planning process; 3) determining how best to engage stakeholders; and 4) facilitating the process.

Getting Started

In **Chapter 4**, *Getting Started,* we describe how to determine if the conditions are "right" within an organization for launching a planning process. Through the use of a strategic audit, an organization can determine what planning has been performed, what gaps currently exist within the organization's planning framework, and what needs to be accomplished through the anticipated planning effort. Two additional tools are provided to assess whether the organization is culturally and attitudinally ready to initiate a strategic planning effort. Circumstances that may impact and stall the timing of a planning effort are reviewed and potential organizational responses are offered.

Defining Roles

In **Chapter 5**, *Defining Roles,* the roles of key stakeholders in the planning process are described. Those stakeholders who are direct participants in the planning process are the executive director, strategic planning facilitator, board of directors, strategic planning committee, staff and may include a strategic planning working group and strategic planning consultant(s). Those stakeholders who provide input to the planning process and who need to be informed about the results of such an effort are clients, donors, funders, community leaders, other agencies and potential partners, and other experts. In addition, when and how to engage an external consultant is discussed.

Engaging Stakeholders

In **Chapter 6,** *Engaging Stakeholders,* communications terminology is defined. It illustrates by way of a communications spectrum the four phases in an organization's evolution toward strategic management of their communications. The components of a communications plan and how to recognize and respond to various types of organizational resistance to the planning effort are discussed.

Facilitating the Process

In **Chapter 7**, *Facilitating the Process,* the concept of facilitation is introduced. It describes the role of the facilitator and provides guidelines for facilitating a planning group. In addition, the frequent challenges faced by a facilitator when working with diverse groups and suggestions for possible techniques to overcome these difficulties are discussed.

Generic Steps in the Strategic Planning Process

A simple overall planning process, illustrated in **Figure 3-1**, *Steps in the Process,* has four steps: 1) situation assessment, 2) strategy definition, 3) agree on action, and 4) implementation and monitoring performance. Each step can be highly customized depending upon the degree to which various elements of the planning model have already been addressed. It may not be necessary to use all steps of this framework in all cases. The greatest benefit is realized, however, when *all* steps have been addressed to some degree. In this way people can more clearly understand how all the pieces of the puzzle fit together and where the weaker elements exist. The weaker elements can then be addressed in greater detail.

Regardless of the type of plan (that is, strategic plan or unit plan) being developed or updated, the steps, as presented here, remain the same.

FIGURE 3-1
Steps in the Process

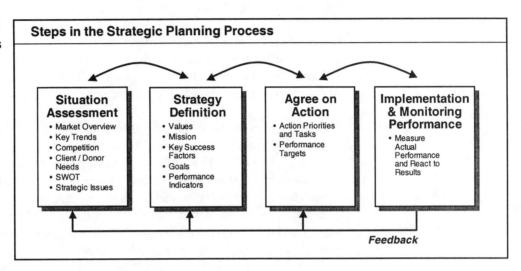

Steps in the Strategic Planning Process

Situation Assessment	Strategy Definition	Agree on Action	Implementation & Monitoring Performance
• Market Overview • Key Trends • Competition • Client / Donor Needs • SWOT • Strategic Issues	• Values • Mission • Key Success Factors • Goals • Performance Indicators	• Action Priorities and Tasks • Performance Targets	• Measure Actual Performance and React to Results

Feedback

Step 1 - Situation Assessment

The intent of a situation assessment is to provide information about the external environment in which the organization is operating, assess the organization's internal strengths and weaknesses, and identify the major issues and implications that may impact long-term success. Recognizing that most organizations in the social service sector do not consider themselves to be "selling" services into a "market" in the same way that private sector companies focus on markets to generate revenues, the term "market" is used here for convenience. The situation assessment includes market overview, key trends, competitors, client/donor needs, SWOT analysis, and strategic issues.

Market overview — clarifies how the organization defines the marketplace it is in, and describes that market's size, historical and projected growth, and the key dynamics and drivers shaping the market. **Chapter 8,** *Situation Assessment,* describes how to perform a market assessment in more detail. It also discusses how the term "market" is used in this social service context for convenience.

Key trends — summarizes the key developments unfolding in the market and which have the potential to impact the organization in some way. Trends may be economic, socio-political, demographic, technological (including information and electronic commerce) and/or philanthropic. They may also capture changing skill requirements and availability, changing regulation and so on. The most important consensus to reach at this time is what trends have the potential to impact the organization the most. **Chapter 8**, *Situation Assessment,* describes how to perform a trend analysis in more detail.

Competition — helps participants understand the distinctive market positioning of key alternative service providers, the threats and opportunities these players create, and the implications for the organization's own distinctive place in the market. Parameters such as services, size, relative strengths and weaknesses, performance, alliances and partnerships with other organizations, funding ability and sources are all helpful in describing alternative service providers and determining their distinctive place in the market. **Chapter 8,** *Situation Assessment,* describes how to perform a competitor assessment in more detail.

Client/donor needs — helps participants understand the current and evolving needs of clients and donors, categorizes clients and donors into segments of common needs and identifies what segments the organization can best serve. **Chapter 8,** *Situation Assessment,* describes how to perform a client/donor needs assessment in more detail.

Strengths, weaknesses, opportunities, threats (SWOT) analysis — identifies the internal strengths and weaknesses of the organization relative to other players within the same sector or market. The SWOT analysis also surfaces the external opportunities and threats within that market which may or may not be specific to the organization. This analysis helps the organization identify its competitive advantages. Strengths are internal advantages, usually a skill, process or organizational capability, that set the organization apart from others and which the organization should seek to leverage. Weaknesses are internal disadvantages that may impede success. Once identified, a decision must be made as to whether resources should be allocated to overcome specific weaknesses. Opportunities are external advantages that an organization could choose to seize. This decision is usually based on whether the opportunity leverages an existing organizational strength. Threats, or risks, are usually uncontrollable external events that may exert a significant impact on the organization's performance. Becoming aware of potential threats and discussing ways in which the organization could alter its course in response to any one of several key threats, is an essential part of the planning process. **Chapter 8**, *Situation Assessment,* describes how to perform a SWOT analysis in more detail.

Strategic issues — a limited, prioritized list of the critical questions the organization must address in its strategic plan. They are a distillation of all the information presented and discussed with respect to the situation assessment and the SWOT analysis. Because these issues provide the basis for defining the subsequent action priorities, the total number of issues should be between three to five. **Chapter 8**, *Situation Assessment* describes how to identify strategic issues in more detail. The focus here should be on strategic rather than operational issues. Strategic issues are those that fundamentally impact the organization's ability to meet the needs of its key stakeholders. Changing demographics and attitudes towards giving, charitable competition, and government funding cutbacks are all examples of strategic issues. Issues related to building and maintaining the human organization, standard setting, service/program delivery and so on tend to be more task-focused, that is operationally-focused, and are outside the scope of the discussion here.

The outcome of the situation assessment, step one of the planning process, is an understanding of the critical issues requiring a response from the organization as well as a factual information base that will support those making strategic choices and establishing priorities.

Step 2 - Strategy Definition

In the second step of the planning process, the results of the situation assessment are used as the context for reconfirming or revising the organization's values, mission, key success factors, goals and performance indicators. These elements of the planning model change infrequently. They do so only if there is a major shift in the environment or a change in senior leadership. Consequently, it is more common to reconfirm rather than fundamentally rethink these elements of the planning model each year. This text focuses on the initial definition of these strategy components, with suggestions for revisiting them on an annual basis.

The outcome of step two of the planning process is a renewed or revised statement of the organization's strategic framework — a clear articulation of what is to be accomplished, why, for whom and with what expected result. It is at this point in the process that the planning document is actually produced. An effective document will briefly summarize the situation assessment (about 10-12 pages) and the strategic issues to be addressed and the strategic framework (about 10-12 pages). **Figure 3-2**, *Table of Contents of a Strategic Plan*, illustrates how the table of contents of such a document might appear. Once prepared, the document needs to be circulated to key decision-makers to ensure that it accurately reflects the issues, agreed-to strategy and priorities. Keep in mind that the document is less important than the quality of the discussion and thinking, and the degree of understanding and commitment to the strategic priorities by the organization.

From here, the organization is ready to discuss specifically how to get the job done.

Step 3 - Agree on Action

Once an organization's strategic framework has been reaffirmed and the critical issues identified, it is time to figure out what to do about them. Action plans record not only how to address these issues but also the specific tasks to be completed by whom, by when and at what cost. At this stage in the process, discussion is often intense and frequently prolonged. The end result, however, is a limited, prioritized list of specific action steps agreed to by senior leadership and the staff and volunteers responsible for implementing them.

New insights frequently emerge at this stage. Be willing to revisit earlier steps in the process in order to take advantage of and integrate this new wisdom and information into the plan. New ideas, information and insights will emerge in all four steps of the planning process. Effectively and efficiently synthesizing and weaving these inputs into the ongoing dialogue will significantly strengthen the strategies and the organizational commitment to those strategies.

In defining action, the planning team often generates a long list of tasks it expects to accomplish within a one-year time horizon. Experience, practice and an objective perspective from someone outside the organization can help the team establish priorities, thereby ensuring that limited resources are targeted to the right areas.

You are now ready for implementation. At this point it is helpful to engage participants in thinking about maintaining momentum in the strategic planning process. **Worksheet 3-1**, *Maintaining Momentum*, is a helpful tool in getting participants to articulate next steps.

FIGURE 3-2
Table of Contents
of a Strategic Plan

Table of Contents of a Strategic Plan

Executive Summary
(One Page Summary)

1. **Situation Assessment**
   Market Overview
   Key Trends
   Competitive Analysis
   Client / Donor Needs and Segmentation
   SWOT Analysis
   - Strengths
   - Weaknesses
   - Opportunities
   - Threats
   Strategic Issues

2. **Statement of Strategy**
   Values
   Mission
   Goals
   Key Success Factors
   Performance Indicators

3. **Action Priorities**
   Objectives
   Prioritization Framework

4. **Performance Targets and Monitoring**
   Performance Targets
   Pro Forma Financial Statements

   Appendices
   Glossary of Planning Terms
   Planning Model
   Value Chain

Step 4 - Implementation and Monitoring Performance

Implementation is the critical element of any successful planning effort. Do not expend limited resources trying to craft the perfect plan. Instead, get to action quickly because implementation provides the necessary feedback on the relative success of a chosen strategy.

It is through this ongoing performance monitoring that feedback is provided to leadership. This provides leadership with signals to determine if remedial action or a comprehensive strategy renewal is required. For the monitoring and evaluating process

FIGURE 3-3
Example of a
Strategic Planning
Process

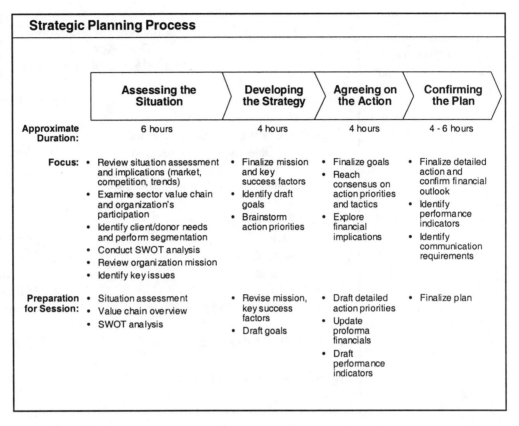

Strategic Planning Process

	Assessing the Situation	Developing the Strategy	Agreeing on the Action	Confirming the Plan
Approximate Duration:	6 hours	4 hours	4 hours	4 - 6 hours
Focus:	• Review situation assessment and implications (market, competition, trends) • Examine sector value chain and organization's participation • Identify client/donor needs and perform segmentation • Conduct SWOT analysis • Review organization mission • Identify key issues	• Finalize mission and key success factors • Identify draft goals • Brainstorm action priorities	• Finalize goals • Reach consensus on action priorities and tactics • Explore financial implications	• Finalize detailed action and confirm financial outlook • Identify performance indicators • Identify communication requirements
Preparation for Session:	• Situation assessment • Value chain overview • SWOT analysis	• Revise mission, key success factors • Draft goals	• Draft detailed action priorities • Update proforma financials • Draft performance indicators	• Finalize plan

to be successful, senior management and key volunteer leadership need to be involved in the discussion. Measuring results is the topic of **Chapter 11,** *Implementation and Monitoring Performance.* **Figure 3-3,** *Example of a Strategic Planning Process,* illustrates a typical planning process in terms of meeting focus, duration and preparation tasks. **Figures 3-4** to **3-7** are example agendas for each of the four meetings proposed in **Figure 3-3**, *Example of a Strategic Planning Process.*

The Ongoing Cycle of Planning

The strategic planning process is never actually finished. As illustrated in **Figure 3-8,** *Planning Cycle,* different types of planning activity occur at different times. While the budget is typically updated on an annual cycle at a particular time of year, strategic and unit plans may follow a different cycle yet still provide input to the budget. It is up to each individual organization to determine how often each level of planning occurs and when each step in the process needs to be scheduled. Operational realities, such as staff and key volunteer availability, major fundraising campaigns and service delivery commitments, will influence when planning initiatives can be successfully undertaken by the organization.

A three-year planning cycle for strategic planning is practical and best suited to organizations operating within the social service sector. In the first year, the situation assessment, strategy definition and action priorities are updated and the strategic plan is produced with a three-year time horizon. In years two and three, the organization evaluates the progress it has made toward its stated goals and revises the action priorities as

**Assessing the Situation
Draft Agenda**
(suggested length of time: 6 hours)

<u>Suggested Topic</u>	<u>Approximate Timing</u>
Establish Context and Ground Rules	
• State Objectives of the Session	15 minutes
• Outline Process	
• Identify Roles and Responsibilities	
Review Situation Assessment	
• Market	30 minutes
• Clients / Donors	60 minutes
• Competition	30 minutes
• Trends	45 minutes
• Sector Value Chain	45 minutes
Perform SWOT Analysis	30 minutes
Review Organization Mission	60 minutes
Identify Strategic Issues	30 minutes
Next Steps	15 minutes

**Developing the Strategy
Draft Agenda**
(suggested length of time: 4 hours)

<u>Suggested Topic</u>	<u>Approximate Timing</u>
Finalize Strategic Direction	
• Mission	
• Key Success Factors	60 minutes
Identify Draft Goals	60 minutes
Brainstorm Action Priorities and Tactics	90 minutes
Next Steps	30 minutes

Agreeing on the Action
Draft Agenda
(suggested length of time: 4 hours)

Suggested Topic	Approximate Timing
Finalize Goals	45 minutes
Finalize Action Priorities/Tactics	120 minutes
Explore Financial Implications • Define financial implications of action priorities/tactics • Review pro formas	 60 minutes
Next Steps	15 minutes

Confirming the Plan
Draft Agenda
(suggested length of time: 4-6 hours)

Suggested Topic	Approximate Timing
Confirm Components of the Plan • Mission • Key Success Factors • Goals • Action Priorities	60 minutes 60 minutes
Confirm Financial Outlook	60 minutes
Identify Performance Indicators	60 minutes
Identify Communication Requirements	60 minutes
Contingency	120 minutes

required. At the end of year three, the strategic planning process begins again with a scan of the external and internal environment. The strategic renewal effort will vary in its extensiveness depending upon the degree of change within the environment, senior management team and/or Board of Directors. What is most important, however, is that the planning process is ongoing and remains responsive to these changes.

FIGURE 3-8
Planning Cycle

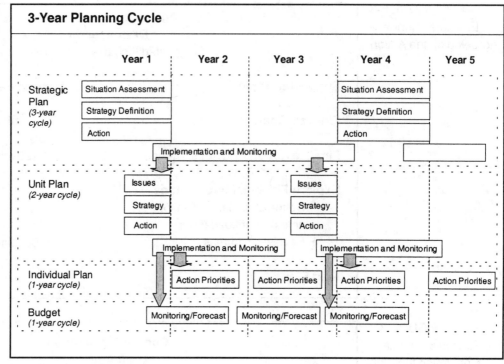

Process Tips: *Focus on developing a first draft of the strategic plan in year one. Focus on building or enhancing individual sections of the strategic plan in subsequent planning cycles.*

Figure 3-9, *Example of Strategic Planning Process,* illustrates the actual steps undertaken by United Way of Calgary and Area and how these planning steps were spread out over a period of time.

FIGURE 3-9
Example of Strategic
Planning Process

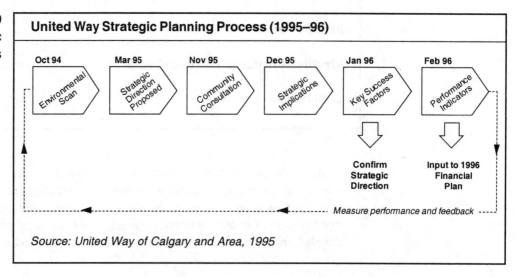

The Link to Unit Plans

The organization's unit plans will be influenced by the priorities set in the strategic plan as well as the organizational structure of the units themselves. The essence of these unit plans are the same as the strategic plan: a clear, brief statement of the critical issues to be addressed within the planning period, a description of the mission, key success factors, goals and performance indicators for the unit, and a limited, prioritized list of specific action to be undertaken usually within a 12 to 18 month horizon. Unit plans are typically prepared and updated annually. The operational nature of these plans and their closer link to budgeting activities requires that they be updated more frequently than the strategic plan. These unit plans are useful when they provide clear guidance for implementation as well as how results need to be monitored.

As introduced in this chapter, the four key components to ensuring a successful planning environment is established and maintained are situation assessment, strategy definition, agree on action and implementation and monitoring performance. **Figure 3-10**, *Successful Planning Checklist*, is a convenient list of success elements to consider when designing a planning process. The next four chapters discuss in greater detail each of the four components introduced here, starting with assessing the organization's readiness to embrace the process.

FIGURE 3-10
Successful Planning
Checklist

Successful Planning Checklist
A successful planning process will: • clarify expectations about end results at the outset of the planning process   • be planned out prior to its initiation   • move quickly so that changes in the environment do not pass by the organization   • be managed   • involve people from all levels of the organization   • develop concepts about the future direction — not the details   • not stop once the vision and strategy are defined — concrete actions must also be defined   • not stop once the strategic plan has been produced — results are achieved through implementation, not the planning itself   • integrate plans across all levels of the organization   • periodically review implementation progress

Summary

A well thought-out strategic planning process encompasses the efforts required to establish and maintain an environment that engages stakeholders in meaningful ways, promotes consensus building, and leads to the sequential steps of a basic strategic plan. Planning is an ongoing management responsibility, not a one-time project to be completed. It is an iterative activity focused on discussion and consensus building that clarifies and builds commitment to the organization's future direction and priorities within a changing environment. The objectives and key success factors of the strategic planning process are presented. The steps for establishing and maintaining a successful planning environment as well as the four generic steps in the strategic planning process are introduced. The process of planning is ongoing, with aspects of the plan being revisited regularly but at varying intervals.

WORKSHEET 3-1
Maintaining Momentum

Maintaining Momentum Worksheet
In your opinion, as a Board member or senior manager, what are the next three action steps required to maintain the momentum of the strategic planning process? 1. _____ _____ _____ 2. _____ _____ _____ 3. _____ _____ _____

Section 2

Establishing and Maintaining the Environment for Successful Planning

Establishing and Maintaining the Environment for Successful Planning describes, in four chapters, the key ingredients required to establish and maintain an environment for successful planning.

CHAPTER 4

Getting Started

Is the organization ready?

The saying "timing is everything" could never be more true than when undertaking strategic planning. Before embarking on any strategic planning effort, consider answering the following key questions: Are the required conditions of leadership support, a clear reason for change and clear expectations satisfied? What are the gaps in the current strategic framework? Is the organization ready to plan? Combined, these three questions and the tools associated with them determine how well prepared and willing the organization is to commit to a planning process. The purpose of this chapter is to introduce each of these tools and describe how they can be applied in a social service context. The chapter concludes with a discussion about how to establish the purpose and expected outcomes for an organization's planning process based on its "readiness" to plan.

Conditions of "Readiness"

As with any major effort, a strategic planning process has its proper time and place in the lifecycle of an organization. Certain conditions must exist for the planning to be effective. It is not uncommon for a planning process to be initiated (often by an overly exuberant planning leader or Board Chair) before an organization is ready to meet the challenges and demands of the task. If launched prematurely, the planning process can stall, deliver less than satisfactory results or stop altogether. Once this has happened, it becomes even more difficult to restart the process at some time in the future.

Three essential conditions must exist within an organization for planning to be successful: 1) leadership support, 2) a clear reason for change, and 3) clear expectations. Here is how to recognize and characterize each of these conditions.

Leadership Support — The most important condition is leadership support. It is essential that the Executive Director, the Board Chair and other informal leaders of the board recognize the need for planning and are willing to devote the time and energy necessary to make the effort worthwhile. If these leaders are not enthusiastically committed at the outset, then the wisest choice is to delay the planning initiative until leadership support exists.

37

Leadership support is described as a willingness to champion the planning process and fight for the resources (both financial and human) necessary to see it through. These leaders must also demonstrate and model a willingness to question the status quo, to look at new ways of doing things, to ask hard questions, face difficult choices and make difficult decisions. Most of all, they must be persistent in their drive to achieve visible results.

Regardless of an organization's need to plan, no one individual is able to initiate a planning process that reaches a successful outcome as a solo activity. This does not preclude, however, an individual from working to amass leadership support over time.

Clear Reason for Change — A second condition is the existence of a clear driver or issue that demands organizational attention. The more urgent the driver or issue, the more likely the organization is to recognize the need for, respond to and actively support a planning initiative. There is nothing like 'panic' for galvanizing a group of managers and leaders into some serious, dedicated and thorough planning discussions and decisions.

Clear Expectations — A third condition is a board and staff that understand the purpose of planning and appreciate what it can and cannot accomplish. Consensus around the desired outcomes of the process is an important aspect of clear expectations. In addition, leaders must acknowledge the need to allocate resources to the planning process. These resources include, but are not limited to staff time, board time, consultant time, systems and processes, and market research.

Of these three conditions, leadership support is the most critical. If this condition does not exist within the organization, delay strategic planning efforts and redirect those efforts to developing leadership support instead. Strong, committed leadership will help create and sustain the second two conditions of "readiness," a clear imperative and clear expectations. Ideally, the organization needs to have all three of these conditions in place before it commits to a planning effort.

The Strategic Audit

Once it has been determined the conditions are right for launching a planning process, it is time to evaluate what planning has been performed within the organization, identify where the gaps lie within the organization's planning framework and prioritize what needs to be accomplished through the anticipated planning effort. Performing a strategic audit will clarify for the organization where it stands on each of these parameters.

The strategic audit is simply a questionnaire. It can be answered verbally or written by a small group of senior managers with the results presented to the board for their review and action. Alternatively, the questionnaire can be administered to cover a broad spectrum of staff, management and volunteers so that potentially a broader variation in perspectives can be compared and contrasted. Gaps in expectations, focus and information will emerge through the discussion and the systematic analysis of that discussion. Armed with this information, the planning team can then design a planning process that best addresses the gaps.

The added benefit of seeking broader input to the strategic audit is that the participants are being prepared, ahead of the formal planning process, to think about the issues, the clarity of the imperative and the expectations. For all intents and purposes, the planning process may be considered launched once the questions of the strategic audit are being asked.

All organizations, regardless of their planning sophistication, would benefit from undertaking a strategic audit periodically. An organization will not pass or fail such an assessment, but it will gain critical information about where misalignment or competing priorities and expectations exist.

Figure 4-1, *Basic Strategic Audit Questionnaire*, outlines a simplified questionnaire for those who wish to undertake a quick and informal approach to a strategic audit.

Figure 4-2, *Comprehensive Strategic Audit Questionnaire,* outlines the key questions to be asked in a comprehensive strategic audit.

Organizational Readiness Assessment

An organizational readiness assessment is a self-evaluation focused on the culture and attitudes of the staff and volunteers. Two organizational readiness tools are included in this section. The first tool, presented in **Figure 4-3,** *Organizational Readiness Assessment,* is a series of questions that are typically asked prior to commencing a strategic planning effort. This tool may be used in whole or in part; conducted by internal staff or external parties; and if required, can be repeated upon completion of a strategic planning or change effort. The second tool discussed in **Chapter 6**, *Engaging Stakeholders*, is presented in **Figure 6-5A**, *Temperature Check,* and is used to gauge ongoing staff and volunteer reaction to broad or specific issues relevant to the strategic planning effort. The power of both assessments is that reactions to specific issues, perception gaps and competing priorities are identified and defined for all stakeholders to see and understand.

The organizational readiness assessment tools are most effective when broad organizational representation is desirable. Ideally, the assessment questionnaires should

FIGURE 4-1
Basic Strategic
Audit Questionnaire

Basic Strategic Audit Questionnaire	Yes	No
1. Do internal stakeholders agree on and support the purpose and values of the organization?	☐	☐
2. Is there a shared understanding of what the organization is trying to accomplish?	☐	☐
3. Is there agreement regarding which clients should be the focus of organizational efforts?	☐	☐
4. Is there agreement regarding which donors should be the focus of organizational efforts?	☐	☐
5. Are the organization's planning efforts strategic?	☐	☐
6. Are the organization's planning efforts operational?	☐	☐
7. Are roles clear within the organization?	☐	☐
8. Are action plans clearly articulated and prioritized?	☐	☐
9. Are resources allocated randomly to activities and projects without thought to overall integration and efficiency?	☐	☐

FIGURE 4-2
Comprehensive
Strategic Audit
Questionnaire

Comprehensive Strategic Adult Questionnaire

Strategic Plan Understanding

1. Are you aware of your organization's strategic plan? If yes, what time horizon does the plan cover?
2. How would you describe the organization's mission, goals and objectives?
3. Are the mission, goals and objectives understood?
   Board perspective   _____
   Staff perspective   _____
   Volunteer perspective _____

Organization Structure and Culture

4. How is the organization currently structured? Describe the decision making process.
5. How well does the present organizational structure fit the organization's goals and objectives, policies and programs?
6. Who are the senior leaders and what are their chief characteristics in terms of knowledge, skill, background and style?
7. What is the senior leaders' involvement in strategic planning?
8. Describe the organizational culture. How is it consistent / inconsistent with the current goals, objectives, policies and programs?

Environmental Factors

9. What are the key environmental (external) factors affecting the organization and its strategies? Which of these factors are the most important in the short term? In the long term?

Stakeholder Perceptions

10. Who are the organization's major stakeholders?
11. To what extent do each of these stakeholders impact the organization?
12. How do you think these stakeholders perceive the organization's goals and objectives?

Improvement Initiatives

13. What concepts and techniques are managers using to evaluate and improve organizational performance? Can you identify specific initiatives that are underway?
14. Are critical characteristics of key processes defined and are these processes consistent and capable in terms of the strategy?

Donors and Clients

15. Are donor and client requirements defined and translated into a process for delivery?
16. Is there opportunity for donors and clients to provide feedback that can be used to improve service delivery?

Measuring Success

17. How is overall success of the organization measured? Are there specific measures in place?

Individual's Perspective

18. What are your strengths in terms of knowledge, skill, background and style?
19. Are the resources allocated to your area adequate relative to attaining what is contemplated by the goals and objectives?
20. What are your recommendations for achieving improved performance in your area?
21. Compared to other similar organizations, what level of risk would you associate with your current goals and objectives?

Assessing the Strategy

22. What strengths exist that will enable your organization to achieve its strategic direction?
23. What short and long-term challenges are facing your organization?
24. Is the current strategy adequate to address these challenges?
25. If the strategy is not adequate, what changes do you recommend?
26. Are adequate control measures in place to ensure organizational alignment with the strategic plan?

be administered to capture representative opinions from board members, staff and volunteers at all levels and within all functions of the organization. Conducting a readiness assessment at the outset of the planning effort provides baseline data that can be used for comparison with subsequent assessments, making it possible to gauge progress and changing attitudes throughout the duration of the planning initiative.

FIGURE 4-3
Organizational
Readiness
Assessment

Organizational Readiness Assessment

1. Do you know what you are expected to accomplish in the next 1, 2 and 3 years (related to the organization's strategic direction)?
2. How long do you think it will be before you will be able to say the organization has achieved its strategic direction?
3. The pace of change in my area is (about right, too fast, not fast enough).
4. Is the organization ready and willing to recognize individual and team contributions?
5. How does senior management communicate with staff and volunteers?
6. How frequent are these communications?
7. What kinds of communications are used (formal or informal)?
8. Is the climate right to begin a strategic planning initiative in your organization?
9. What will the barriers to success be (prioritized)?

Circumstances Impacting the Readiness to Plan

Several circumstances may impact and stall the timing of a planning effort within an organization. Once these circumstances have been identified (as they usually are through the process of conducting a strategic audit and an organizational readiness assessment) the planning team needs to determine how best to design or modify the planning process and the desired outcomes within the realities of these circumstances. The potential pitfalls to be aware of, and the possible response of the organization facing each circumstance, are in the scenarios described below.

Scenario 1

Pitfall: Senior management and/or staff are distracted by a current operating crisis or major commitment (such as a major fundraising campaign).
Response: Bring the operating crisis under control or complete the commitment before initiating a strategic planning effort.

Scenario 2

Pitfall: Leadership of the organization (either senior management or board) is in transition.
Response: Use the planning effort to determine what type of leadership is required to lead the organization towards its vision. Alternatively, delay the planning process until the new leader is onboard and can be an integral part of the initiative.

Scenario 3

Pitfall: Senior leadership assumes that strategic planning can be delegated to staff, volunteers or consultants.
Response: Without committed and involved leadership, delay planning until there is a change of heart in the leadership or a change in leadership. Planning efforts that are delegated quickly lose credibility and commitment within the organization.

Scenario 4

Pitfall: Senior leadership is not willing to accept the decisions that evolve from the process.
Response: Actively involve key leaders and people of influence in the process every step of the way. Assign these individuals to be key spokespersons, decision-makers and network builders.

Scenario 5

Pitfall: Board or senior leadership is unwilling to be inclusive.
Response: Significantly scale back the planning effort or delay planning until there is a change in the approach and style of the leadership or a change in the leadership itself. One way to introduce and encourage leadership to be more inclusive in their planning is to schedule opportunities for leaders from other organizations to share their planning experiences in a confidential setting. Learning directly from those who have worked through the process will help less experienced leaders gain the courage and perspective they require to open the process to more diversified input. A strategic plan is considerably stronger when the input is from a variety of sources and perspectives.

Scenario 6

Pitfall: The organizational climate does not inspire forward thinking or reward creativity and strategic thinking.

Response: Create frequent, small opportunities for key stakeholders to provide their input to the process. Introduce tools such as brainstorming, puzzles and games to help open up the possibilities and stimulate creativity. Bring in external speakers who can offer new perspectives and challenge the organization to think in new directions. Offer mechanisms for people to provide their ideas anonymously, such as a comment box, so that the organization can begin to discuss new ideas in non-threatening environments.

Scenario 7

Pitfall: The planning process gets bogged down, failing to reach consensus on a limited, prioritized, clear set of action steps.

Response: The planning team needs to keep moving the process forward, either through a highly visible schedule, or by focusing and refocusing discussion on the most relevant and important issues. This is where a strong facilitator is worth their weight in gold. It is easy to get off on tangents in the course of planning discussions. The tendency is to solve the issues that are raised in the course of the discussions immediately, rather than to determine:

- when the discussion should be scheduled,
- who should be involved,
- what information is required,
- what outcomes are expected.

A facilitated process will increase the likelihood of reaching clear action priorities within the timeframe allotted.

How to Measure Readiness

The merits and organizational readiness for a strategic planning effort are best reviewed by conducting a facilitated board and staff planning session. This session can be used as a way of evaluating the results of the strategic audit and organizational readiness assessment. At this stage, an outside facilitator can be of particular benefit in posing the readiness questions and facilitating a discussion that will surface and explore underlying issues and concerns. The objectivity and skill of the facilitator involved will ensure that all pertinent information is surfaced in an attempt to assist the organization to determine if this is the right time to undertake a strategic planning effort. The session can also be used as a way of exploring what other issues may need to be addressed before a planning effort can be initiated. **Chapter 5,** *Defining Roles*, provides a detailed perspective on the role of outside assistance in the planning process.

Delaying is an Option

There is danger in launching a planning process unless the necessary conditions can be met and there is agreement to proceed from senior management and the board. Even under the right conditions, there may be other reasons to question an organization's readiness. The trick is not to hesitate, but to delay before you start! Strategic planning is immensely useful but it can easily be sabotaged by a lack of honesty on behalf of the organization in terms of organizational readiness. One negative experience can turn an organization off planning forever, when a delay can make all the difference in timing and result in ultimate success.

How to Prepare the Organization

Once it has been decided that a strategic planning effort is going to be undertaken, it is important to start communicating with employees and other key stakeholders as soon as possible. This communication should be focused on ensuring that participants, as well as those likely to be affected by the process, are aware of the planning effort, what to expect and how it might involve or impact them. In addition, this communication needs to clearly set the context for the effort and create a compelling case for change.

While communication planning is dealt with in more detail in **Chapter 6,** *Engaging Stakeholders*, several suggestions for how this communication can be accomplished include:

- a kick-off event for all employees and key stakeholders hosted by senior management and the board,
- a feature in the organization's newsletter,
- employee/stakeholder workshops,
- a question-and-answer web site on the organization's intranet.

Resistance to Change

Strategic planning involves fundamentally rethinking all aspects of the organization's direction and how it delivers value. This means an open and objective examination of what things are done for what purpose, how these things are done and by whom. This assessment requires participants, many of whom have been responsible for designing and managing the existing systems and processes within an organization, to actively consider how these same systems and processes can be improved or changed in often significant ways or maybe even discarded altogether.

In some instances, change or improvement implies that the old or existing is not good enough. In other instances, change implies an unknown or uncertain future. In either case, it is human nature to resist change before embracing a new reality. **Figure 4-4,** *Emotional Cycle of Change*, illustrates this resistance/acceptance cycle and describes how participants in a planning effort may feel as the process unfolds.

Leading organizations acknowledge, up-front, that there will be a natural resistance/acceptance change cycle associated with the planning process. They spend time actively and consistently communicating this understanding throughout the organization at the start, middle and end of the planning process. This continuous education effort makes it easier for people to recognize and manage resistance when it happens in themselves or within their teams.

Anticipate where pockets of employees or stakeholders may feel particularly threatened by the planning process and the change it brings. Create safe places and circumstances where these people can communicate their concerns and issues with leaders, either directly or anonymously. **Chapter 6,** *Engaging Stakeholders*, provides

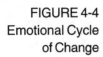
FIGURE 4-4
Emotional Cycle
of Change

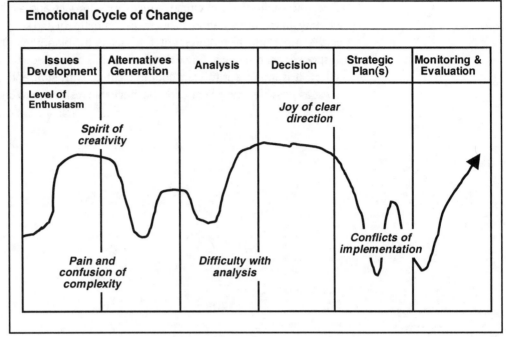

more information about effective communication planning while **Chapter 7,** *Facilitating the Process,* suggests tools and approaches which may prove helpful if you are faced with resistance.

Process Tips: *People are usually open to change as long as they can continue to perform their jobs well and have a feeling of security. Inherently, people just want to be able to do a good job.*

Continuous Improvement

By continuously asking questions and assessing the answers, an organization is able to pinpoint where incremental improvements can be made in its services and the processes and systems related to the delivery of those services. Organizations that routinely go through self-evaluations of this nature will discover that they can identify and readily eliminate unneeded activities. It is these types of organizations that tend to involve their staff in all levels of decision making and problem solving.

Assessing the organization's readiness for planning is the first of the four chapters in **Section 2,** *Establishing and Maintaining an Environment for Successful Planning.* Determining which key stakeholders should be involved and what are their roles (the second chapter in this section) is discussed in **Chapter 5,** *Defining Roles.*

Summary

Strategic planning results depend greatly on the cultural and attitudinal "readiness" of the organization to launch and sustain a strategic planning effort. The state of readiness can be measured and evaluated using an Organizational Readiness Assessment and a

Strategic Audit. Several circumstances may impact and stall the timing of a planning effort within an organization. Leadership commitment and support of the planning initiative is the most critical requirement for successful planning. Other pitfalls and possible responses are discussed. Once the decision has been made to initiate a strategic planning effort, it is important to start communicating with staff and other key stakeholders as soon as possible, and prepare for the inevitable resistance to change that will undoubtedly arise.

CHAPTER 5

Defining Roles

Who does what?

Communication and broad engagement of key stakeholders are two essential components of a successful strategic planning effort. The planning leader faces the difficult task of identifying and engaging the organization's stakeholders in ways that allow those stakeholders to contribute in meaningful ways. This task is a tricky one, particularly if the organization is large or has many complex networks of interested people. This chapter focuses on who should be involved in the planning process and describes their respective roles and responsibilities.

Inclusive Process

For best results, strategic planning should be an inclusive process that engages the right stakeholders in a meaningful way. Although a truly inclusive process demands more time and resources, the benefits to be gained from this approach are significant and more likely to be sustainable in the long-term. A few of the benefits likely to be experienced from undertaking an inclusive approach include:

- commitment to the organization's strategic direction and its implementation since involvement and contribution build understanding leading to commitment,
- open lines of communication among stakeholders including staff, management, board, clients, donors and others,
- diversity of perspectives and skills that are better able to challenge traditional thinking and approaches resulting in a more robust strategic direction,
- stronger internal and external relationships as a result of working together in a process of discovery and consensus building.

Social service organizations play a direct role in providing service to their communities. However, they typically have multiple communities when it comes to responsiveness and accountability. Consequently, social service organizations need to take into account the perspectives of many stakeholders, including the opinions of those not usually sought.

47

This inherent need for an inclusive process must be balanced against the limited resources available to consult and fully engage stakeholders and make timely decisions.

Regardless of the degree to which the input of multiple stakeholders is sought and incorporated into the planning process, Board and senior management leadership remains important. For this reason, a planning process that combines Board and senior management direction (sometimes referred to as top-down) and multiple stakeholder input (sometimes referred to as bottom-up) is the most successful approach to use in social service organizations.

Key Stakeholders

A stakeholder is defined as anyone internal or external to the organization who has an interest, or stake, in the organization and its future, including those responsible for creating, approving, communicating and implementing the strategic direction. Individuals and groups affected by the strategic direction or those who could impact its successful implementation should also be considered as stakeholders.

Stakeholders who are considered peripheral, or outside the immediate circle of the organization, frequently have unique and valuable perspectives to offer about the organization, its services, style and future direction. In designing the planning process, it is helpful to determine who these players are in the community and how best to consult with them.

When identifying who the stakeholders are and how they should be included in the planning process, it is also important to identify who should *not* be, or cannot be, included. Persons or groups may be bypassed for political reasons, budget or time constraints, a negative attitude towards the organization, a reluctance to devote sufficient time and effort to the initiative, or if it is anticipated that the challenges they will cause outweigh the benefit of their involvement. It is best to be clear up-front about whose input will and will not be sought in the process.

This section describes the role of key stakeholders in the planning process. Those stakeholders who are direct participants in the planning process are the executive director, strategic planning facilitator, board of directors, strategic planning committee, and staff; and, may include a strategic planning working group and strategic planning consultant(s). Those community stakeholders who should be consulted during the planning process and who need to be informed about the results of such an effort include clients, donors, funders, community leaders, other agencies and potential partners, and other experts.

Key Stakeholders Directly Involved

Executive Director

The leadership and commitment of the executive director is essential for the success of any strategic planning initiative. It goes without saying that if the executive director is not behind the effort, the effort will fail because there will likely not be sufficient commitment to implementation. S/he is frequently the instigator behind the effort and the prime contact between the board's strategic planning committee and the staff. The most important roles an executive director can play are:

Champion:
- be accountable for leading the planning effort,
- remove obstacles to the process and make sure that the necessary resources are available to support the planning effort,
- ensure ongoing organizational commitment to planning for the long-term,
- demonstrate commitment to the organization's values through action, words and behavior,
- accept responsibility for making hard decisions.

Process Manager:
- select and support a strategic planning facilitator,
- ensure integration across functional lines during the development and implementation of the plan.

Communicator:
- foster enthusiasm and support for the planning effort,
- make it safe to question, take risk, have and express positive and negative feelings, be innovative and make mistakes,
- communicate the results of the planning process frequently, clearly and with passion.

The executive director does not need to be the source of 'all the answers'; rather, this pivotal leader is most helpful when s/he acts in a facilitating capacity, nurturing and promoting full discussion and ensuring the environment is such that ideas are freely generated and exchanged.

Strategic Planning Facilitator

The strategic planning facilitator may be internal to the organization, for example a designate of the executive director, or external to the organization, for example, a consultant. It is preferable to have someone who does not have a vested interest in the outcome. Although a member of the senior management team may have the skill to perform this role, s/he should avoid doing so in order that all members of the team be able to take advocacy positions on certain issues and express personal convictions freely during discussions.

The strategic planning facilitator needs to have personal confidence and the respect of participants in order to surface and resolve underlying conflicts when required. This is a role that is frequently difficult for an internal person to perform. The strength of an internal person is that s/he brings an in-depth knowledge of the organization and generally is more accessible than an external consultant. On the other hand, an external consultant brings a broader and more diverse experience and is usually perceived to be more objective than an internal person. An effective option is to create an internal/external team that brings the best of both worlds.

The strategic planning facilitator's primary role is to enable groups and organizations to work more effectively; to collaborate and achieve synergy. S/he is a "content neutral" party who by not taking sides or expressing or advocating a point of view during the meeting, can advocate for fair, open and inclusive procedures to accomplish the group's work. The role of the strategic planning facilitator is to:

- guide and manage the systematic development of the strategic plan components,
- ensure clear action results from each planning session,
- provide tools and techniques as required,
- establish meeting ground rules and group norms, making it safe for everyone to participate,
- challenge traditional assumptions and provide objectivity,
- build group consensus.

In **Chapter 7**, *Facilitating the Process*, the role of facilitator and the challenges s/he faces are described in greater detail.

Board of Directors

Social service boards tend to be larger than corporate boards because they need to represent the organization's many stakeholders and have broad-based community leadership support for fundraising. The overall responsibilities of the board of an organization specifically related to strategic planning are:

- approve the mission of the organization and review it at least every three years,
- ensure a common vision exists,
- align policies with strategic direction,
- guide the planning process and approve the strategic direction and priorities,
- ensure adequate financial resources for the planning effort,
- understand the sector in which the organization is operating in order to have a fact-basis from which to make strategic decisions,
- monitor external relations with key external stakeholders to gauge the impact of strategic change,
- communicate the results of the planning process frequently, clearly and with passion.

Working in partnership with senior management, the board has a vital role to fulfill in providing input to the organization's priorities and future direction. Either directly, or through its Strategic Planning Committee, the board needs to be involved or at least kept informed throughout the planning process. Prior to the Toronto Stock Exchange's (TSE) Dey Report of 1994 recommending that boards be accountable for setting organizational strategy, corporate board involvement in strategic planning was inconsistent. This pivotal report has resulted in the current trend toward working boards (that is, those that take on strategy accountability) rather than purely advisory boards (that is, those that delegate the strategy accountability to senior management) in the corporate sector. This trend is also evident in leading social service organizations. Given this accountability, board members need a meaningful way to contribute their external, broader view of the organization, its mandate, strengths, weaknesses, opportunities and threats. A well-designed planning process is the logical vehicle for the work of the Board.

Strategic Planning Committee

The Strategic Planning Committee of the board may be either a standing committee or an ad hoc committee (which may also be known as a task force). Standing committees are permanent subcommittees of the board, while ad hoc committees have a pre-defined task and timeframe within which to accomplish that assignment. They both derive their authority from and report regularly to the board of directors. Given the need for continuity in the strategic planning process, a standing committee is the preferred approach.

The role of the Strategic Planning Committee is to:

- define, manage and communicate the process for strategy development and review,
- remove obstacles to the process,
- collect data, synthesize findings and prepare draft materials and recommendations for the board,
- identify opportunities to integrate across the organization,
- maintain momentum in the process,
- foster enthusiasm and support for the planning effort.

In addition to directors, the Strategic Planning Committee would benefit from senior management input as well as high-profile community leaders willing to contribute their knowledge, expertise and network. A significant side benefit of community leader participation is the advocacy role they can assume for new initiatives and related funding in the implementation phase of the planning process.

Strategic Planning Committee membership size depends upon the extent of the Committee's role, size of the organization and the scope of the planning initiative(s) underway. When the scope, sophistication and magnitude of the planning effort justifies the need for additional resources, a Strategic Planning Working Group may be used to support the work of the Strategic Planning Committee.

Strategic Planning Working Group

In larger organizations or in more extensive strategic planning efforts, additional resources may be required to support the Strategic Planning Committee. These resources can be assembled in a Strategic Planning Working Group. When such a Working Group is assembled, the role of the Strategic Planning Committee is elevated to focus on formulating recommendations for the Board and managing the planning process, leaving the data collection and synthesis to the Working Group. More specifically, the role of a Working Group is to:

- make recommendations to define and evolve the planning process as obstacles and issues arise in the course of performing the work,
- collect data, synthesize findings, prepare draft materials, and draft recommendations for the review of the Strategic Planning Committee,
- identify opportunities to integrate across the organization,
- make suggestions and recommendations to maintain momentum, enthusiasm and support for the planning effort.

One common mistake when organizing to undertake a strategic planning initiative is to assemble a Working Group that is fully representative of all the stakeholders. The result of this action is usually a large, cumbersome, bureaucratic structure that is slow to define priorities and make decisions. Participants tend to gravitate to, and then solidify, their representative positions and fail to evolve their perspectives for the best of the overall organization. At best, consensus is time consuming to achieve and at worst consensus is impossible to reach.

It is much more effective and helpful to assemble a Working Group that is competency-based ("competency-based" implies special skills or knowledge, such as client or donor knowledge, community knowledge, media/public relations expertise), reflecting the skills and capabilities from across the organization and drawing from the organization's informal leaders. The best results are produced when the Working Group is kept to no more than 12 team members that are a combination of visionaries and doers with diverse backgrounds. Although desirable in some circumstances, any more than 15 people on the Working Group becomes difficult to manage. Team members have considerably less "airtime" to discuss and evolve key issues, concepts and actions not to mention the logistical difficulty of scheduling meetings and sticking to timelines. The primary requirement for each member of the Working Group is a commitment to the overall direction of the organization and a positive attitude. The Working Group is a good place to incorporate external consulting expertise.

Staff

Staff has program expertise, knowledge about clients and ultimate responsibility for implementing the plan. Consequently, their early involvement in the discussions and decisions increases the likelihood of organizational buy-in and commitment. The benefit of having staff interact with the Strategic Planning Committee is enhancement of organizational memory of the subtle choices made as a result of complex and frequently lengthy discussions. Always keep in mind that staff has a vested interest in the practicality of the outcome because they remain with the organization through the struggles of implementation. Volunteer board members also have a vested interest in the outcome but their livelihood does not depend directly on the success of the organization, nor are they impacted by the complexities and stresses of implementation.

The role of staff in strategic planning is to:

- take accountability for implementation and integration across the organization,
- freely contribute ideas and suggestions in a positive manner,
- take responsibility for getting involved, asking questions and remaining informed,
- nurture and support each other,
- externally communicate a positive attitude about the organization,
- communicate information to key stakeholders,
- walk the talk.

Strategic Planning Consultant(s)

Not all social service organizations possess the expertise, experience or special knowledge required to design and manage a strategic planning effort. In addition, social service organizations are complex and political because of their extensive volunteer networks, connections into other community agencies and funding sources. Consequently, knowing when and how to use external assistance for strategic planning is a sign of leadership strength not weakness. In the long run such a decision saves the organization time, stress and money.

A good case could be made for the decision to hire external consultants. Consultants can play several roles:

- *Project manager* – design, implement and facilitate the strategic planning process; design and facilitate strategic planning meetings; and perform tasks that the organization simply does not have time to undertake.
- *Expert* – provide tried and true tools and methods for strategic planning; research and analyze information; and provide objective, expert opinions.
- *Coach* – train individuals within the organization involved in the planning process.
- *Catalyst* – challenge traditional ways of thinking; and surface and manage conflict.

A Word About Leadership

The foregoing discussion about the key stakeholders directly involved in the process has identified the need for leadership at many levels. Two distinct leadership roles, strategic and operational, are required during a strategic planning process. Both leadership roles are important and their differences need to be recognized and understood.

Strategic Leaders

Strategic leaders are skilled in understanding existing markets as well as selecting future markets and opportunities in which to invest the organization's limited resources in order to sustain, and in some cases grow, the organization. They are able to create and nurture a common vision across the organization. Strategic leaders initiate, support and provide leadership to change initiatives and create an organizational environment that is so exciting people want to be a part of the adventure.

Operational Leaders

Operational leaders are skilled at managing resources already invested to maximize benefits and outcomes. They provide stability in the midst of change and keep the organization focused on the mission. Operational leaders maintain the excitement in the adventure.

Community Stakeholders to be Consulted and Informed

Clients and Donors

Clients are the recipients of the service provided by the social service organization and donors are the source of time, money and talent provided directly or indirectly to the organization. The role of both clients and donors in strategic planning is to provide critical input to, rather than to participate directly in, the strategic planning process. Through focus groups, interviews, surveys and other similar mechanisms, information about past, current and potential clients and donors and their needs, as well as their unique first-hand experience of the organization can be gathered. **Chapter 8**, *Situation Assessment,* provides greater detail about how client and donor input can be obtained.

Funders

Funders play a role similar to clients and donors in the planning process in that they provide input rather than participate in the process. Their perspective regarding sectoral trends as well as an organization's relative strengths and weaknesses is valuable because of their broader view of the social service sector and experience with individual social service organizations. In addition, funders can be helpful sounding boards and sources of feedback to test and validate straw-model strategies and "fundability" of new programs.

Community Leaders

In addition to the potential involvement in the Strategic Planning Committee described above, individual community leaders can provide opinions and perspectives about an organization's strengths and weaknesses. Similar to funders, community leaders often have broad knowledge of community needs and alternative service providers. Therefore, the role of community leaders is usually to provide input to the planning process.

Other Agencies and Potential Partners

For organizations new to strategic planning, the input from other agencies and potential partners is not necessary. With time and increased planning sophistication, it may be worthwhile to solicit the input of these groups.

Experts in the Field

Experts in the field may also provide an informed external view of the environment in which the organization is operating. Their objectivity can help to identify the organization's key strengths and weaknesses, opportunities and threats. Importantly for the organization, experts can identify emerging competitors and sources of non-traditional competition.

Establishing Accountability

With an extensive strategic planning effort, it is also necessary to be more specific and rigorous about the definition and assignment of roles. Every organization wants to be effective at what it does, and the importance of clarifying roles and responsibilities to assure this effectiveness cannot be overstated.

Simply stated, identifying *What has to be done?* and *Who must do it?* helps clear up ambiguities and redundancies within the organization as it struggles to implement a new direction or refocused priorities. Answering these two questions clarifies relationships among staff and volunteers, and motivates staff and volunteers to work together in new and more effective ways. When roles and responsibilities are clearly understood, a function or activity is moved to the most appropriate level within the organization.

Responsibility Framework

The process of identifying responsibilities provides a straight forward way for the Strategic Planning Working Group to resolve what has to get done and who will do it throughout the strategic planning effort. The components of a clear responsibility framework are:

Responsible

Do the Job (R) individuals are the doers or those who actually complete tasks. These individuals are responsible for implementation; consequently, responsibility can be shared amongst several individuals. The degree of responsibility is determined by the individual with the accountability.

Accountable

Make the Decision (A) individuals are ultimately responsible; they hold the 'yes' or 'no' authority and veto power.

Consulted

Communicate Before, No Veto Power (C) individuals must be consulted before a final decision or action is taken. They usually provide input to and support for the activities being performed. They cannot unilaterally change a decision or stop an action but they can convince or persuade an A to rethink.

Informed

Let Know, but Does Not Change the Decision (I) individuals need to be informed once a decision has been made or action has been taken. It is important that these individuals are kept in the loop and hear it directly rather than read it in the news, or learn about it on the street.

In smaller social service organizations, it may not be reasonable to differentiate between the 'R' and 'A' individuals because the two roles are performed by a single individual.

A responsibility chart is typically developed collectively as a team. The greatest benefits are derived by the team members going through the process of developing the chart, not the resulting chart itself. The following steps outline how to complete a responsibility chart. To expedite the process and focus team member effort on defining and clarifying roles and responsibilities, prepare a list of activities and functional roles prior to the initial team meeting.

Steps in Developing a Responsibility Chart

1. *Activities* — List, in sequential order, the set of activities and tasks that must be performed (vertical axis).
2. *Functional Roles* — Define the individuals, groups or departments who play a part in performing the activities identified in Step 1. Identify the functional responsibilities by title and, as required, by the name of the individual if a high level of detail is required (horizontal axis).
3. *Title* — Describe the group of activities/tasks by assigning it a label (decision).
4. *Assignment* — Assign R, A, C or I to each activity/task (squares of the matrix).

Refer to **Figure 5-1**, *Example Responsibility Chart*, for an example of a completed Responsibility Chart.

A few simple guidelines will assist you and your team in completing a Responsibility Chart.

- there can be only one A (accountability) per activity,
- authority must accompany accountability,
- assign accountability (A) and responsibility (R) at the lowest feasible level in the organization,
- minimize the number of consults (C) and informs (I),

FIGURE 5-1
Example
Responsibility Chart

Example Responsibility Chart

RESPONSIBILITY CHART R = Do the Job A = Make the Decision C = Consulted I = Informed	Functional Role/Individual					
	Executive Director	Program Manager	Administration Team	Communications Team	Board Programming Committee	Program/ Service Team
Activities:						
1. Identify gaps in current program/service offerings	C	A				R
2. Develop new program/service framework to address gaps	C	A		I		R
3. Secure funding for new program/service	R				A	
4. Develop communications plan to support new program/service		A	I	R		C
5. Develop, or modify, internal processes required to deliver program/service	C	A	R			C

- keep in mind the organization's culture when defining roles and responsibilities:
  — eliminate "checkers checking checkers,"
  — encourage teamwork,
  — 100% accuracy is not always required or desirable.
- all roles and responsibilities must be documented and communicated.

Once the organization's readiness for planning has been assessed (**Chapter 4**, *Getting Started*) and roles and responsibilities have been defined (**Chapter 5,** *Defining Roles*), attention is placed on how to meaningfully engage stakeholders, the topic of **Chapter 6,** *Engaging Stakeholders*.

Beyond the Basics: Working with Consultant(s)

Defining the Role

While outside expertise can be very useful, it is important to think carefully about who needs to be engaged and for what purpose. Consultants are most effective when the organization can outline exactly what it wants a consultant to do; however, consultants can also be very helpful in assisting the organization in determining what actually needs to be accomplished and how. A good consultant recognizes the importance of the organization developing the internal capability to continuously analyze itself and oversee the ongoing strategic planning effort. Over time, this enables the organization to become less reliant on external assistance. After all, the organization must assume ownership of the strategic direction for it to be meaningful and sustainable in the long-term.

Consultants should not relieve the organization from making its own tough decisions. While the consultant can assist the organization in articulating alternatives and identifying the implications of various choices, it is the organization's responsibility to actually make the decisions.

In order to establish and maintain an effective working relationship with the consultant, agree up-front who the consultant will report to and take direction from. Similar to managing a staff member, provide positive and constructive feedback to the consultant throughout the course of his/her work. Remember, consultants generally work within many different organizations, situations and assignments, often simultaneously, and they may be unaware of your organization's internal procedures.

Process Tips: Watch out for consultants who tend to dominate the process either by being too prescriptive or rigid in approach or methodology used, or in personal style.

Selecting a Consultant

Interview more than one consultant particularly if the task is a substantial one. The contrast in style and approach between different consultants will provide members of the planning team additional ideas to consider in the course of their work. In addition, it is always a good idea to request references and to follow-up with recent or current clients of the consultants. Try to find out through your network of contacts if anyone else has experience with the consultant and inquire what their impressions are regarding the consultant's work ethic, style, delivery, strengths and weaknesses. Do not be afraid to be direct about the questions you have regarding the consultant. This investment of time will pay off in the long run.

The best way to find an external consultant that is right for your organization is to seek the advice of other agencies, board members and staff members. Social service organizations are rich with people from diverse backgrounds and experiences. Many of these people have direct experience working with a range of consultants within the context of a strategic planning initiative. The advice of these people is important. Follow the interviewing steps outlined above and you will be able to gauge for yourself if the fit will be the right one for your needs.

From the initial interview with the consultant you will be able to record observations that reflect first impressions. The incoming detailed proposals will contain more substantive material on which to base a more thorough evaluation. **Worksheet 5-1**, *Evaluating Potential Consultants*, provides a more detailed scoring sheet for assessing the capabilities of potential consultants.

Is a Request for Proposal Really Necessary?

A Request for Proposal (RFP) is not always necessary. Although a RFP can generate detailed input to the planning process and help to widen the number of potential candidates, preparing and circulating a RFP can also delay the start of the process.

Should discussion lead to a request for a written, formal proposal from the consultant, such a RFP could contain, but not be limited to:

- qualifications or previous experience relevant to this initiative,
- general approach to strategic planning,
- detailed structure, work plan, and schedule,
- specific role(s) and work arrangements of consultants,
- biographies of the consultants,
- proposed budget including expenses and invoice schedule.

Steps for Selecting a Consultant when the Planning Initiative is of a Substantial Size

The procedure for selecting external assistance becomes a more important task when the planning initiative is of substantial size. A few simple steps can help make this task easier to complete.

1. Prepare and distribute an information package to potential consultants. The package should clearly and briefly outline the context, scope and timing of the initiative you wish to undertake, as well as provide background information about your organization.
2. Schedule an initial interview with several potential consultants as an opportunity for the consultant to clarify scope and expectations and for you to gain a preliminary feel for the consultant's fit with your organization and his/her qualifications.
3. As an outcome of the interview, invite a limited number of consultants to submit a detailed proposal to you by a pre-determined date. To assist consultants in the development of their proposals, provide them with any additional pertinent background documents after signing a confidentiality agreement.
4. Draw upon the diverse perspectives of a small team to individually review, and rate/rank the incoming proposals and identify the short-list of consultants. This team's recommendation may identify the "top" candidate if there is a clear winner or the top two to three candidates if there is little to differentiate between them.
5. Solicit the input of the Board or Strategic Planning Committee on the short-list of candidates with respect to:
   - their experience with any of the consultants,
   - any significant concern with using any of the consultants, and
   - any preference for any of the consultants.
6. Check the references.
7. Finalize any outstanding issues or concerns, such as affordability and availability.

Cost and Remuneration of Consultants

While some may consider the use of consultants to be an unnecessary expense or even expensive, the hidden costs associated with duplication of effort, unnecessary tasks and incorrect sequencing can be eliminated by having the appropriate expertise on board. Regardless of these benefits, the dollars spent on external assistance need to be managed carefully to avoid the false perception that the strategic planning effort is diverting resources away from social service programs. Finally, if it is perceived that the consultant has sold a pre-defined, generic solution to the organization, significant issues related to the effectiveness of the process and outcomes may arise. This in turn may stall the overall process and reinforce any resistance to change.

Once the decision has been made to hire a strategic planning consultant, the next decision is the method of remuneration. Consultants can be paid on an hourly rate, a per diem rate (that is, a fixed rate per day) or a fixed fee basis (that is, a pre-determined amount usually based on an established set of defined outcomes). The choice of remuneration can be a point of negotiation between the organization and the consultant.

If the organization is able to offer an intangible benefit to the consultant, such as referrals or joint promotion on each other's web site, the consultant may be willing to further reduce his/her rates or even be willing to provide services at no charge. Explore this opportunity and work in partnership with the consultant.

Unfortunately, consultants and contractors cannot receive partial payment in the form of a charitable receipt because only materials, not services, are eligible as charitable donations in Canada. Regardless of the approach selected, agree in advance how the consultant fees will be paid, including any overruns. It is always best to have a written contract with the consultant with payments based on the consultant's performance of agreed tasks.

Summary

For best results, strategic planning should be an inclusive process that engages the right stakeholders in a meaningful way. This approach typically improves commitment, opens communication lines, incorporates a more varied and diverse perspective and set of skills, and establishes stronger internal and external relationships leading to consensus building. The need to be inclusive must always be balanced against the limited resources available to the social service organization. Roles of the various stakeholder groups are defined in this chapter, as well as what is involved in establishing the strategic planning working group and accountabilities. Consultants, although an incremental expense, can provide invaluable experience and expertise that will make the planning effort considerably more effective.

WORKSHEET 5-1
Evaluating Potential
Consultants

Evaluating Potential Consultants

TASK

1. *Score each potential consultant against all criteria (1 = weak and 5 = strong)*
2. *Total the scores*

Experience and Qualifications of Consultant

	Project Management	Proven Approach/ Methodology	Understand Organization's Issues	Meet Schedule	Cultural Fit	Meet Budget	Experience in the Sector	TOTAL
Consultant A								
Consultant B								
Consultant C								

Comments:

_____

_____

_____

_____

_____

_____

_____

_____

_____

_____

CHAPTER 6

Engaging Stakeholders

Is the organization involved and committed?

Organizations may evolve impressive strategic plans, but all too often find their implementation undermined by inadequate communication. Effective communication within an organization and with key stakeholders is critical to the success of any strategic planning initiative. As more social service organizations undergo fundamental restructuring because of funding cutbacks and increasing competition for resources, the need for effective communication of how an organization adds value to society is greater now than ever before.

People must understand and believe in the organization's strategic direction and action priorities if they are to be successfully implemented. This calls for well-planned interactive two-way communication.

This chapter describes how to communicate effectively and how to plan communications in the context of strategic planning.

Definitions

Communications and its terminology can be confusing to people unfamiliar with the discipline. For the purposes of this book, key terms have been defined to simplify the approach. **Figure 6-1,** *Contrasting Communication and Communications,* and **Figure 6-2,** *Elements of a Communications Plan,* help to clarify the definitions below.

Communication — is a function that encompasses what we say, how we behave and how we reinforce our words and actions through the use of policies, infrastructure and support systems.

Communications — are the tools or the operational aspects of communicating; for example, the medium used, timing, sequencing.

Communication Strategy — provides the overall context for communication planning including an assessment of why we need to communicate and the communication needs of the target audiences. The strategy provides direction and context for decision making

FIGURE 6-1
Contrasting
Communication and
Communictions

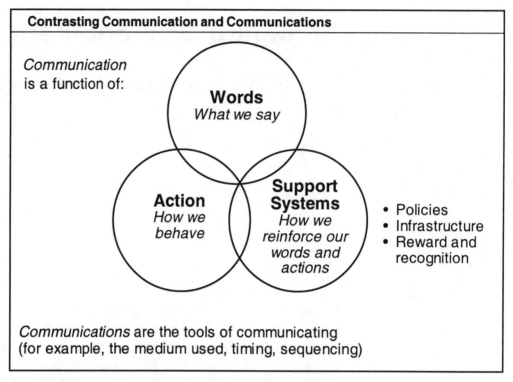

Contrasting Communication and Communications

Communication is a function of:

Words
What we say

Action
How we behave

Support Systems
How we reinforce our words and actions

- Policies
- Infrastructure
- Reward and recognition

Communications are the tools of communicating
(for example, the medium used, timing, sequencing)

FIGURE 6-2
Elements of a
Communications Plan

Elements of a Communications Plan

The Communications Plan

COMMUNICATION STRATEGY

Components:

- Strategy statement
- Guiding principles
- Target audiences
- Organizational core messages
- Goals
- Performance indicators
- Strategic communication issues

Accountability:
Strategic Planning Committee

COMMUNICATIONS TACTICS

Milestone Specific:

- Prioritized audience(s)
- Purpose of communicating
- Key message(s)
- Communications approach
- Timing
- Roles and responsibilities
- Measures/feedback
- Budget

Accountability:
Internal Marketing and Communications function

regarding communications and articulates the guiding principles for a consistent organizational image. The internal communications function is responsible for developing the organization's communication strategy while the Strategic Planning Committee is accountable for approving that strategy.

Communications Tactics — are milestone-specific actions that implement the communication strategy. They summarize what needs to be communicated, when and with whom, and how to assess whether the expected outcome of that communication has been achieved. The organization's internal marketing and communications function is accountable for developing and approving the organization's communications tactics.

Communications Plan — is a document that includes the communication strategy and milestone-specific tactics.

Benefits of Effective Communication

In essence, effective communication is the act of negotiating differences and aligning interests to reach consensus. Some of the benefits realized from effective communication are:

- helping to facilitate integrated planning through a coordination of efforts,
- encouraging understanding, engaging audiences and enhancing commitment for organizational goals and action priorities,
- identifying possible synergies,
- facilitating the development of consensus throughout the community of stakeholders,
- having better information to make decisions,
- minimizing the risk of leaving out important contributions,
- helping to ensure planning remains in alignment with expectations of stakeholders.

Despite all these benefits, achieving understanding and committing to a strategic direction is no easy task particularly if there are numerous stakeholders involved. The three most common barriers to effectively communicating a strategic direction are:

- leadership's assumption that everyone knows the strategic direction already or that they have already been told once,
- staff's assumption that the strategic direction is only in the purview of the senior management and board,
- unclear, incomplete messages resulting from the use of inappropriate forums, formats, mediums or messengers.

Good communication depends on thoughtful planning and design to overcome these barriers. In addition, communication must be ongoing, two-way and reinforced. The messages and delivery mechanisms must evolve as the organization's needs and priorities change.

Spectrum of Communication

Organizations are typically at different levels of sophistication with respect to communication. It is important for the Strategic Planning Committee to identify where on this spectrum their organization resides because it helps them plan the process and approach for their strategic planning. For example, sophisticated communications tools and techniques will not be successfully applied in an organization having no formal communication function or in an organization that takes a crisis management approach to communication.

Figure 6-3, *Communications Spectrum*, illustrates the four phases in an organization's evolution towards strategic management of their communications.

Phase 1: No Communications — An organization with no formal communication function in place.

Phase 2: Reactive Issues Management — An organization that reacts to issues as they arise, often known as a crisis manager. These organizations do not identify potential issues in advance, nor do they undertake to perform any research or information gathering prior to an issue erupting. They tend to have no networks in place upon which they can draw for support, information or guidance once an issue has arisen.

Phase 3: Proactive Issues Management — An organization that has proactively identified and researched the issues it may need to address and has established the positions it will assume should the situation warrant. To further assist the organization in the proactive management of issues, it has sought out and established a foundation of key relationships upon which issues can be identified and managed.

Phase 4: Strategic Communications — These organizations are most advanced in their communications because they have an overall communication strategy and communications plan in place that is tied directly to organizational strategy. In addition, these organizations have a high-level of commitment to communications objectives, an integrated strategy for all organizational requirements (not project driven) and a process for continuously analyzing results. They seek to maximize relationship opportunities and they are continuously making strategy adjustments.

FIGURE 6-3
Communications
Spectrum

Communications Spectrum

Phase 1	Phase 2	Phase 3	Phase 4
No Communications	Reactive Issues Management	Proactive Issues Management	Strategic Communications
	• Waits for issue to arise before acting • No advance preparation or information • No networks in place • Crisis management	• Identifies issue at some point prior to need for action • Prepares background/positioning on specific issue • Builds network proactively	• Overall communications plan in place and aligned with organizational strategy • High-level commitment to communications objectives • Integrated strategy for organizational requirements • Established process for continuously analyzing results • Maximizes networks • Makes ongoing strategy adjustments

Components of a Communications Plan

A Communications Plan consists of two components, the communication strategy and related tactics required for implementation. At the highest level, the communication strategy provides direction to all planning-related communications efforts. A typical strategy is made up of the following elements (as summarized in **Figure 6-2,** *Elements of a Communications Plan):*

Strategy Statement — briefly describes the overall purpose of the communications efforts.

Guiding Principles — state the beliefs and expectations the organization has with respect to how it will conduct its communications efforts. Refer to **Figure 6-4,** *Example of Communication Guiding Principles,* for an example of guiding principles.

Target Audiences — lists, in order of priority, the individuals and/or groups to which communications efforts are directed and provides a brief analysis of each audience.

Organizational Core Messages — summarizes the three or four main ideas to be reinforced throughout all communications efforts.

Goals — lists the areas for longer-term emphasis.

Performance Indicators — lists a limited number of measures to be used in determining the effectiveness of the communications efforts.

FIGURE 6-4
Example of
Communication Guiding
Principles

Example — Communication Guiding Principles	
• We are guided by our values • We integrate our communications efforts across the organization • We measure and evaluate our communications with a view to improve our effectiveness • Time is of the essence, and pace is an important factor • We seek high quality not perfection	• We use existing networks and expertise to provide technical communications support and assist with integration and timing of communications • We need external expertise, who can also develop internal expertise • Timely release of information is important to maintain trust in the process • Maintain consistent support of leaders

Communications tactics operationalize the communication strategy into milestone-specific actions. For each communications milestone, a worksheet is developed which includes the following components (refer to **Worksheet 6-1,** *Communications Tactics):*

Communications Milestone — identifies a major event.

Prioritized Audience(s) — lists the prioritized groups or individuals to engage.

Purpose of Communicating — identifies the reason why the communication needs to take place.

Key Message(s) — states the few ideas to be reinforced to each targeted audience.

Communications Approach — outlines the mechanism(s) to be used to convey the key messages to the target audience.

Timing — indicates when and how frequently the communication needs to occur.

Roles and Responsibilities — lists who is involved in the creation, delivery and evaluation of the communication.

Measures/Feedback — lists a limited number of measures to be used in determining the effectiveness of the communications efforts. **Figure 6-5A,** *Example of Temperature Check,* described below, is an example of a simple tool which can be used to assess the organization's current and evolving state regarding a particular issue or milestone.

Budget — estimates the cost of the milestone-specific communications.

FIGURE 6-5A
Example of
Temperature Check

Temperature Check					
Audience: _____	**Definitely Yes**				**Definitely No**
1. I believe a major step change is required for the organization to be successful in the future	5	4	3	2	1
2. My understanding of what the strategic planning process is about has improved	5	4	3	2	1
3. I found this session to be useful	5	4	3	2	1
4. I feel I have had the opportunity to be included in the planning process	5	4	3	2	1
5. I have sought out information from people in the planning process	5	4	3	2	1
6. I know what the planning process will deliver	5	4	3	2	1
7. I know how the action priorities will be implemented	5	4	3	2	1

A temperature check, as illustrated in **Figure 6-5A**, is a series of simple questions that can be asked of participants and other stakeholders directly or indirectly involved in the planning process to gauge their response to and perceptions about various issues.

The example used in **Figure 6-5A** includes questions about the overall strategic planning process as well as specific questions about a planning or communications session. These questions need to be customized to the circumstances of each organization.

Figure 6-5B, *Example of Temperature Check Planning*, used in conjunction with the temperature check, helps the planner/planning team record baselines, establish targets and measure perceptions over a period of time. This tool can be used for particular audiences or across the entire organization. The tool is used to record baseline perceptions of an audience, by calculating the average of individual responses, against a defined set of questions. For subsequent milestones/events, targets can be set to help manage leadership expectations about the highs and lows in perceptions that are anticipated through the project. As the temperature check is administered for each milestone/event the average actuals are recorded on the planning tool and, if required, the targets can be revised for subsequent milestones. In **Figure 6-5B**, *Example of Temperature Check Planning,* notice the questions have been aligned with key success factors. In this example, key success factors for the process were established initially, then temperature check questions were developed to measure results against these key success factors.

Process Tips — *When attempting to complete Worksheet 6-1,* Communications Tactics, *a little trick to test the appropriateness of the content, delivery and timing is found within the sentence,* Why are you telling me this now? *While the aspects of communications planning may be easily forgotten, the sentence is relatively easy to remember.*

What is the purpose of the communication?	*__Why__ are you telling me this now?*
Why are you the messenger?	*Why are __you__ telling me this now?*
What is the appropriate method of communication? now?	*Why are you __telling__ me this now?*
Why am I the audience?	*Why are you telling __me__ this now?*
What is the information/communication about?	*Why are you telling me __this__ now?*
What do you want me to do?	*Why are you telling me this __now__?*

Communication Issues and Watch-outs

Strategic planning requires that the right mechanisms be used at the right time to engage key stakeholders. Much of this effort can be anticipated and planned; however, you will inevitably run into individuals who will resist supporting the planning process. Recognizing and managing this resistance is an important element of the strategic planning process and its related communications. By identifying the symptoms of resistance early, the planning team can adjust the process without being sidetracked in having to defend the integrity of the process.

Resistors tend to focus on what is wrong rather than contribute to and help build solutions. The planning team must stay above the criticism of resistors, maintain focus on the desired end result, and constantly reinforce the positive aspects of the process and the accomplishments to date. Some common symptoms of resistance to watch out for are:

Temperature Check Planning

Audience: *Staff*

Performance Targets and Actuals

Process Key Success Factors	Questions		Baseline Jan. 20, 2003	Feb. 14, 2003	Mar. 25, 2003
Knowledge of need for change	1. I believe that a major change is required for the organization to be successful in the future	*Target: Actual:*	3.7	3.6	4.3
Understanding of the change itself	2. My understanding of what the planning process is about has improved.	*Target: Actual:*	2.6	2.7	2.8
Relevant, timely	3. I found this planning session to be useful.	*Target: Actual:*	2.8	3.0	3.3
Buy-in	4. I feel I have had the opportunity to be included in the planning process.	*Target: Actual:*	2.3	2.8	2.6
Shared responsibility	5. I have sought out information from people in the planning process.	*Target: Actual:*	2.5	2.5	2.5
Managed expectations	6. I know what the planning process will deliver.	*Target: Actual:*	1.9	2.3	2.7
Managed expectations	7. I know how the action priorities will be implemented.	*Target: Actual:*	1.9	2.2	2.8

Intellectualizing — characterized by attempts to over-complicate the task or demonstrate superior knowledge.

Critique of methodology — characterized by continual criticism of the way things are being done.

Requests for more details — characterized by demands for more and more detail.

Personal or project attacks — characterized by open hostility towards an individual(s) or the project.

Problem avoidance — characterized by not acknowledging that a problem exists.

Silence — characterized by a refusal to communicate.

Confusion — characterized by continually stating that s/he does not understand.

Changing the subject — characterized by redirecting the discussion away from areas of focus.

Compliance — characterized by passively accepting whatever is suggested.

Pressing for solutions — characterized by wanting to hear only about the solutions, and not the rationale or the problem to be addressed.

Low energy/attention — characterized by a lack of enthusiasm and suggestion that the current work is of low value.

Assertions that this has been done before — characterized by a dismissal of the planning objectives as nothing new.

Possible approaches to take when faced with these types of resistance are described in the remainder of the chapter. **Chapter 7,** *Facilitating the Process,* provides more detail about recognizing and managing potentially disruptive behavior.

Plan communications ahead of time — Be realistic in how much communication can occur during the planning process. Balance realism with the fact that you will not be able to communicate enough. Be sensitive to the needs of each target audience; present the same message in a variety of ways; and recognize that different audiences call for different communications vehicles and frequency of repetition. Finally, know when a crisis is a crisis and do not feel compelled to always react immediately.

Have a steady flow of communication — Avoid significant intervals of time when nothing is being communicated. With obvious communication gaps, the rumor mill works overtime and people become concerned that things are happening without them being informed. Realize you cannot communicate enough.

Be open and honest with communication — As soon as you know something, communicate it to the appropriate audiences. Always present good and bad news and admit that you do not know all the answers.

Be prepared for resistance — Recognize the symptoms of resistance and determine ahead of time how you and your planning team might deal with them.

Prepare communicators — Make sure those being asked to communicate messages understand their role and are given appropriate tools and coaching.

Know where your organization is on the communications spectrum — Be cautious about trying new, high-risk communications approaches such as video conferencing, dramatic presentations and other gimmicks.

Articulate a clear imperative — Make sure the core messages are very clear and describe the drivers behind why this initiative is being undertaken at this time.

Provide opportunities for meaningful contribution — Solicit input and feedback and be clear on how this information will be used in the planning process.

Avoid jargon — The planning process is the opportunity to bring groups to a consensus understanding, while the use of acronyms, abbreviations and jargon only creates barriers.

Walk the talk — Be aware that how you act speaks louder than what you say, particularly for leadership.

Honour the past — Avoid unnecessary criticism of leaders and previous decisions.

Timing is everything — If external communication regarding the organization's strategic planning and future direction occurs too soon, external audiences will expect the organization to already have completed the implementation of its strategic direction long before the organization is actually in a position to do so. The organization's credibility may be compromised as a result of this mistiming.

Reinforce deliverables and timing — The planning process always takes longer than you think it should. By having a clear timeline that highlights the milestones that have been met and those still to be met, the planning team will better be able to reinforce that work is actually being accomplished, break a complex task into manageable steps that are also understandable, and keep everyone on track and motivated.

> *Process Tips: Focusing on particular stakeholder groups does not mean that other groups will be ignored. Choose to address the needs of most groups through general communication mechanisms (such as newsletters and ad campaigns) and direct the majority of effort on engaging a limited number of critical stakeholders.*

What is Confidential and What is Not?

This is a controversial topic at best. In these times of increasing competitiveness for funding and resources, it is best to consider what information generated as a result of strategic planning may be considered proprietary to the organization. While financial statements and business plans of social service organizations tend to be readily available to the public, it may be prudent to determine when strategic planning information is released for general public consumption. Timing is everything. Remember, the organization may have expended considerable time and resources collecting, analyzing and synthesizing the information within a strategic planning process. The debate quickly becomes, should this intellectual property be freely shared with other social service organizations? There is no simple answer. Each organization will have to decide for themselves how they wish to deal with this issue. **Figure 6-6**, *Example of a Confidentiality Statement*, is an example of a confidentiality statement included in the first section of some organization's strategic plans where confidentiality was deemed to be an important issue.

FIGURE 6-6
Example of a
Confidentiality
Statement

Example of a Confidentiality Statement

At the present time, to ensure security of this strategic plan and its supporting reference documents, we will adhere to the following steps:

1. Plans and reference documents are CONFIDENTIAL to the organization.
2. Numbered copies will be assigned to all members of the management team, staff and board members, in a manner to be determined by the senior management team.
3. Plans and reference documents will not be shown or otherwise revealed to persons or agencies beyond the organization's staff and the board of directors, unless approved by the Executive Director.
4. Plans are not to be photocopied.

It is the *intent* of the planning document that needs to be widely communicated — not the document itself.

The following chapter deals with the benefits, roles and challenges of facilitating the strategic planning process.

Summary

Meaningful communication is critical to the successful implementation of the strategic direction. Effective communications are strategic and managed on an ongoing basis, rather than reactive and project-based. A communications plan consists of two major components: the communication strategy and the communications tactics. There are a number of potential stumbling blocks to watch out for in strategic planning that may require adjustments in the process and the communications plan.

WORKSHEET 6-1
Communications
Tactics

Communications Tactics Worksheet

Task:
- *Describe the overall communications milestone.*
- *For each audience, identify the purpose, key messages and the communications approach.*
- *For each communications approach, determine and record timing, roles and responsibilities and measures.*

Communications Milestone:

_____

_____

Audiences (Prioritized)	Purpose of Communicating	Key Message(s)	Communications Approach	Timing	Roles and Responsibilities	Measures/ Feedback

CHAPTER 7

Facilitating the Process

How to make it happen

Facilitation is key to establishing and maintaining an environment conducive to strategic planning. This chapter introduces the concept of facilitation, describes the role of the facilitator, and provides guidelines for facilitating a planning group.

Perspectives on Facilitation

Facilitation is a form of *assisted* planning, problem solving, and decision making. A facilitator is a neutral "process champion" who helps groups improve their effectiveness and achieve their goals.

Facilitation assumes that participants are willing, wise and creative. An effective facilitator has a working knowledge of group dynamics, a belief in the power of groups, and respect for individual perspectives. Facilitators require the ability to listen openly and actively, strong personal and collaborative skills and high tolerance for ambiguity.

The Role of the Facilitator

The role of facilitator will vary from organization to organization. In general, the primary role of the facilitator is to enable groups and organizations to work more effectively; to collaborate and achieve synergy.

At the most basic level, a facilitator can assist a group to accomplish its goals by helping the group organize its work, by guiding discussions, and by recording decisions. *Challenge facilitation* goes one step further – the facilitator uses his/her process skills to provoke, challenge and question the status quo in order to unfreeze the organization and open it up to new thinking.

Within the context of strategic planning, the facilitator manages the process, manages the planning sessions and acts as an objective resource.

Manages the Process

The strategic planning facilitator ensures there is clarity and agreement around the goals (or outcomes) of the planning process. S/he guides the systematic development of

73

the strategic plan components. The facilitator anticipates developments for the planning team to address and outlines the next steps in the process. An additional role for the facilitator may be to assist in refining ideas and materials outside the planning sessions and meetings.

Manages the Planning Sessions

In managing planning sessions, the strategic planning facilitator helps to establish group norms and effective ground rules for meetings. S/he ensures clear action results from each planning session by visibly recording group ideas and decisions. The facilitator acts as the timekeeper, refocusing, deferring or terminating discussion where necessary. S/he deals with resistance by making it safe for everyone to participate and employs strategies to overcome barriers. The ultimate goal for the strategic planning facilitator is to help the group achieve consensus.

Acts as an Objective Resource

As an objective resource to the planning team, the facilitator provides tools and techniques and suggests when additional resources or expertise may be required to augment the planning effort. S/he challenges traditional assumptions and provides objectivity and, in this way, helps to both focus the discussion and expand the team's thinking. An objective, external strategic planning facilitator can provide external experience and expertise, as required.

Challenges Faced by the Facilitator

The facilitator faces a myriad of challenges when working with groups, including:

- the diverse professional backgrounds of the participants,
- a range of strategic and operational perspectives,
- divergent and convergent thinkers,
- differences in problem-solving orientation (results-, process-, or relationship-driven),
- differences in formal and informal power and influence,
- a mixture of personalities (extroverts and introverts),
- differences in expectations and commitment to the planning process,
- varying complexity of issues,
- needing to push people beyond familiar opinions and solutions.

Not everyone is suited to the demanding role of facilitator. At a minimum, a facilitator must be seen by all members of the group as a neutral party who will act in the best interests of all participants, and who possesses the basic meeting management skills to keep the work of the group on time and on track.

In addition, an effective facilitator must be able to:

- develop the trust of group members,
- observe and correctly interpret group behavior,

- listen actively and communicate with precision and clarity,
- help the participants articulate their needs and interests,
- understand, paraphrase, summarize and synthesize multiple perspectives,
- model effective behavior, and intervene on ineffective behavior,
- help the participants overcome disagreement and achieve consensus,
- provide support and encouragement,
- demonstrate patience and humility.

Stages of Facilitation

Effective facilitation has five steps as illustrated in **Figure 7-1,** *Stages of Facilitation:* preparation, contracting, facilitating task and process, summary and follow-up.

FIGURE 7-1
Stages of Facilitation

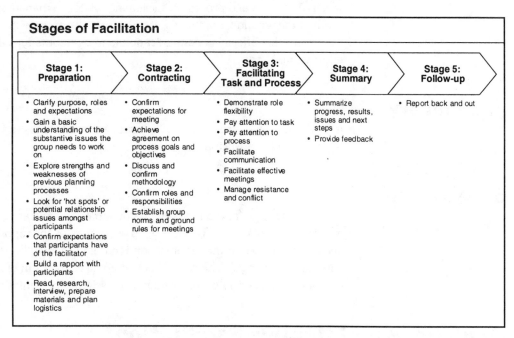

Stages of Facilitation

Stage 1: Preparation	Stage 2: Contracting	Stage 3: Facilitating Task and Process	Stage 4: Summary	Stage 5: Follow-up
• Clarify purpose, roles and expectations • Gain a basic understanding of the substantive issues the group needs to work on • Explore strengths and weaknesses of previous planning processes • Look for 'hot spots' or potential relationship issues amongst participants • Confirm expectations that participants have of the facilitator • Build a rapport with participants • Read, research, interview, prepare materials and plan logistics	• Confirm expectations for meeting • Achieve agreement on process goals and objectives • Discuss and confirm methodology • Confirm roles and responsibilities • Establish group norms and ground rules for meetings	• Demonstrate role flexibility • Pay attention to task • Pay attention to process • Facilitate communication • Facilitate effective meetings • Manage resistance and conflict	• Summarize progress, results, issues and next steps • Provide feedback	• Report back and out

1. Preparation

In this first stage, the facilitator prepares for the task ahead. Initially the purpose of meeting, as well as the roles of all participants, is clarified. The facilitator identifies the expectations of the senior management and Board, while gaining a basic understanding of the content issues — that is, the substantive issues that the groups need to address. In addition, a skillful facilitator will also take the time to explore the strengths and weaknesses of previous planning processes, determining what did or did not work well in these previous efforts. It is important in this stage to build a rapport with the participants while at the same time looking for hot spots or potential relationship issues (for example, the degree of trust and cooperation among the participants). One way to establish rapport is to confirm the expectations that participants have of the facilitator. Finally, the facilitator uses this preparation stage to read, research, interview, prepare materials and plan the logistics of the process.

2. Contracting

Stage two of facilitation is called contracting. At this point, the facilitator confirms the expectations for meeting by developing the agenda and establishing the meeting objectives. S/he works to achieve agreement on what needs to be accomplished. Roles and responsibilities of the facilitator and participants are confirmed and group norms and ground rules for meetings are established by the planning team. The methodology to be used is discussed and confirmed during this stage.

3. Facilitating Task and Process

Stage three relates to the actual task and process of facilitating. Here the emphasis is on demonstrating role flexibility, facilitating communication and running effective meetings. Much of the task and process of facilitating relates to managing resistance and conflict. Much of the remainder of this chapter explores the approaches and tools facilitators can use to facilitate effective communication (and overcome typical problems) and conduct effective meetings.

4. Summary

In the fourth stage, progress, results, issues and next steps are summarized and feedback is offered to the participants.

5. Follow-up

The final stage of facilitation is the follow-up conducted after the meeting or series of meetings has concluded. This follow-up encompasses the report back to the participants and the report out to the organization regarding the key decisions and progress made during the meeting(s). The report back often takes the form of minutes, while the report out may take a variety of forms such as newsletter, presentation or memo.

Guidelines for Effective Facilitation

The Agenda

The agenda defines the course of the meeting and acts as a road map for the discussion. It is one of the most important tools in meeting effectiveness. It helps the facilitator and the participants prepare. The agenda communicates the expectations for the meeting. It provides a mechanism for order and control because it dictates what will and will not be discussed. It divides the meeting time into manageable segments to ensure that all meeting objectives are met in the allotted time. An agenda provides a basis for measuring whether what was accomplished was what you set out to do in the meeting. To be effective, the agenda should always be distributed prior to the meeting. In this way, it may be possible to resolve obvious conflicts prior to the meeting. In addition, some participants may discover that they are not really needed at the meeting and you can save people unnecessary time. Or conversely, someone may see an agenda item and alert you that another resource is needed in order to accomplish the meeting objective.

When developing an agenda, consider the following tips:

- identify the time, date, place and participants,
- tell the participants how to prepare and what to bring,
- make sure everyone understands the purpose of the meeting — state the objectives of the meeting clearly,
- set time limits for each agenda item,
- schedule items, putting the most important item(s) first on the agenda,
- distribute the agenda in advance.

Several items on the agenda that can help improve the effectiveness of a meeting but that you may not always use are:

Agenda Review — a quick review of the agenda at the start of the meeting can accommodate any last minute changes requested by the participants.

Expectations — clarifying what participants hope to accomplish by the end of the meeting provides participants the opportunity to voice their thoughts early enough for the facilitator to adjust the agenda or clarify the objectives of the session.

Next Steps — by concluding every meeting with an understanding and agreement on what action is to be taken, by whom and by when ensures that the process continues to move forward.

Benefits and Concerns — recording what went well in the meeting, that is, *benefits*, and what could be improved for the next meeting, that is, *concerns*, helps the facilitator to understand where and how to improve the process and to surface any issues that are still outstanding.

The final step in planning an effective meeting is arranging the logistics. Consider the room size and set-up, equipment and materials, catering and location. Even if you do an outstanding job in planning the agenda and distributing the information ahead of the meeting, if the room is too small or too large, too hot or too cold, too bright or too dark, or if there are no flip chart pens, the meeting can quickly fall apart.

Meeting Roles and Responsibilities

The leader is responsible for owning the problem, making decisions and assigning actions. The facilitator is responsible for managing the meeting, policing the process, acting as the link between the team and the leader and resources. Team members are responsible for generating ideas, building on others' ideas and adding expertise to the meeting.

Group Norms and Ground Rules

Group norms and meeting ground rules are guidelines that help a team get its work done. They are agreements on how the team members will work and interact together. Group norms and meeting ground rules are suddenly important when not observed.

Example of Group Norms	
Preparation	Distributing agendas and materials in advance; accepting personal responsibility to prepare for the meeting.
Punctuality	Providing advance notice of absences; arriving early to get settled; starting and finishing on time; extending meetings by consensus.
Full participation	Encouraging everyone to participate, not just the vocal few; giving people room to think and get their thoughts out; protecting participants acting in good faith from negative repercussions or recriminations.
Equal voice	Giving everyone equal opportunity to speak and to be heard without interruptions or pre-judging; giving equal weight to each participant's opinion, regardless of their position within the organization.
Mutual understanding	Seeking first to understand, then to be understood; looking at issues from multiple perspectives; allowing opposing viewpoints to co-exist; ensuring that participants can accurately represent each other's points of view.
Respectful treatment	Listening actively; paying attention to the person speaking through eye contact; avoiding distractions such as sidebar discussions and note-passing; focusing on the problem and not the person; avoiding language that provokes or causes defensive reactions.
Confidentiality	Encouraging openness and input on work-in-progress; avoid speculating about possible outcomes; supporting the process by raising concerns within the group; no talking behind people's backs; no disclosure of comments by individuals.
Joint problem-solving	Viewing problem solving as a joint effort between partners and not a contest between adversaries; focusing on interests and not on positions; searching for integrative, mutually acceptable solutions (not a win/lose); placing value on the relationship as well as the outcome.
Decisions by consensus	Arriving at solutions that everyone supports, agrees to or can live with; arriving at decisions that reflect a wide range of perspectives; ensuring that everyone understands the reasoning behind the solution.
Disagreements	Encouraging people to articulate their beliefs, even in the face of opposition; recognizing that conflict is a natural part of the process; committing to working through disagreements in ways that sustain the process and preserve relationships; discussing consequences.
Humor	Recognizing the value of good-natured humor in breaking the ice, building rapport and developing good group dynamics, and helping participants as well as the facilitator avoid taking themselves too seriously.

Source: Spark Consulting Services, 1999

Consensus is defined as a state of affairs where a clear alternative appears with the support of most members, and the others feel that they have been listened to, had a fair chance to influence the decision outcome, and support the final decision. **Figure 7-2,** *Example of Group Norms,* lists examples of group norms. **Figure 7-3,** *Example of Meeting Ground Rules,* lists examples of meeting ground rules.

FIGURE 7-3
Example of Meeting
Ground Rules

Example of Meeting Ground Rules
• Challenge ideas, not people • Participate • Stay focused and in process • Be positive and open • One conversation at a time • Listen generously • Ensure closure on each topic before moving on • Encourage new ideas; build on the ideas of others • Observe time limits; stick to the agenda • Ensure that everyone gets heard

Evaluating the Effectiveness of a Meeting

The effectiveness of any meeting can be quickly assessed by establishing some simple criteria. The list of criteria should be of a manageable size, an example of which is given in **Worksheet 7-1,** *Basic Effective Meeting Checklist.* Occasionally, it may be worthwhile to review the planning session or meeting using a more detailed checklist similar to that presented in **Worksheet 7-2,** *Detailed Effective Meeting Checklist.* As a rule of thumb, in evaluating the effectiveness of a meeting, the majority of time should be spent in preparing for and following up after the meeting, as illustrated in **Figure 7-4,** *Plan, Do, Review.* Note that the more effective meetings have only 10 to 20% of the time devoted to conducting the actual meeting.

FIGURE 7-4
Plan, Do, Review

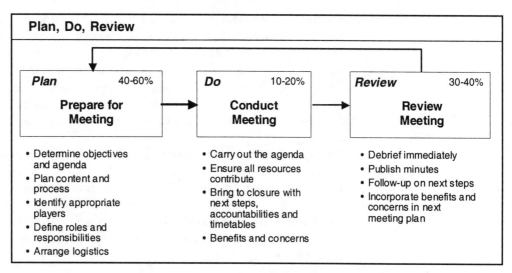

Typical Problems

Several problems typically arise when facilitating groups, such as individuals who dominate the discussion, block ideas, nit-pick details, joke and mock other's contributions, engage in side conversations or withdraw. A skillful facilitator will recognize these problems early and address them in a number of ways.

Running behind schedule — As soon as you are aware that the meeting is behind schedule, announce to the group that it is behind schedule and either reconfirm and/or redefine the time contract with the group. Limit the discussion on some of the points and/or consider shortening the agenda by postponing some of the discussions for another time. Record digressions in the "parking lot" of issues to be dealt with at a later date.

If you are running well behind schedule, determine the cause: is it because the discussion has wandered off track or have you, as the facilitator, underestimated the time required for each agenda item? Decide which items can be next steps, carried over to the next meeting or captured in the "parking lot" to be dealt with at another time. Reprioritize the remaining agenda items.

Working the issue during information sharing — Reinforce that information sharing involves only questions for clarification. If the information-sharing item needs to be worked through to resolution, make it an agenda item for discussion at a subsequent meeting.

Going around in circles — Inform the group that it is behind schedule and summarize the discussion while noting relevant points on a flipchart. Offer a proposal for getting the meeting going again by identifying and assigning next steps to be undertaken to advance the discussion.

Shutting out quiet and passive members — Have each person in the room make points or offer their opinion in rotation. Inform those at the end of the queue that their turn will come.

Members dropping out of discussion — Bring the person into the discussion by asking a question or seeking an opinion on the topic being discussed.

Disruptive behavior — Initially use nonverbal techniques such as making eye contact or giving a dissatisfied glance to the person exhibiting disruptive behavior. Noticeably reinforce positive behaviors. If the disruptive behavior continues, confront the behavior in a firm but friendly manner by suggesting alternative behaviors, for example, "Do you think you could hold your messages until the break?" Keep in mind to focus on the behavior and its effect on the group; do not focus on the person or his/her personality. If all else fails, talk privately to the members who continually exhibit disruptive behaviors.

Disruptive differences of opinion — Define the areas of agreement and disagreement and record them visibly on a flipchart. Identify what next steps should be taken to resolve the differences and determine if the discussion should be taken off-line outside the meeting.

Not identifying next steps — Use the flipchart to record *item*, *who*, and *when*. At the start of each meeting, make it a practice to follow-up on the action items from the previous meeting.

Major Breakdowns

Difficult dynamics manifest themselves in a variety of ways. For example, participants may lose focus or engage in sidebar conversations. Low group participation, withdrawal, a lack of follow-up or preparation are all signs of process breakdown. Grandstanding, personal tests of will, repetition/stridency, personal attacks, such as non-verbal behaviors, discounting a person's opinion, condescending behavior, sarcasm, provocations, accusations, threats and ultimatums, are disruptive behaviors or potential power imbalances that demand intervention by the facilitator. Evidence of deferring to authority or attacking the process present barriers to getting the job done effectively.

In many cases, these obstacles and difficult dynamics may be overcome by employing one of several general strategies including:

- anticipating the potential for difficulties during preparation,
- discussing your role as facilitator and intervenor with the full team,
- establishing ground rules and group norms,
- co-facilitating or engaging a "process monitor" from the team,
- ordering the agenda to deal with contentious issues at the appropriate time.

Other more specific approaches to take are:

Disseminating information — the productivity of the meeting is greatly improved if everyone comes together with basic knowledge of the issues to be discussed.

Pre-positioning — if the facilitator anticipates opposition from one of the participants, talk to him/her prior to the meeting. Sometimes s/he just needs a chance to vent feelings; sometimes you can help him/her to see things in a more positive light. Although an opposing position is not always possible to change, the facilitator will be better prepared for the discussion if s/he meets with the opposer prior to the meeting.

Limiting the objective — if the group has no authority for decision making, restate the objective of the meeting (for example, "develop a recommendation for...").

Canceling the meeting — due to a lack of information, lack of authority, it may be best just to not meet at all.

Initial Response to Major Breakdowns

If during the course of a planning session a major breakdown in process occurs, the facilitator needs to:

- manage his/her own reaction,
- avoid panicking or assuming it is the fault of the facilitator,
- avoid over reacting,
- take time to think about underlying dynamics by taking a break,
- address the problem, not the behaviour of the person,
- consider a one-on-one discussion with the person involved.

Process Feedback

One of the roles of the facilitator is to provide a forum for feedback to the organization on the efficacy of the planning process and the facilitation used. Immediately following the conclusion of the planning effort, an evaluation of the process should be undertaken to measure the effectiveness of the process and the facilitation services utilized. This information will be fed back into the planning cycle in order to improve subsequent iterations of the process. **Worksheet 7-3**, *Strategic Planning Process Evaluation*, is an example of a process and facilitator evaluation tool. The results of the evaluation should be input to improving the process, as well as reference data in retaining a future facilitator.

The discussion moves now to the details of the strategic plan. **Chapter 8**, *Situation Assessment*, describes the first stage of the strategic planning process.

Summary

This chapter introduces the novice planning participant to the role and responsibilities of an effective process facilitator. Starting with a clear understanding of what effective facilitation is and can do for a planning process, the chapter moves into defining the facilitator's role, stages in facilitating and then guidelines for effective facilitation.

When the process is complete an evaluation of the process and facilitator/facilitation should be undertaken using a questionnaire to poll the participants. This information should be reference in retaining future facilitation support and when charting upcoming planning processes.

WORKSHEET 7-1
Basic Effective
Meeting Checklist

Basic Effective Meeting Checklist

ACTIVITY	Yes	No
Was an agenda sent out ahead of time?	☐	☐
Were handouts and meeting aids prepared in advance and presented at the meeting?	☐	☐
Were objectives of the meeting clear?	☐	☐
Was the meeting room set up properly?	☐	☐
Were time contracts observed?	☐	☐
Did participants understand what was expected of them?	☐	☐
Was there active participation?	☐	☐
Did facilitator(s) practice good interpersonal skills, such as active listening, paraphrasing?	☐	☐

WORKSHEET 7-2
Detailed Effective
Meeting Checklist

Detailed Effective Meeting Checklist

Date: _____   **Purpose**
of Meeting: _____

ACTIVITY	Yes	No
1. Was an agenda sent out ahead of time?	☐	☐
2. Were objectives clear?	☐	☐
3. Were handouts and meeting slides prepared in advance and presented at the meeting?	☐	☐
4. Was the meeting room set up properly?	☐	☐
5. Did the meeting start on time?	☐	☐
6. Was the agenda followed?	☐	☐
7. Did participants understand what was expected of them during the meeting?	☐	☐
8. Did the meeting end on time?	☐	☐
9. Was there good participation in the meeting?	☐	☐
10. Was the meeting summarized?	☐	☐
11. Were participants' problems, concerns, and needs sought?	☐	☐
12. Were differing opinions acknowledged and was a consensus arrived at?	☐	☐
13. Were decisions made or action items assigned to resolve problems?	☐	☐
14. Were follow-up reporting times established?	☐	☐
15. Did facilitator(s) practice good interpersonal skills: active listening, paraphrasing, and recognizing non-verbal behavior?	☐	☐
16. Will participants receive minutes from the meeting?	☐	☐
17. Were the time and place of the next meeting established?	☐	☐

WORKSHEET 7-3
Strategic Planning
Process Evaluation

Strategic Planning Process Evaluation Worksheet

TASK   *Please complete this evaluation by circling the number that best reflects your response, and return it in the self-addressed envelope.*

	Strongly Agree	Agree	Disagree	Strongly Disagree	Don't Know	Not Applicable
The Process						
• Clearly articulated objectives of planning initiative	4	3	2	1	0	N/A
• Clearly described process steps	4	3	2	1	0	N/A
• Outside facilitation valuable	4	3	2	1	0	N/A
• Effective tools and methodologies supplied	4	3	2	1	0	N/A
• Sufficient time allocated to each step in process	4	3	2	1	0	N/A
The Results						
• Common vision exists	4	3	2	1	0	N/A
• Consensus reached on key issues	4	3	2	1	0	N/A
• Limited, prioritized objectives linked to key issues	4	3	2	1	0	N/A
• Clearly articulated action steps	4	3	2	1	0	N/A
• Clearly defined accountabilities and responsibilities	4	3	2	1	0	N/A
• Clearly defined indicators and targets	4	3	2	1	0	N/A
• Easy to read format of planning document	4	3	2	1	0	N/A
The Facilitator						
• Had an in-depth understanding of the planning process	4	3	2	1	0	N/A
• Challenged thinking without being threatening	4	3	2	1	0	N/A
• Motivated the team	4	3	2	1	0	N/A
• Had an adequate understanding of the organization	4	3	2	1	0	N/A
• Was skillful in conflict resolution	4	3	2	1	0	N/A
• Moved the process forward at the correct pace	4	3	2	1	0	N/A
• Involved all participants	4	3	2	1	0	N/A

Activity   Yes   No

Did the process meet your expectations?   ☐   ☐

If no, please indicate why not.

_____

_____

What was your greatest learning from this planning initiative?

_____

_____

Do you have any suggestions for improvement?

_____

_____

	Yes	**No**
Did the facilitator meet your expectations?	☐	☐
If no, please indicate why not.		

_____

_____

	Yes	**No**
Would you recommend the facilitator be used again?	☐	☐
If no, please indicate why not.		

_____

_____

Section 3

The Steps Leading to a Practical Strategic Plan

The Steps Leading to a Practical Strategic Plan details the four major steps of the strategic planning process, beginning with understanding the organization's internal and external environments and identifying the critical issues. The second step, defining the organization's strategy, involves identifying the organization's unique purpose and position in the sector. Step three addresses how to turn the strategy into implementable action. The fourth step discusses how to implement the strategy and action and how to gauge progress and performance.

CHAPTER 8

Situation Assessment

What strategic issues must be addressed?

The situation assessment provides a common fact base from which strategy and implementation choices can confidently be made. Assessing the organization's situation, or scanning the environment as it is sometimes referred to, involves assessing current trends, issues, and anticipated developments that have the potential to impact the organization.

A situation assessment is typically undertaken at the outset of a strategic planning effort. Its ultimate purpose is to bring all decision makers and all those involved in the process to a common level of understanding about the facts and factors that could impact the organization's success. An important byproduct of undertaking a situation assessment is the broader perspective leadership develops about the organization, the context in which it is operating and the implications for its future direction. This chapter describes what to include in the situation assessment and how best to conduct the assessment.

Conducting a thorough situation assessment can be a time consuming exercise. The critical task is not gathering and dumping large quantities of data on the decision-makers, but collecting, analyzing and synthesizing the right data into meaningful and succinct conclusions. More in-depth approaches and techniques for conducting components of a situation assessment are outlined in **Section 4: *Beyond the Basics***: *Tools and Techniques for Advancing Strategic Thinking and Planning.*

Situation Assessment Framework

The situation assessment encompasses an evaluation of the internal situation and the external environment in which the organization is operating, leading to the identification of key strategic issues and their associated implications for the organization. **Figure 8-1**, *Situation Assessment Overview,* illustrates this framework.

The objectives of a situation assessment include:

- Increasing participant's understanding about their key stakeholders and clients: who they are, their needs, and their relative importance to the organization.

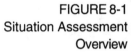

FIGURE 8-1
Situation Assessment
Overview

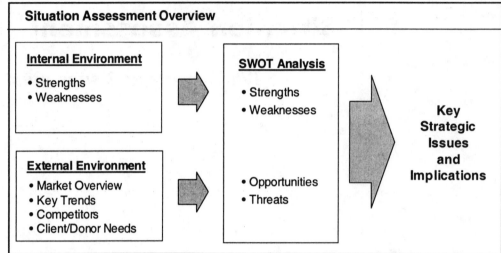

- Gaining an appreciation for the existence of competition and developing a broader understanding of the "competitive environment," including the performance and strategies of alternate service providers.
- Identifying and analyzing key trends with potential to impact the organization.
- Identifying opportunities and threats arising from the external environment.
- Assessing the organization's strengths and weaknesses relative to other similar or alternative service providers.
- Identifying the issues of strategic importance facing the organization.

The time horizon of the situation assessment can vary but a three to five year outlook is best. Shortening the term of the outlook to any less than three years tends to result in an assessment that is an extension of the current situation, focusing more on already identified issues and challenges. A longer-term outlook lends itself better to considering emerging ideas and issues and allows the organization to consider broader perspectives about how its sector may evolve.

The components covered by a situation assessment vary depending on the particular circumstances and needs of the organization. The topics helpful to address in the context of the social service sector are discussed in the remainder of this chapter and include market overview, key trends, competitor analysis, client/donor needs analysis, internal assessment, SWOT analysis, and key strategic issues and implications.

Market Overview

Recognizing that most organizations in the social service sector do not consider themselves to be selling services into a market in the same way that private sector companies focus on markets to generate revenues, the term "market" is used here for convenience. The market overview consists of two components: an assessment of the size and growth of the organization's market and a value chain analysis to provide information about the dynamics of the playing field in which the social service organization provides service.

Market Size and Growth Assessment

At a macro level, the organization's marketplace needs to be clarified and the historic and projected growth in this marketplace needs to be determined. Market size is assessed by:

- Identifying the characteristics that define the organization's marketplace, for example, geographic, demographic, psychographic, needs or other relevant characteristics. Is the market clearly defined? Is the market readily accessible?
- Describing the size of the market, historical and projected growth in number of clients and their utilization and needs of the service(s). What is the basis for the projected market growth? Is it reasonable? What could impact future market growth positively or negatively?
- Drawing out implications, including any opportunities and/or threats, by defining the potential impact of the market information on the organization.

Value Chain Analysis

The value chain provides a visual foundation for the structure of the sector and its participants. The value chain describes the sequence of activities through which value is created and added as a service is delivered to meet the needs of one or more clients. Understanding the value chain helps provide insight into how a service is delivered, who is involved in its delivery and what opportunities there may be to improve service delivery. **Figure 8-2,** *Example of a Value Chain,* illustrates a value chain developed and used by United Way of Calgary and Area early in their planning process. The value chain illustrates the various activities involved in the raising and distribution of funds to a wide variety of social service agencies.

The value chain is used as a framework to answer the following questions and to facilitate discussion related to these topics in a planning session:

- What are the value adding activities/services that comprise the value chain from an initial client need through to satisfaction of the client need?
- What related value chains need to be understood, that is, which activities are also components of other value chains used to satisfy completely different client needs or what other value chains are used to satisfy the same client needs?
- In what elements of the value chain does the organization participate? Where does the organization wish to participate?
- What is known about costs and revenues and how they are distributed across the value chain?
- What are the cost drivers or regulatory drivers that are important to the organization's participation in the value chain?
- What opportunities exist to consolidate/separate elements of the value chain or reconfigure the value chain to generate new value or better service?
- What are the organization's sources of differentiation relative to other service providers? How can the organization better differentiate itself from other service providers?
- Conclude the value chain discussion summarizing or drawing out any conclusions or implications, including opportunities and threats, for the organization and

FIGURE 8-2
Example of a
Value Chain

United Way Value Chain

Define Needs	Set Funding Priorities	Develop Revenue Tactics	Recruit/ Train Staff/ Volunteers	Raise Funds	Perform Advocacy Role	Mktg & Communi- cation	Relation- ship Building	Data Mgmt	Financial Mgmt	Distribute Funds	Customer Service	Evaluate Success
• Request proposals • Planning, visioning • Financial definition of need • Research • Consultation	• Set campaign targets • Review agencies case-by-case • Reaffirm principles • Set distribution priorities	• Perform SWOT analysis • Consult with volunteers • Assess current environ- ment • Set focus	• Identify skills, knowledge, connection required • Recruit- ment strategy • Training strategy • Assign tasks	• Corporate gift campaign • Employee campaign • Direct mail campaign • Leadership campaign • Planned giving • Capital campaign • Special events • Grants • Annual campaign • Endow- ment	• Knowledge base • Represent community needs • Encourage people to give time and money • Promote needs of voluntary sector	• Develop key messages • Advertising • Sales support material	• Recognition program • Face-to- face • Events • Involvement strategies • Provide expert advice • Friend raising	• Pledge tracking • Segmen- tation • Historical funds distribution • Giving history • Contact names	• Pledge collection • Audit • Account- ability • Manage invest- ments • Distribute receipts	• Final decisions regarding distribution • Mail check	• Answer queries	• Onsite analysis process • Celebrate • Personal reviews • Resources reviews • Analyze feedback • Benchmark

Source: United Way of Calgary and Area used in initial planning stages, 1994

agreeing on any additional information required to complete this piece of the analysis.

The Value Chain Analysis is an invaluable tool to help participants gain a broader understanding of the marketplace and how value is delivered to their clients. Invariably, the discussion helps participants learn more about the organization and the sector. The value chain, once documented, is a useful visual tool to explain the 'service' to others, including new staff members and volunteers to the organization.

> ***Process Tips:*** *Either include development of a value chain and related discussion as a component of a planning session, as laid out above, or ask one participant or a small group of participants to prepare a straw model value chain in advance of the session and discuss and revise the straw model during the planning session.*

Key Trends

Key trends are those known or emerging factors that have the potential to impact the organization's future, positively or negatively. Key trends need to be identified and their potential impact on the organization need to be understood. Thinking through trends and their implications helps participants understand how the external environment affects the organization and provides a glimpse of what the future may hold in store.

Key trends typically include such topics as:

- demographic trends such as aging of the population, migration and regional relocation, urban growth, and others,
- economic factors such as employment rates, interest and inflation rates, and leading economic indicators,
- government policy and legislation, and anticipated changes to that legislation,
- philanthropic trends,
- technology developments, including information and electronic commerce,
- community and social issues such as crime rates, homelessness, urban development, volunteerism and local government funding,
- political issues at the local, regional and national levels,
- human resource issues such as changing skill needs and availability.

Figure 8-3, *Example of Trends*, lists key trends associated with the fundraising environment. **Figure 8-4,** *Giving Trends,* is an example of a diagram prepared to help participants in a planning process understand the history, evolution and evolving trends regarding giving.

Worksheet 8-1, *Key Trends,* is a convenient tool to record and organize key trend information. A suggested process to develop key trends using this worksheet is summarized below:

1. As a component of a planning session early in the process, conduct a brief brainstorming session to identify trends potentially important to the organization.

FIGURE 8-3
Example of Trends

Key Trends

- Increased competition for charitable dollars
- Increasing demand for accountability
- Increased diversity of community
- Pressure on community to offset decreases in government services and funding
- Donors seeking more recognition; closer connection with recipients
- Donors demanding more customization and flexibility
- Community and agencies needing new solutions as well as funds

FIGURE 8-4
Giving Trends

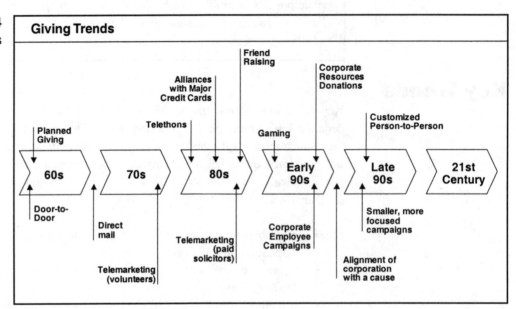

Giving Trends

2. Once a brainstorm list has been produced, circle back to each idea on the list and have a brief group discussion about each topic to ensure all participants understand the trend and potential implication to the organization.

3. Using a simple voting scheme, ask participants to select which trends they believe are most important and therefore worthy of additional investigation to ensure the trends are more thoroughly understood and a fact-base is established for decision-making.

4. Select the three to five trends thought to be most important and assign participants or groups of participants to conduct further investigation. Have these participants report back at a subsequent session with their findings. The report back would include the same information as requested in **Worksheet 8-1**, *Key Trends*, that is, a description of each trend and identification of the implications to the organization, but more thoroughly described. The implications should draw out the opportunities and threats for the organization.

Process Tips: *Provide* **Worksheet 8-1**, *Key Trends, and a list of possible categories of trends drawn from the list above to session participants in advance* *and ask them to give some thought to trends prior to the session. Alternatively, the planning leader/team could assign subject areas to individuals or small working groups for data gathering and preliminary synthesis prior to the session.*

Competitor Analysis

In business sectors, competitive analysis allows management to gain a better understanding of the dynamics of an industry and the opportunities and threats that exist or may exist for their company based on the activity of competitors. In a social service context, competitive analysis has varying degrees of relevance. While there is typically not profit-motivated competition for social services, there are often alternate sources of service that constitute increasing competition. In recent years the downloading of government services has necessitated a closer examination of who provides what services to whom and who funds those services. In addition, private for-profit service providers have emerged. From this perspective, analyzing alternative service providers and their funders, that is, competitive analysis is an important tool for planners in the social service sector.

Competitive analysis helps participants in the planning process understand the strategies and market positioning of key competitors, the competitive threats and opportunities created by these strategies and the resulting implications or potential impact for the organization.

The following topics should be covered when considering competition:

- Identify the nature of competition faced by the organization. Are there direct service competitors, substitute services/products, other forms of indirect competition?
- Identify and characterize key sources of competition. Define generic competitor types or groupings based on similarities in their funding model, client base, service, or other such criteria.
- Describe the positioning and strategy of key competitors (or the generic groups of competitors defined in the step above). Who are their target clients? How successful are they at satisfying the needs of these clients? How has their client base been changing? What are their key strengths and weaknesses? What can be implied about your organization's strategy given the strategy of these competitors?
- Describe what key competitors are likely to do differently in the future that may have a significant impact on the marketplace, that is, value chain? Or your organization?
- What will the competitive playing field look like in two years? Five years? If practical, create a competitive map by developing a quadrant diagram that positions your organization against key competitors (or generic groups of competitors) using relevant axes such as client focus, size, and service breadth/focus.
- Stepping back with a better overall view of the competitors, what opportunities and threats exist for your organization?
- Do any competitors represent alliance opportunities for the organization?
- What are the overall implications of this competitive analysis for your organization?

As is the case with all components of the situation assessment, different levels of effort and sophistication can be used when conducting assessments. **Worksheet 8-2,** *Competitive Assessment,* provides a relatively quick and efficient approach for sizing up the competition and capturing some of the information listed above.

> *Process Tips: Worksheet 8-2,* Competitive Assessment, *can be used in a planning session to work the competitive assessment as a group or can be assigned to participants to think about or complete in advance of the planning session. The worksheet can be used to record the characteristics of individual competitors, or with enough information, used to record information about generic competitive groups.*

More detailed information about competitors can be accumulated and organized and used to make more informed decisions relative to the competition. A competitor profile, as outlined in **Figure 8-5**, *Competitor Profile Template,* is useful for organizing competitive information in a consistent fashion. It is most helpful to complete competitor profiles for at least the major competitors in the sector.

FIGURE 8-5
Competitor Profile
Template

Competitor Profile Template

1. Identify the organization's head office and its geographical coverage.
2. Describe the key people behind the organization at the management and board level.
3. Describe the competitor's target clients and their perceived strategies related to such areas as volunteerism, funding, partners/collaborators and service.
4. Estimate the size and growth of the market the competitor is targeting and identify the drivers of the market's growth.
5. Identify how the competitor communicates with, attracts and retains clients.
6. Determine the competitor's source of funds, revenues and financial health.
7. List the services typically offered by this competitor.
8. Identify key service delivery partners.
9. List the strengths and weaknesses of this competitor relative to other providers of similar services.

Client/Donor Needs Analysis

Of fundamental importance to any organization operating in the private or public sector, is understanding the needs of current and potential clients (referred to throughout this section as "clients") and current and potential donors. While this has always been true, it has become increasingly important for social service organizations as they attempt to carve out a clear niche that enables them to appeal to a focused and interested group of clients and donors.

Understanding client needs is an ongoing process of direct interaction and inquiry with clients. Front-line staff dealing with clients are very able to articulate the needs of their clients from the perspective of the services currently being offered and delivered. However, it is helpful to obtain alternate perspectives on client needs that are not tied to the services currently being provided by the organization in order to assess what the right services ought to be.

The needs of clients can be categorized into those needs that are common to most clients and those needs that are unique to some clients. Generic client segments are defined by clusters of one or more unique needs. Identifying these generic client segments provides valuable insight about how best to optimize service delivery.

A better understanding of client needs is obtained by:

1. Brainstorming the current and emerging needs of clients.
2. Categorizing this list of needs as those that are common to all or most clients versus those that are unique to individual or individual groups of clients.
3. Use the differentiating needs as the basis for creating a small number of three to five client segments. Name and describe each of these client segments. Identify representative clients for each segment.

For each client segment consider:

- What needs are currently being met? What needs are not being met? Where is there opportunity to improve needs satisfaction?
- How are needs changing and what is influencing the change?
- What is the size and growth prospects for each segment? What is driving the growth?
- What other characteristics (for example, geography, demographics, psycographics) can be used to identify and reach the needs-based segments?
- Which needs is your organization best able to satisfy?
- What services does your organization currently or propose delivering to satisfy the needs of each client segment?
- What is your organization's performance at satisfying key needs?
- Which client segment has your organization historically targeted?
- Based on the availability of alternate service providers and the organization's current and/or potential ability to satisfy client needs, which segment(s) should the organization strive to best serve (that is, target)?
- What are the implications, including opportunities and threats, that this analysis presents to your organization?
- Identify any new services that will be needed to address the current and emerging needs of your targeted clients.

Answering the questions posed above will help the organization obtain a thorough understanding of their clients and their needs. **Worksheet 8-3,** *Client Needs and Segmentation Assessment,* is a convenient tool to help prepare for and summarize the results of a client needs and segmentation discussion.

Process Tips: When no or limited preparation time is possible, conduct this client analysis during a planning session and answer as many of the questions laid out above as possible. Assign follow-up work to complete the analysis and quickly review results at the next planning session. When preparation time is possible, distribute **Worksheet 8-3,** Client Needs and Segmentation Assessment, *and the list of questions above (or a subset) to all or some process participants prior to the planning session. Ask these participants to complete the worksheets and questions in order to prepare for the session, or ask them to be prepared to present their findings.*

Now that you have worked through the steps of a client needs analysis, these same steps can be repeated for donors, and the same worksheets can be used to capture donor information.

Internal Assessment

The internal assessment is used to gauge the organization's capabilities relative to its purpose and mission and the environment in which it is operating. For this reason, the internal assessment is best completed after the external assessment is completed. However, fully assessing an organization's capabilities and identifying the gaps to be addressed can be an extensive undertaking. The practical approach proposed here focuses instead, on identifying the organization's strengths and weaknesses as a proxy for a more extensive internal assessment. A more in-depth assessment of capabilities and core competencies can be a useful undertaking once strategic planning is successfully underway.

Using this practical approach, strengths and weaknesses are identified relative to other service providers. The following steps are suggested to quickly identify the organization's strengths and weaknesses:

1. Review the organization's current mission/vision and the work completed to date on the external situation assessment.
2. Adopt a client perspective. This may involve inviting selected representative clients or proxies for clients (that is, people from other organizations familiar with your clients and the services you deliver) to participate in a discussion of your strengths and weaknesses. If unable to include this external perspective, use people from within the organization who have a good appreciation for your organization's abilities as well as that of similar service providers.
3. Adopt a donor perspective.
4. Brainstorm and record a list of the organization's strengths and weaknesses.
5. Review and shorten the list of strengths and weaknesses by considering if each is truly a strength or weakness relative to alternate service providers. What is it that your organization does better than anyone else? Where are you at a disadvantage relative to the competitors? For example, a social service organization that is good at fundraising would only claim this as a strength if they were better at it than most organizations in their sector.

This assessment of strengths and weaknesses helps the organization determine its source(s) of competitive advantage and its areas of competitive vulnerability.

SWOT Analysis

Strength, **W**eakness, **O**pportunities, **T**hreats (SWOT) Analysis is a framework used to synthesize the positive and negative elements of an organization and its environment.

The SWOT analysis is based on the information obtained from the situation assessment and from participants' perceptions of the relative strengths and weaknesses of the organization. The positive and negative elements need to be identified relative to the current situation as well as the anticipated future situation. Strengths and weaknesses are defined in **Figure 8-6,** *SWOT Definitions.*

FIGURE 8-6
SWOT Definitions

SWOT Definitions	
Strengths	• Internal advantages on which an organization should try to capitalize • What we do well that could give us a competitive advantage
Weaknesses	• Internal disadvantages that may impede success • Once identified, a decision must be made as to whether resources should be allocated to overcome specific weaknesses
Opportunities	• External advantages that an organization should exploit • Capitalize on opportunities based on strengths
Threats	• External events that may exert a significant impact on an organization's performance • Similar to risks • Be aware of in order to take appropriate action when required

Strengths and weakness are defined from the client's perspective, (and if important from a donor's perspective), not that of the organization

The degree to which the situation assessment is analyzed depends upon the *level* of planning (i.e. strategic, tactical) being undertaken

The organization's strengths and weaknesses are identified during the internal assessment discussed above. Opportunities and threats are based on a synthesis of the situation assessment and are identified for each component of this external analysis, i.e., market overview, key trends, competitor analysis and client (and donor) needs/segmentation.

> **Process Tips**: If the organization is overwhelmed with the number of identified opportunities and threats, it may be helpful to conduct a separate brainstorm session to surface and group ideas. **Figure 8-7,** Opportunity and Threat Affinity Process, is a simple approach to accomplish this in a group setting.

At this point the SWOT elements can be summarized onto **Worksheet 8-4,** *SWOT Table.* Completing the SWOT Table is often a sufficient level of SWOT analysis for many social service organizations, particularly those with limited time and resources. The SWOT Table provides a useful summary view of the organization and its situation and is a valuable reference point when considering changes in strategic direction and identifying action priorities.

FIGURE 8-7
Opportunities and
Threats Affinity
Process

Opportunities and Threats Affinity Process

1. Take 5 minutes to think of additional opportunities and threats and record these on yellow (opportunities) and blue (threats) sticky notes.
2. Post the yellow notes on one wall and the blue notes on another wall.
3. Break into two teams, one for opportunities and one for threats:
   - group opportunities/threats into categories
   - label the categories
   - record categories on a flipchart
   - select spokesperson to present findings
4. Review first team's summary of opportunities.
5. Review second team's summary of threats.
6. Identify any additional work required:
   - clearer definition of opportunities/threats?
   - information to validate the opportunities/threats?
   - assign tasks for follow-up.

If desired, an additional level of SWOT analysis can be undertaken by aligning the relevant strengths and weaknesses with each opportunity and each threat. This alignment helps the organization to categorize each opportunity and threat as:

- an investment opportunity where strengths support the opportunity and provide advantage to the organization,
- a decision area where significant weaknesses may impede the organization's ability to realize the opportunity requiring the organization to decide how to proceed,
- an area to be defended where the organization has strengths that can be mobilized to counter the threat,
- a high risk area where the threat corresponds with significant weaknesses requiring the organization to take dramatic action or prepare to manage the consequences.

Worksheet 8-5, *SWOT Analysis,* can be used to record this alignment of strengths and weaknesses to the opportunities and threats.

Key Strategic Issues and Implications

Key strategic issues are the few high priorities that must be addressed within the current planning horizon. These three to five issues are a distillation of all the implications arising from the situation assessment.

A practical approach for identifying key strategic issues is outlined below.

1. Ask all participants to identify what they believe to be the three strategic issues that need to be addressed as the organization moves forward over the next three to five years. The resulting list is ideally a half dozen or so in length.

Identifying ten or more issues usually indicates that participants are identifying important tactical issues rather than strategic issues.

2. Because these issues provide the basis for the subsequent action priorities, the total number of issues should be kept to no more than five. This can be accomplished by letting each participant vote on what they consider to be the top three issues. This simple process usually results in an approximate priority ranking of the issues.

Alternatively, identifying key strategic issues can be conducted without the benefit of a full situation assessment and by relying on the collective knowledge of board members, management and staff. The process outlined in **Figure 8-8,** *Key Issue Identification Process,* is a convenient way to surface the key strategic issues from the organization's perspective, but relies on the intuition of participants and, therefore, lacks the rigor of a fact-based approach required for robust strategic planning. **Figure 8-9**, *Sampling of Key Strategic Issues*, illustrates several key strategic issues identified by United Way of Calgary and Area in their planning efforts.

Dealing with Scope: How much detail is enough?

In an ideal world, organizations would have all the information they require to make informed decisions about their strategy and direction. Of course, we do not live in a perfect world and often have to make decisions without having the benefit of all the facts and information we would like. Managing the balance between the resources expended to conduct a situation assessment against the value of the information acquired is an important task for the planning team/leader to resolve. A number of trade-offs must be considered particularly when the organization is new to the process of strategic planing:

Participant Engagement — It is important to clarify the organization's strategy and start setting action priorities quickly in order to keep participants engaged in the process. Participants in any planning process are invariably busy people with many priorities. They must see immediate, tangible benefits of a planning process if they are to maintain commitment to the effort.

Avoid Speculation — Organizations new to planning efforts often lack succinct information and organizational knowledge about their environment (for example, clients, donors, other stakeholders, competitors). Investing time up-front to increase the understanding of the environment allows the organization to establish a new strategic direction based on fact and well researched conclusions rather than speculation.

Inject New Thinking — Without the injection of new thinking about the organization and its environment, the organization will tend to default back to its existing strategy and will not adequately consider a break through in strategic direction.

Incremental Resource Commitment — Resource commitment to the planning process must be commensurate with the benefits realized. An organization new to planning is unlikely to commit significant resources until it is clear that worthwhile benefits can be achieved.

FIGURE 8-8
Key Issue
Identification
Process

Key Issue Identification Process

1. Through informal discussions or a few interviews, identify a list of key issues facing the organization. Prepare a list of these issues and describe each one in two or three words.
2. Conduct formal interviews with individuals across the organization to perform an assessment of these issues.
3. Ask the interviewee to think about the organization's strategic direction and then ask them to sort the issues on the list into two categories:
   - issues critical to achieving the organization's strategic direction
   - issues relatively less important to achieving the strategic direction
4. Record the critical issues.
5. Now ask the interviewee to number the list of critical issues from most critical to least critical. Record the rankings.
6. Ask the interviewee to rank the organization's current performance against each critical issue using a scale from 1 to 10 where 1 means organizational performance is poor relative to where it needs to be, and 10 means organizational performance is strong relative to where it needs to be to address the issue. Record the results.
7. Select the highest scored critical issue. Ask why this issue was scored the highest and record the answer.
8. Select the two lowest scored critical issues and ask the following questions for each:
   - What are the two or three things about this issue that are most in need of improvement?
   - What are the principle barriers to achieving the needed improvement?
   - How would you approach the task of achieving the required improvement?
9. Tabulate the results from this assessment and produce the following:
   - A qualitative summary of the findings.
   - A four-quadrant diagram to illustrate the areas of highest impact as illustrated in the Key Issues Map.

Key Issues Map

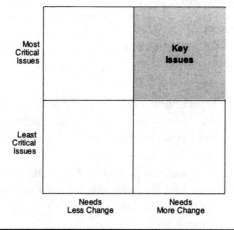

FIGURE 8-9
Sampling of Key
Strategic Issues

Key Strategic Issues

- Corporate restructuring favouring growth in small and medium sized companies
- Rekindling workplace spirit
- Significant rise in other fundraisers' activity
- High demand for professional, experienced fundraisers
- Corporations seeking more recognition
- Volunteerism decreasing

Source: United Way of Calgary and Area, 1995

Avoid Reworking — Without adequate information and development of a common view of the environment up-front in a planning process, the effort can become bogged down. Those involved in the planning effort become reluctant to make decisions with long-term ramifications without the benefit of sufficient market data. This can result in reworking previously reached conclusions, frustration for those involved in performing the work, and significant delays in the process.

There is no straightforward answer to these trade-offs. Success lies in walking a tight rope between keeping the situation assessment process manageable while maximizing the injection of new thinking and knowledge about the organization and its environment. Initially, keep the assessment focused on the most urgent or core issues. As the organization gains knowledge about its environment and experience in conducting this type of assessment, other important issues and topics will surface and can be introduced and dealt with in subsequent planning cycles. This incremental approach to assessing the situation is most effective in producing the required results in an organization with limited resources.

Three suggested approaches to consider when conducting a situation assessment, depending on the time and resources available, are:

1. Establish working teams to investigate and prepare summary conclusions about each component.
2. Assign individuals to investigate and prepare summary conclusions about each component.
3. Conduct a planning session and draw from the knowledge in the room.

The facilitator's role throughout the situation assessment discussions is to ensure participants obtain a broad understanding of the marketplace, trends, competitors, donors and client needs and segments by avoiding unnecessary investigation of details. If additional information is required, note these issues as parking lot items for off-line resolution and review at a subsequent planning session. Throughout ask questions that help participants understand these topics and how they are likely to impact the organization.

Having completed this situation assessment, the planning team is well prepared to set its organization's strategic direction, the subject of **Chapter 9**, *Strategy Definition*.

Summary

The situation assessment provides a common fact base from which strategy and implementation choices can confidently be made. The situation assessment increases the organization's awareness of its stakeholders' needs, the environment in which it operates, including the identification of trends affecting the organization and organizations competing for the same resources or clients. This information is utilized in a SWOT (Strengths, Weaknesses, Opportunities, Threats) analysis to ultimately derive a limited number of strategic issues and their implications for the organization.

WORKSHEET 8-1
Key Trends

Key Trends Worksheet

Task 1. Identify and describe the key trends, external to your organization, with potential to impact your success over the next 3 to 5 years. Possible trends to consider: technological, regulatory, political, economic, social, legal, demographic, human resources.

2. Identify the implications to your organization for each of these key trends.

Key Trends	Description	Implications
1.		
2.		
3.		
4.		
5.		
6.		

WORKSHEET 8-2
Competitive
Assessment

Competitive Assessment Worksheet

TASK
1. Identify the key competitor groups that deliver service/value to your clients.
2. For each group, identify one or two representative organizations.
3. Complete the table by identifying the perceived generic strengths and weaknesses for each competitor group to develop a profile for each.

Competitors	Focus/Services Provided	Typical Clients	Perceived Strengths	Perceived Weaknesses
Competitor Group 1: _____				
Competitor Group 2: _____				
Competitor Group 3: _____				
Competitor Group 4: _____				

WORKSHEET 8-3
Clients Needs and
Segmentation
Assessment

Client Needs and Segmentation Assessment Worksheet

Task
1. Identify the significant client groups/segments based on their needs.
2. For each segment, identify one or two representative clients.
3. Complete the table by listing the prioritized needs and identifying the program/services delivered to develop a profile for each group.
4. Finalize the table by ranking your organization's performance in satisfying each of the key needs identified.

Representative Customers	Key Needs (prioritized)	Programs/Services Delivered	Your Performance Satisfying Key Needs			
Client Segment 1: _____			1 Poor	2 Fair	3 Good	4 Excellent
Client Segment 2: _____			1 Poor	2 Fair	3 Good	4 Excellent
Client Segment 3: _____			1 Poor	2 Fair	3 Good	4 Excellent
Client Segment 4: _____			1 Poor	2 Fair	3 Good	4 Excellent

WORKSHEET 8-4
SWOT Table

SWOT Table Worksheet

TASK   1. Identify your organization's strengths and weaknesses relative to others providing similar services in your sector.
       2. Identify external opportunities and threats that could impact your organization over the next 3 to 5 years.

Internally Focused	Externally Focused
Strengths:	Opportunities:
Weaknesses:	Threats:

WORKSHEET 8-5
SWOT Analysis

SWOT Analysis Worksheet

TASK
1. Insert opportunities and threats in the first row of the chart.
2. Insert key strengths and weaknesses in the left column of the chart.
3. Check off the key strengths and weaknesses that are relevant to each opportunity and threat.
4. Select from one of two categories for each opportunity and each threat:

Opportunity Categories:	Investment	— opportunity with significant supporting strengths
	Decision	— opportunity with significant weaknesses; decision required
Threat Categories:	Defend	— threat that can be mitigated using strengths
	High Risk	— threat complicated by significant weakness

	Opportunities			Threats		
	Opportunity #1	Opportunity #2	Opportunity #n	Threat #1	Threat #2	Threat #n
Key Strengths Strength #1 . . . Strength #n						
Key Weaknesses Weakness #1 . . . Weakness #n						
Category						

CHAPTER 9

Strategic Definition

How is your organization unique?

As defined in **Chapter 2,** *The Planning Model,* an organization's mission statement defines the distinctive identity or purpose that the organization seeks within the social service marketplace. The mission clearly, concisely and simply states what value the organization provides and establishes a unique and distinguishing position. This distinctive identity allows an organization to be successful because the organization is able to differentiate itself from others who provide the same or similar services in an increasingly cluttered social service market. Clearly communicating a distinct value attracts clients, funders and potential partners.

An organization's unique position can really only be defined once a situation assessment has been completed and the organization understands the clients it can best serve. (Refer to **Chapter 8,** *Situation Assessment,* for how to conduct a situation assessment.) This chapter assumes a situation assessment has been completed and describes simple approaches for developing a mission statement as well as the other components of the planning model: values, key success factors, goals and performance indicators.

Developing the Value Statement

Values are fundamental principles and beliefs that serve as implicit criteria guiding all actions and decision making. They are far reaching, applying not only to how staff should treat each other, but also to how the organization interacts with all its stakeholders, that is clients, donors, funders, community leaders, other social service agencies, government and potential partners.

The process of developing a value statement can take many forms and depends upon the size and management style of each organization. The most successful approach, however, involves all levels of the organization (not just senior management) and a clearly defined series of steps.

A simple approach for generating a value statement centers on the use of discussion groups, also known as focus groups, to solicit representative input from across the organization. Focus groups are a practical method for interested individuals to participate actively. Focus groups are most effective when participation is limited to eight to twelve people, no more than two hours in length, guided by an experienced facilitator and reflective of the diversity of the organization (for example, gender, age, expertise, and tenure with the organization).

In this particular situation, individuals involved in the focus groups are expected to:

- Learn what values are and why they are important to the organization's success.
- Solicit ideas from the units within the organization they represent.
- Identify the organization's core values.
- Commit time to the identification, validation and communication of the value statement.

Suggested steps to generate a value statement are:

1. Establish a clearly defined series of steps and timetable for developing a value statement.
2. Have the Executive Director communicate, both verbally and in written form, the organization's commitment to the development and use of a value statement.
3. Solicit volunteers or assign staff representative of the various units of the organization to participate in focus group sessions. It may be necessary to hold multiple focus groups to extend organizational representation beyond eight to twelve participants.
4. In parallel to step 3, prepare and distribute materials to focus group participants that include:
   - definition of values and why values are important to an organization (refer to **Chapter 2**, *The Planning Model*),
   - selected recent articles describing values, their use and the impact they have on organizations,
   - draft value statements or list value statements that are currently in use in the organization,
   - a variety of examples of value statements from other organizations (these are easily found on the internet).
5. Conduct a one-hour orientation session (or include as a component of the initial focus group) with participants to:
   - confirm senior management's support for this initiative,
   - discuss the definition of values, why values are important and the impact values have on an organization,
   - review and evaluate examples of value statements from other organizations and record what is and is not desirable about each.
6. Conduct an initial focus group to brainstorm a list of values and prioritize these to the five or six key values for the organization. As follow-up to the session, integrate and consolidate the input collected and prepare one or two draft value statements to be critiqued at a follow-up focus group session.
7. Conduct a follow-up focus group discussion to review the draft value statement(s), identify the pros and cons, and if time permits, reach consensus on the preferred wording.

8. Validate the wording of the proposed value statement with senior leadership. Revise wording as required.
9. Think creatively about how to present and communicate the value statement to all key stakeholders.

Example: The focus group participants from one organization felt so strongly aligned with the value statement resulting from their work that they insisted on posting a signed copy of the statement throughout the organization. In another setting, senior management fully endorsed the wording suggested by the focus group participants and supported the participants desire to communicate their authorship of the statement.

Developing the Mission Statement

The mission communicates the distinctive identity or purpose that the organization seeks within the social service sector. It clearly and concisely conveys what overall value the organization generates for its clients and stakeholders. It is this clarity and distinctiveness of purpose as well as the alignment of everything about the organization around this purpose that allows clients and stakeholders to be able to understand and therefore support exactly what the organization stands for.

An organization needs to be deliberate about creating and communicating its uniqueness; distinctiveness does not just happen. In defining uniqueness, the following key questions need to be answered:

- Is the organization willing to be a leader or follower, and what does this actually mean?
- Is the organization a small or large player and what implications does this have for the delivery of service to clients and interaction with and solicitation of support from funders?

Unique positioning is not about strengths, but rather, about how the sector perceives the organization relative to other providers. Unique positioning evolves over time in response to changes in the external environment (such as government policy) and the evolving needs of key stakeholders.

A mission is best developed once the situation assessment has been completed and the environment in which the organization is and will be operating is more fully understood. Defining the mission is the role of senior leadership (that is, the board and senior management) with the support of the organization.

A simple approach for developing a mission statement is:

Independent Work Prior to a Group Planning Session:

1. Prepare and distribute materials to participants in the planning process that include:
   - definition of mission and why a mission statement is important to an organization (refer to **Chapter 2**, *The Planning Model*),
   - selected recent articles describing mission statements, their use and impact they have on organizations,

- key findings and conclusions from the situation assessment,
- any mission statement that is currently in use in the organization,
- a variety of examples of mission statements from other organizations (these are easily found on the internet).

2. Based on this background material, ask participants in the planning process to prepare a draft mission statement that captures their view of the organization's purpose.

In a Group Planning Session:

3. Ask each participant to present and explain his or her draft mission.
4. Discuss the pros and cons of the various draft statements presented. Identify all the common purposes or concepts among the mission statements, as well as the one or two unique concepts that may have surfaced.
5. Reach agreement on the two or three concepts that need to be included in the mission.
6. Using these agreed to concepts as the basis, draft a proposed mission statement in the session or ask one or more individuals to draft a mission statement outside the planning session for subsequent review, discussion and agreement by the group. Each of the key concepts in the statement should be briefly defined.

A slight variation on this process eliminates steps 1 and 2. Instead, in the planning session, participants are asked to brainstorm the organization's key purposes. Once the key purposes have been agreed to, one or more groups are asked to prepare draft mission statements outside of the planning session. These drafts are then reviewed at the next planning session and the preferred alternative is selected or a hybrid is developed.

> ***Process Tips:*** *In order to stimulate people's thinking about a mission statement, ask people to visualize success by drawing a picture of what "success" looks like. For example, generate a newspaper headline or the front cover of a magazine. These pictures will surface valuable concepts for the mission statement.*

As the mission is being developed, the following questions are a useful checklist to ensure a clear and worthwhile mission is being developed:

- Is it clear what the focus, direction and uniqueness of the organization are?
- Is it clear what the organization will do and will not do?
- Is the client focus of the organization clear?
- Is the statement inspiring? Will it captivate the interest of funders, donors, staff and volunteers?
- Does the statement provide direction for day-to-day decision making?
- Is the mission viable/realistic in the context of the situation assessment?
- Is the organization adequately differentiated from alternate service providers?

Once developed and articulated, an organization's mission does not need to be redeveloped every year. Typically, the strategic direction of an organization is stable over time, changing only in response to changes in the external environment or internal leadership. As a result, the mission does not need to be revisited unless issues are raised by the situation assessment or leadership decides to change the organization's direction.

For more advanced planning, refer to **Chapter 12**, *Developing a Vision*. For a lighter look at mission statement development, try Dilbert's "Mission Statement Generator" at the Dilbert web site (http://www.dilbert.com).

Developing Key Success Factors

Key success factors (KSFs) are the characteristics, conditions, or variables that when properly sustained, maintained or managed can have a significant impact on the success of an organization competing in a particular sector. They are defined in terms of output, not input or ends, not means, and they are often similar within organizations that provide similar services. Key success factors help leadership direct the organization's limited resources to where the greatest impact will be realized relative to the organization's mission. Key success factors are also used as the basis for identifying performance indicators in subsequent steps of the planning process.

Similar to the mission, key success factors are best developed after a situation assessment has been completed and the organization has a broader and refreshed view of the external environment. Because key success factors are a function of both the external environment and the particular strategic direction the organization has chosen, it is important to have a clear understanding of the organization's mission before identifying or revising the key success factors.

A simple approach for developing key success factors within a group planning session is:

1. Given the direction implied by the organization's mission, ask the participants to brainstorm the areas where results must be achieved and will likely be measured, keeping in mind the guidelines for key success factors introduced in **Chapter 2**, *The Planning Model*.
2. Describe each key success factor with two or three words (although, in some situations a clarifying sentence may be helpful).
3. If there are more than six proposed key success factors, probe the group about why each factor is thought to be important and use the guidelines from **Chapter 2**, *The Planning Model* to eliminate some. For example, the natural tendency is to identify the activities required to achieve an end result rather than to identify the end result. Resist the temptation to accept "client satisfaction" as a key success factor. While this is a common end result that all organizations must achieve, it is much more helpful to the organization to dig deeper to understand what makes up "client satisfaction" to discover the underlying key success factors.
4. Reach agreement on the five or six key success factors that adequately reflect the areas of fundamental outcomes to the organization.

If any difficulty is encountered, remember that key success factors are usually similar for organizations with similar services and clients. Consider obtaining other organization's views of their key success factors as a source of ideas for thinking about your own key success factors.

Like the mission, key success factors should be stable over time and only revisited when the organization changes its strategic direction or changes in the external environment necessitate a review.

Developing Goals

Goals are the longer-term areas targeted by the organization for emphasis. They provide direction for fundamental change and extend beyond the time horizon of the annual budget cycle.

The goals and mission, when articulated together, should provide a clear picture of the organization's focus and priorities over a multiple year period. They will not, however, articulate how these priorities will be achieved or what specifically needs to get done.

A simple approach for developing goals within a group planning session is:

1. For each purpose included in the mission, identify one, two or three potential goals, keeping in mind the guidelines identified in **Chapter 2**, *The Planning Model*.
2. Articulate each goal as a short statement that excludes mention of when it will be achieved and how it will be accomplished.
3. If significantly more than five or six goals are proposed, consider asking the following questions about each goal to help eliminate goals that are not adequately strategic:
   - Is the goal too tactical and specific about what will get done?
   - Will the goal be accomplished within a year or two?
   - Is the goal relatively easy to accomplish, not challenging or stretching the organization or implying some degree of risk for the organization?
   - Does the goal support one or more of the purposes included in the mission?
4. Reach agreement on the five or six goals that reflect the organization's desired direction and priorities.

Goals are likely to change more frequently than the mission and key success factors. As goals are accomplished, new goals need to be identified to clarify the organization's priorities and direction in the context of the mission.

Developing Performance Indicators

Performance indicators are the measures used to gauge actual results against the key success factors. For each key success factor, one or more performance indicators are typically defined.

Performance indicators are used by leadership to assess the organization's implementation progress and overall achievement of its strategic direction. Like the mission, key success factors, and goals, senior leadership defines performance indicators with the support of the organization.

A simple approach for identifying performance indicators in a group planning session is:

1. Confirm with the participants that the key success factors are understandable and comprehensive.
2. For each key success factor, have participants brainstorm possible ways to measure organizational results against each key success factor. Record these initial ideas in **Worksheet 9-1**, *Potential Performance Indicators*.

3. Using the performance indicator characteristics outlined in **Chapter 2**, *The Planning Model*, filter and refine the initial brainstormed ideas into potential performance indicators.

4. Reach agreement on the eight to ten performance indicators that best and most practically measure results across all key success factors.

5. Use **Worksheet 9-2**, *Performance Indicator Validation,* to validate that all key success factors are adequately measured by these eight to ten indicators. Make modifications to the indicators, if required, to ensure all key success factors will be measured. **Figure 9-1**, *Example of Performance Indicator Validation,* is included to illustrate how Worksheet 9-2 was used by United Way of Calgary and Area.

6. Review the performance indicators and categorize each as a leading indicator (that is, a gauge of where the organization is going and its likelihood of success) or a lagging indicator (that is, a gauge of how well the organization achieved its priorities after the fact).

7. Modify the performance indicators as required to ensure an adequate balance of leading and lagging indicators.

8. Consider testing the appropriateness of the draft performance indicators within the organization and with external partners.

FIGURE 9-1
Example of
Performance
Indicator
Validation

Performance Indicator Validation	1 KSF	2 KSF	3 KSF	4 KSF	5 KSF	6 KSF
Donor Satisfaction Index	✓	✓		✓	✓	
Volunteer Satisfaction Index			✓			✓
Dollars Raised	✓	✓	✓	✓	✓	✓
Number of Donors	✓	✓				
Number of Donors Retained	✓	✓				
Consistency of Giving History (year/year)	✓	✓				
"Wow" Factor	✓			✓	✓	✓
Number of Volunteers			✓			✓
Dollars per Donor Raised (average gift)	✓	✓				
Percent Increase in Average Gift		✓		✓		
Employee Satisfaction Index	✓	✓	✓	✓	✓	✓

Source: United Way of Calgary and Area; Resource Development Plan, 2000

A somewhat more elaborate process can be used to develop performance indicators and establish baseline information by following **Worksheet 9-3,** *Performance Indicator Development*. The sequence of steps used with this worksheet is:

1. Performance Indicators — As a team, brainstorm four or five possible performance indicators (fill in one per line) for each key success factor.

2. Information Sources — For each potential performance indicator, assign a small working group to seek out information sources within the organization. An information source is the place where information about the performance indicator is created. There are three possible outcomes of this activity:
   a) One source of information found (ideal). Move to step 3.
   b) Multiple sources of information found (usually the case). If possible, rationalize the sources of information, otherwise select one source of information and use it consistently.
   c) No sources of information found (frequently the case). Verify that the performance indicator is reasonable and then identify where within the organization the information to support that indicator will be created.

3. Other Organizations' Performance — For each indicator, identify the performance level of two or three other organizations. These organizations should be classified as "best in class" and need not be within the same sector.

4. Baseline Data — Using the information from step 2, identify the organization's current level of performance for each indicator. **Note**: In some cases, it may not be possible to report baseline data if an information source is not readily available. In this case, refer to step 2c above.

5. Reporting Frequency — As a team, decide what an appropriate reporting frequency would be (for example quarterly, annually, biannually, as required) for each indicator.

6. Short List — Once the worksheet is completed, the team must decide which two or three indicators per key success factor promote the desired behavior. This short list of indicators becomes what the organization will track on an ongoing basis.

7. Accountability — Identify one individual accountable for tracking each indicator.

Performance indicators, once correctly identified, should not change unless the key success factors change.

The planning team has now completed development of the strategic elements of the planning model. **Chapter 10**, *Agree on Action*, assists the team in turning that strategy into action.

Summary

An organization should attempt to define its strategy only after it has completed a situation assessment, as described in **Chapter 8**, *Situation Assessment*. An organization's strategy includes its values, mission, key success factors, goals and performance indicators. With the values as the fundamental principles or beliefs that serve as criteria or a foundation, the mission statement clearly, concisely and simply states what value the organization provides and establishes a unique and distinguishing position in the market. Key success factors, which may be common to organizations providing similar services in similar circumstances and markets, are the characteristics, conditions or variables that when properly sustained, maintained or managed can have a significant impact on the success of an organization. Goals provide direction for fundamental change and extend beyond the time horizon of the annual budget cycle. While performance indicators are the measures used to gauge actual results against the key success factors.

WORKSHEET 9-1
Potential
Performance
Indicators

Potential Performance Indicators Worksheet

TASKS:
1. *Fill in the key success factors along the top of the table.*
2. *Record brainstormed performance indicator ideas for each key success factor.*

	Key Success Factor #1	Key Success Factor #2	Key Success Factor #3	Key Success Factor #4	Key Success Factor #5
Potential Performance Indicators					

WORKSHEET 9-2
Performance
Indicator
Validation

Performance Indicator Validation Worksheet

TASKS:
1. List the key success factors along the top of the chart.
2. List the performance indicators down the left side of the chart.
3. Under each key success factor, check off each performance indicator that supports and measures that key success factor.

	Key Success Factor #1	Key Success Factor #2	Key Success Factor #3	Key Success Factor #4	Key Success Factor #5
Performance Indicator #1					
Performance Indicator #2					
Performance Indicator #3					
Performance Indicator #4					
Performance Indicator #5					
Performance Indicator #6					
Performance Indicator #7					
Performance Indicator #8					
Performance Indicator #9					
Performance Indicator #10					

WORKSHEET 9-3
Performance
Indicator
Development

Performance Indicator Development Worksheet

TASKS:
1. List the key success factors in the left column.
2. Identify performance indicators for each key success factor.
3. Identify information sources to support measuring results for each indicator.
4. Assess the performance of other organizations and your own organization for each indicator.
5. Determine the reporting frequency and accountability for each indicator.

Key Success Factor	Performance Indicators	Information Sources	Other Organizations' Performance	Baseline Data	Reporting Frequency	Accountability
KSF #1						
KSF #2						
KSF #3						
KSF #4						
KSF #5						

CHAPTER 10

Agree on Action

How do you turn strategy into action?

Turning the strategy into action requires the development of clear action priorities and performance targets. Action priorities are the specific steps, or tasks, required to achieve the goals. Performance targets are the pre-determined end results to be achieved in a given period of time and are a useful means to communicate performance expectations to the organization.

This chapter describes how action priorities and performance targets are identified in the strategic planning process and how current work can be prioritized and rationalized given the addition of these strategic action priorities. Identification of action priorities that align with the organization's strategic direction and goals are described first. A process to rationalize these action priorities with current initiatives is then introduced. Finally, an approach to develop performance targets is discussed.

Action Priorities Framework

In the strategic planning process, action priorities are generated from two sources:

- the three to five strategic issues identified as a result of the situation assessment as outlined in **Chapter 8**, *Situation Assessment*,
- the goals of the strategic plan as outlined in **Chapter 9**, *Strategy Definition*.

Consequently, the action priorities reflect both the high-priority issues facing the organization as well as the organization's longer-term strategic direction.

Brainstorming action is the easiest and most prolific part of the planning process. Without fail, pages of ideas for action are quickly generated. The resources required to implement these many ideas for action during the time horizon of the strategic plan usually far exceed what the organization can realistically make available. The resources required to implement these action priorities are over and above those resources already dedicated to existing organizational commitments. Evaluating the relative importance and urgency of current initiatives relative to those action priorities generated by the strategic planning process allows the organization to shift its focus and resources to actions with the highest strategic significance.

Worksheet 10-1, *Action Priority Template,* is a convenient tool designed to organize objectives and action plans. As illustrated in the worksheet, each action plan includes who is accountable for implementation, by what target completion date, and any other relevant comments.

The process to develop action priorities is:

Brainstorming Initial Action Ideas (in a group planning session)

1. For each goal, brainstorm and record initial action ideas that would help the organization accomplish the goal. Remember that the elements of the SWOT analysis discussed in **Chapter 6**, *Situation Assessment,* are an excellent source of action ideas.

2. Using the list of strategic issues previously identified in the situation assessment, review the list of brainstormed action ideas to ensure sufficient action has been proposed to address each of the strategic issues. If not, continue to brainstorm and record additional action ideas to address the strategic issues.

Organize Ideas into Objectives (independent or group work)

3. This initial brainstorming effort typically produces ideas in a wide variety of forms, frequently from very broad, long-term objectives to very specific, short-term action details. Outside of any group planning session, delete redundant action ideas and cluster or organize the remaining brainstormed action ideas into objectives and supporting action plans.

4. Complete the objective and action plan components of **Worksheet 10-1**, *Action Priority Template,* for each proposed objective, leaving the accountability, target completion date and comments section until later.

5. Distribute the draft objectives and action plans prior to the next planing session with instructions for individuals to review and be prepared to comment on the draft materials circulated.

Finalize Action Plans (group planning session)

6. During a group planning session, review and revise the draft objectives and action plans, making sure they align with the characteristics outlined in **Chapter 2**, *The Planning Model*. Start identifying the accountable person and approximate target completion date for each action plan as each objective is reviewed. Do not let the process become bogged down if the answers to these two parameters are not immediately obvious.

7. At this stage, it is wise to once again ensure that sufficient action exists to address all the goals and each of the strategic issues.

8. Ensure the accountable person and target completion date are clearly recorded and agreed to for each action plan. If possible, get each of the people designated as "accountable" to confirm that they support the action plan as defined and agree to its implementation under their leadership.

9. Ensure action plans cover the entire timeframe of the plan. Not all actions can, or should, be completed in the first six months or year of a plan. It may be helpful to create a large wall-sized timeline and actually map out all the tasks identified to determine where the schedule may be unrealistic.

10. As a final check, consider the following questions for each action priority:
    - Is the objective of strategic importance?
    - Can the implementation of each objective and action plan be measured?
    - Are the actions clear and specific?
    - Are the action plans realistic given the target completion date and resources available?
    - Is the accountability assigned to the right person?

Figure 10-1, *Example of a Personal Strategic Plan,* is a simple example of a complete strategic plan as applied to an individual. This example illustrates how the values, mission, key success factors and goals comprise the strategic focus of the plan while the action priorities comprise the tactical focus of the plan and support the achievement of the strategic focus.

FIGURE 10-1
Example of a
Personal Strategic
Plan

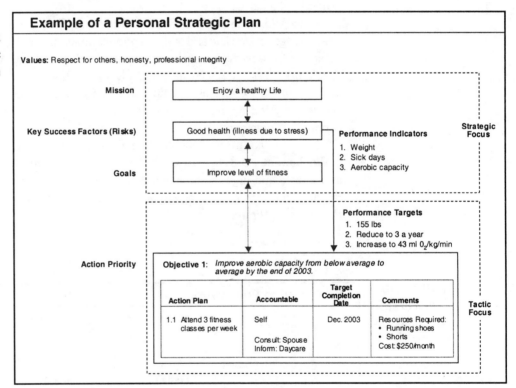

Example of a Personal Strategic Plan

Values: Respect for others, honesty, professional integrity

Mission — Enjoy a healthy Life

Key Success Factors (Risks) — Good health (illness due to stress)

Performance Indicators
1. Weight
2. Sick days
3. Aerobic capacity

Goals — Improve level of fitness

Strategic Focus

Performance Targets
1. 155 lbs
2. Reduce to 3 a year
3. Increase to 43 ml O_2/kg/min

Action Priority

Objective 1: *Improve aerobic capacity from below average to average by the end of 2003.*

Action Plan	Accountable	Target Completion Date	Comments
1.1 Attend 3 fitness classes per week	Self Consult: Spouse Inform: Daycare	Dec. 2003	Resources Required: • Running shoes • Shorts Cost: $250/month

Tactic Focus

Prioritization Framework

Developing action priorities usually produces many ideas for action that must be considered in the context of existing initiatives already underway or planned by the organization. An "initiative" is defined as any non-routine activity that requires an expenditure of a pre-defined amount of money and human resources with a defined start and end date. It is not an ongoing activity. For example, an initiative might be considered to be a non-routine activity that has not been budgeted for and requires an expenditure of $1,000 or more and/or 50 person hours of effort within the next 12 months.

Having just developed a strategic direction and related action priorities, some organizations believe these strategic action priorities must be implemented and existing initiatives need to be reviewed and rationalized to ensure sufficient resources are available for implementing the strategic action priorities. Other organizations, overwhelmed by the quantity of action priorities and initiatives, believe it is necessary to review all action priorities and initiatives together to ensure their resources are committed to only the highest priority activities, whether these activities be generated by the strategic planning process or be initiatives already underway.

In either situation, a prioritization framework can be used to define the organization's overall priorities. This framework provides a method for reviewing and rationalizing existing initiatives. The greatest benefit of this process is the discussion that occurs amongst those individuals or teams that must implement the action. Merely by defining the action and describing its priority, implementation teams form a better understanding about how the action contributes to the organization and how it integrates or needs to coordinate with other initiatives.

Using **Worksheet 10-2**, *Basic Prioritization Framework,* individually or in a group planning session, review and assign a priority ranking of 'must do', 'should do', 'consider doing' or 'nice to do' to each initiative and action priority. Upon completion of this simple prioritization, review each initiative and action priority again to determine if the implementation effort and timing should be adjusted by accelerating the timing, decelerating the timing, stopping the effort altogether, delaying until next year, or continuing implementation as currently planned.

For more advanced planning, a more detailed version of this framework presented in **Worksheet 10-3**, *Initiatives and Action Priority Ranking,* may be used to rank the importance and urgency of all existing initiatives and proposed action priorities. The results of this priority ranking are best presented visually as illustrated in **Figure 10-2**, *Prioritization Framework.*

FIGURE 10-2
Prioritization
Framework

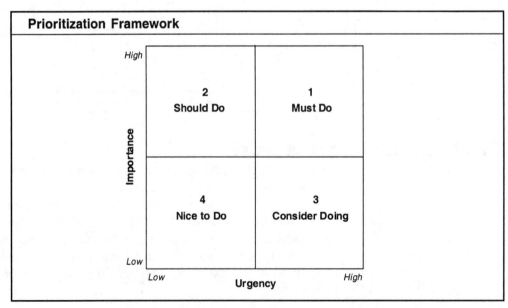

Performance Targets

Performance targets communicate the organization's desired level of performance relative to each performance indicator. If, for example, the performance indicator is "distance in meters," a possible performance target might be "200 meters." Performance targets are a powerful tool to set expectations and thereby motivate the organization, but can have the opposite effect if unachievable targets are set.

Performance targets are developed based on an assessment of current performance and expected emphasis and desired results during the planning period. The following process is used to establish performance targets with the participants in the process.

For each performance indicator:

1. Establish baseline data; that is, what is the organization's current performance level?
2. Determine what is acceptable and "best-in-class" performance (based upon a comparison to other organizations serving the same client group). The organizations to consider for this type of best practice review should not be limited to those in the social service sector.
3. Consider the action priorities and existing initiatives that will have a direct or indirect impact on results relative to the performance indicator.
4. Consider the organization's strengths and weaknesses relative to achieving the desired results.
5. Based on this review of current performance, other organization's performance, proposed actions and strengths and weaknesses, define achievable performance targets that stretch the organization.

Now the Organization is Ready to Produce a Planning Document

At this point all the elements of the strategic plan have been developed. The details of the situation assessment and planning model can now be incorporated into a document, commonly known as the strategic plan, as outlined in **Figure 3-2**, *Table of Contents of a Strategic Plan*.

In addition to the strategic planning document, summarizing the organization's strategic direction and action priorities on one page is an effective method for communicating and reinforcing the key elements of the strategic plan to key stakeholders, particularly those accountable for implementation. This summary means that stakeholders do not need to carry around an actual document but can remind themselves of pertinent organizational priorities by referring to the one-page summary. **Worksheet 10-4**, *One-Page Summary of a Strategic Plan,* is a template for organizing the organization's strategic plan onto one page. **Figure 10-3** provides an example of a one-page summary of a strategic plan.

Beyond the Basics: Prioritizing Action with Greater Rigor

Worksheet 10-3, *Initiatives and Action Priority Ranking,* is a helpful tool for ranking action priorities and current initiatives based on their relative importance and urgency.

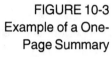

FIGURE 10-3
Example of a One-
Page Summary

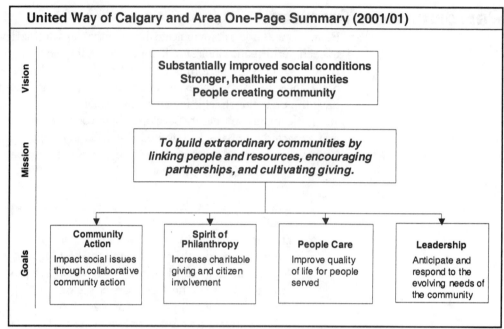

United Way of Calgary and Area One-Page Summary (2001/01)

Vision

Substantially improved social conditions
Stronger, healthier communities
People creating community

Mission

*To build extraordinary communities by
linking people and resources, encouraging
partnerships, and cultivating giving.*

Goals

| **Community Action** | **Spirit of Philanthropy** | **People Care** | **Leadership** |
| Impact social issues through collaborative community action | Increase charitable giving and citizen involvement | Improve quality of life for people served | Anticipate and respond to the evolving needs of the community |

The worksheet is completed in eight steps:

1. Establish Definitions — Determine how the organization will define an initiative.

2. Document all Action — Document all initiatives and action priorities with respect to:
- external resource requirements,
- key employee utilization, that is supervisors and/or senior staff,
- degree to which the task is non-routine in nature,
- timing requirements,
- dependencies on the outcome.

3. Establish Urgency Criteria — Define the urgency criteria to be used to rank the relative urgency of each initiative and action priority. One to three urgency criteria are usually sufficient. Sample urgency criteria may include:
- required to comply with a prescribed timetable
- required to avoid impacting other important activities

4. Establish Importance Criteria — Define the importance criteria to be used to rank the relative importance of each initiative and action priority. Three to five importance criteria are usually sufficient for this task. Any more than five criteria and the ranking process can become too onerous. Sample importance criteria may include:
- required to comply with legislative or regulatory requirements,
- required to satisfy a board or senior management directive,
- strategic impact; that is, degree to which the needs of target clients are met, or degree to which the initiative aligns with the organization's strategic direction,
- impact on efficiency; that is, degree to which the initiative or action priority reduces costs or resource requirements,

- meets stakeholder (staff, volunteer, senior management, board) expectations,
- financial impact; that is, degree to which the activity increases revenues or decreases costs.

5. Rank Initiatives and Action Priorities — Using **Worksheet 10-3**, *Initiatives and Action Priority Ranking*, conduct a group review of each initiative and action priority to establish the importance and urgency ranking for each. A simple ranking scheme is implied by this worksheet. Each criterion has a weighting of *one*. If the initiative or action priority satisfies the criteria, one point is assigned. The points are totaled to obtain an importance and urgency ranking for each initiative and action priority. While more sophisticated ranking schemes can be used, this simple approach has proven effective.

6. Plot all Activities — Use the urgency and importance rankings determined in steps 3 and 4 above to plot all of the initiatives and action priorities on a quadrant diagram as described in **Figure 10-2**, *Prioritization Framework*.
- The urgency axis, or horizontal axis, begins at zero on the left side of the diagram and extends to the total number of urgency criteria identified in step 3 above on the far right side of the diagram.
- Similarly, the importance axis, or vertical axis, begins at zero at the bottom of the diagram and extends to the total number of importance criteria identified in step 4 above at the top of the diagram.

7. Rank Activities — Determine which initiatives and action priorities fall into the categories of "must do," "should do," "consider doing" and "nice to do" from the quadrant diagram. If necessary, adjust the midpoint line on each axes to increase or decrease the size of the various quadrants so that the priorities assigned reflect the resources available.

8. Determine Implementation Schedule — The individuals participating in this process must then reach a decision about how to proceed with each initiative and action priority. For each initiative and action priority, determine if the implementation schedule should:
a) *accelerate* the timing of the initiative or action priority,
b) *decelerate* the timing of the initiative or action priority,
c) *stop* the effort altogether,
d) *delay* (until next year when the initiative or action priority will once again be evaluated in the planning process along with all other identified action), or
e) *continue* as currently planned.

Having turned the strategy into action, it becomes necessary to implement the plan and monitor the results. This becomes the subject of **Chapter 11**, *Implementation and Monitoring Performance*.

Summary

This chapter details how the organization's strategy is turned into action with the development of clear action priorities and performance targets. It describes how action priorities and performance targets are identified in the strategic planning process and how current work can be prioritized and rationalized given the addition of these strategic action priorities. Action priorities are the specific steps required to achieve the goals. They reflect both the high-priority issues facing the organization as well as the organization's longer-term strategic direction. Performance targets communicate the organization's desired level of performance relative to each performance indicator. When used wisely, they are powerful tools to set expectations and thereby motivate the organization.

WORKSHEET 10-1
Action Priority
Template

Action Priority Template Worksheet				
Goal 1				
Objective 1.1				
	Action Plans	**Accountability**	**Target Completion Date**	**Comments**
1.1.1	Xx a) xx b) xx			
1.1.2	xx a) xx b) xx			
1.1.3	xx a) xx b) xx			
1.1.4	xx a) xx b) xx			
1.1.5	xx a) xx b) xx			
1.1.6	xx a) xx b) xx			
1.1.7	xx a) xx b) xx			
1.1.8	xx a) xx b) xx			
1.1.9	xx a) xx b) xx			

WORKSHEET 10-2
Basic Prioritization
Framework

Basic Prioritization Framework Worksheet

TASKS   *For each initiative and action priority:*
1. *Review and assign a priority ranking.*
2. *Determine if the implementation effort and timing should be adjusted.*

Initiatives *non-routine activity planned or currently underway*	Priority Ranking				Implementation Effort and Timing				
	Must Do	Should Do	Consider Doing	Nice to Do	Accelerate	Decelerate	Stop	Delay	Continue as Planned
1.	☐	☐	☐	☐	☐	☐	☐	☐	☐
2.	☐	☐	☐	☐	☐	☐	☐	☐	☐
3.	☐	☐	☐	☐	☐	☐	☐	☐	☐
4.	☐	☐	☐	☐	☐	☐	☐	☐	☐
5.	☐	☐	☐	☐	☐	☐	☐	☐	☐

Action Priorities *as generated by the strategic planning process*	Priority Ranking				Implementation Effort and Timing				
	Must Do	Should Do	Consider Doing	Nice to Do	Accelerate	Decelerate	Stop	Delay	Continue as Planned
1.	☐	☐	☐	☐	☐	☐	☐	☐	☐
2.	☐	☐	☐	☐	☐	☐	☐	☐	☐
3.	☐	☐	☐	☐	☐	☐	☐	☐	☐
4.	☐	☐	☐	☐	☐	☐	☐	☐	☐
5.	☐	☐	☐	☐	☐	☐	☐	☐	☐

WORKSHEET 10-3
Initiatives and Action
Priority Ranking

Initiatives and Action Priority Ranking Worksheet

TASKS
1. List the importance and urgency criteria along the top of each chart.
2. List the initiatives and action priorities in the left column.
3. For each initiative and action priority, place a 1 in each column when the initiative or action priority satisfies the criteria and a 0 if it does not satisfy the criteria.
4. Sum the 1s and 0s to get an importance and urgency rank for each initiative and action priority.

Initiatives *non-routine activity planned or currently underway*	Importance					Urgency				
	Criteria #1	Criteria #2	Criteria #3	Criteria #4	Total Points "Rank"	Criteria #1	Criteria #2	Criteria #3	Criteria #4	Total Points "Rank"
1.										
2.										
3.										
4.										
5.										

Action Priorities *as generated by the strategic planning process*	Importance					Urgency				
	Criteria #1	Criteria #2	Criteria #3	Criteria #4	Total Points "Rank"	Criteria #1	Criteria #2	Criteria #3	Criteria #4	Total Points "Rank"
6.										
7.										
8.										
9.										
10.										

WORKSHEET 10-4
One-page Summary
of a Strategic
Plan

One-Page Summary of a Strategic Action Plan

Values
Fundamental principles and beliefs that serve as implicit criteria guiding all actions and decision-making

- •
- •
- •
- •

Mission
The distinctive identity or purpose which the organization seeks

_____
_____
_____
_____

Key Success Factors
Five or six critical areas an organization must sustain, maintain or manage for long-term success.

KSF 1 _____
KSF 2 _____
KSF 3 _____
KSF 4 _____
KSF 5 _____

Goals
The longer term areas targeted for emphasis.

Goal 1 _____
Goal 2 _____
Goal 3 _____
Goal 4 _____
Goal 5 _____

Performance Indicators
The measures used to gauge actual results against the key success factors.

Leading Indicators — *gauge the likelihood of future success*

Indicator 1 _____
Indicator 2 _____
Indicator 3 _____

Lagging Indicators — *measure how well the organization has performed*

Indicator 4 _____
Indicator 5 _____

Situation Assessment
The areas of the environment that are analyzed annually

- Conclusion/ Trend #1
- Conclusion/ Trend #2
- Conclusion/ Trend #3
- Conclusion/ Trend #N

Events/factors that are expected to have significant impact on the organization

Strategic Issue #1
Strategic Issue #2
Strategic Issue #3

Action Priorities
The specific steps, or tasks, needed to implement the goals and address the strategic issues.

Action Priority 1 _____
Action Priority 2 _____
Action Priority 3 _____
Action Priority 4 _____
Action Priority 5 _____

CHAPTER 11

Implementation and Monitoring Performance

How do you measure up?

Once an organization has successfully defined its strategic direction and the action priorities required to achieve that direction, its attention must shift to implementation and monitoring of results.

As illustrated in **Figure 11-1**, *The Continuous Cycle of Planning*, the act of developing a strategic plan is only one step in the continuous processing of organizational planning. Upon completion of the strategic plan, the organization must shift its focus to implementation and subsequently to the ongoing monitoring and measurement of results. This chapter introduces tips for implementation then describes a performance measurement system to monitor and track the organization's success at achieving its strategic direction.

FIGURE 11-1
The Continuous
Cycle of Planning

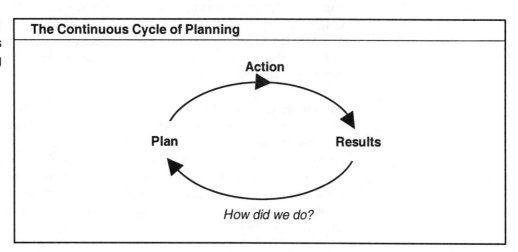

Implementation Tips

Now that the organization has invested substantial time and effort in developing and documenting the strategic plan, the most critical step is its successful implementation.

The following implementation tips provide invaluable guidance to the implementation effort:

Communicate the completed plan to stakeholders and keep people informed of progress. Clearly articulate what and how the organization will change as a result of the strategic direction. Provide stakeholders ample opportunity to inquire about and understand the strategic direction. Post the mission (and if available, the vision) statement(s) in a highly visible location and widely distribute a one-page summary of the plan while respecting the confidentially policy. Regularly communicate results on a quarterly and annual basis; communicate good and bad news as it becomes known.

Provide support to those not directly involved in the process of developing the strategic plan. They will not have had the benefit of the discussion and may not understand how decisions or direction were reached. Ensure that those who did participate in the planning process have an ongoing role in communicating with others. It is best to establish this expectation of an ongoing communication role by participants at the outset of the planning effort. Encourage stakeholder involvement, particularly internal stakeholders, in the implementation of the action plans. Conduct informal surveys to gauge how members of the organization are managing the change and their assessment on the level of improvement/progress that is being made. Periodically check their level of understanding of various components of the plan. Consider using questions from the organizational readiness or temperature check questionnaire introduced in **Chapter 4 —** *Getting Started*.

Establish a mechanism to capture and encourage new ideas for improvement and comments as the year progresses. These ideas should be made available for review at progress review meetings. Be prepared to act if a course correction is required. What seemed like a realistic objective and action plan at the planning stage might become impractical for implementation. Act earlier rather than later to correct this situation. Celebrate success! When action has been taken and results have been achieved, acknowledge the accomplishment and the contribution of those who made it happen. Recognize the need to say goodbye to the old and embrace the new. Help others in the organization to make the same transition.

Leaders in the organization need to demonstrate their support of the strategic direction and action priorities. If roles or functions have been redefined, provide retraining for those impacted. Stay focused on implementing the action plans. The organization's priorities have been defined through the objectives and action plans — stick to them! Leaders need to talk about the direction at every opportunity, visibly support implementation efforts, make tough decisions along the way and show commitment by being willing to stop activities that do not contribute to the organization achieving its strategic direction.

Performance Measurement System

With implementation underway, results must be monitored and used as input to subsequent rounds of strategic plan development. Measuring the results achieved by the organization provides the organization with the opportunity to assess how well it is meeting its stated goals and where changes in effort may be required. Leading organizations use this feedback to adjust their strategic and tactical focus for optimal results. It is this process of monitoring, understanding results and adjusting action that is referred to as a performance measurement system. The primary attribute of a performance measurement system is that it distinguishes *chance* results from *planned* performance.

A performance measurement system is used both as a monitoring device and a diagnostic tool. As a monitoring device, the performance measurement system measures where the organization is relative to where the organization wants to be (that is, it measures relative success). It measures the benefits of change implied by the strategic direction and provides the structure within which performance targets can be developed to drive improvement efforts. As a monitoring device, a performance measurement system facilitates quality decision-making within the organization. As a diagnostic tool, a performance measurement system identifies the areas in need of attention and alerts leadership to those areas that require remedial action.

A performance measurement system helps promote appropriate behaviors and integrate all levels of planning across the organization by clearly defining, in advance, how the organization measures success. If appropriate, a performance measurement system can also be used as the basis for individual compensation and recognition.

Benefits and Concerns of a Performance Measurement System

A performance measurement system is an extremely powerful component of the strategic planning process. It helps to make the strategic direction tangible by monitoring progress towards the attainment of the direction. While a performance measurement system offers a number of benefits for an organization, it needs to be managed with care.

Benefits associated with a performance measurement system are:

- clarifies performance expectations for the organization,
- communicates what is important across the organization,
- motivates the organization to pull together and achieve desired outcomes,
- provides the basis from which to link individual contributions to strategic direction.

Concerns associated with a performance measurement system may include:

- organizational energies being misdirected if incorrect performance indicators are selected,
- organizational discouragement and skepticism of the entire process if unrealistic (either too high or too low) targets are set,
- unnecessary degree of bureaucracy and infrastructure put in place to track performance indicators making the system slow and cumbersome to use and overly complex to manage.

A performance measurement system is composed of three elements: key success factors, performance indicators and performance targets. Each of these concepts is described in **Chapter 2,** *The Planning Model*. Processes to develop key success factors and performance indicators are discussed in **Chapter 9,** *Strategy Definition* and a process to develop performance targets is introduced in **Chapter 10,** *Agree on Action*.

Monitoring Progress and Measuring Results

From a strategic planning perspective, monitoring progress and measuring results are separate, but related activities. Monitoring progress is the process of managing and reviewing the implementation status of the action priorities. Measuring results refers to the process of measuring and communicating the performance achieved against the performance indicators.

Monitoring Progress

Once the action priorities have been finalized and resources committed to their implementation, the various assigned individuals can begin carrying out their action plans. Establishing regular reviews of progress against the action priorities helps emphasize the importance of the action priorities and provides senior leadership an opportunity to make adjustments in action, if required. Regular progress reviews:

- Establish milestones where accountable individuals know they will be expected to report on what has been accomplished and what has been achieved.
- Provide an opportunity to understand how implementation is proceeding.
- Provide an opportunity to surface and resolve resource or organizational hurdles to be overcome.
- Adjust action priorities, if necessary, to reflect new information or evolving conditions.

Progress reviews should be conducted with a frequency that reflects the schedule established for the action priorities. In most cases, quarterly reviews, and in some cases, biennial reviews, are sufficient.

> **Process Tips:** *Implement an annual cycle to review the strategic plan.*

Worksheet 11-1, *Status Report Template*, outlines a template for recording overall implementation status and the status of individual action priorities. Ideally, this template should be distributed and completed in advance of the review session. It may also be helpful to have the completed sheets returned to an individual responsible for synthesizing the information and redistributing prior to the meeting. Participants need to come prepared for the review sessions. Discussion time during the review sessions should focus on items that are really off course. But remember to take some time to celebrate successes!

Figure 11-2, *Example of a Status Report,* is an example of a status report used by the board and the senior management team to review implementation progress of action priorities. In this example, task teams, rather than individuals, were assigned accountability for implementing the action plans.

Measuring Results

Measuring results against the performance indicators helps leadership determine if, together, the action priorities being implemented are achieving the desired strategic results. **Worksheet 11-2**, *Measuring Results,* can be used to record results against the performance indicators and manage their review. This worksheet is best used by following these steps:

FIGURE 11-2
Example of a
Status Report

Status Report		
Task Teams	**Activity**	**Status Update**
Finance	Raise the dollars or resources required to staff the transition stage of strategic change	Discussions with potential funders still in progress
Community Issues	Determine the key issues facing Calgary, and determine United Way area(s) of focus	Continue as planned
Market Research	Identify and prioritize donor segments based on their needs	Proceed with market research only
External Readiness	Work with key external stakeholders to ensure optimum change for both United Way and its stakeholders	Initial meeting will determine feasibility of proceeding at a reduced level
Strategic Transition	Identify current United Way initiatives and determine which of these can be stopped, delayed, expanded, narrowed	Deferred
	Determine high level guiding business principles and tenets which will guide United Way	Mission and values presented at Board Meeting. Other activity deferred
Community Services	Make funding decisions for the 1996 allocation year	Other Board members reassigned for duration of strategic transition task team responsibilities
Resource Mobilization (annual campaign)	Provide leadership to the 1996 Campaign Cabinet	Other Board members reassigned for duration of strategic transition task team responsibilities
Nominating		Deferred to later start date
Audit		Deferred to later start date

Source: United Way of Calgary and Area, 1996

1. Complete columns 1 through 3, Performance Indicators, Performance Targets and Actual Results prior to a review meeting.
2. Distribute the worksheet to participants for review prior to the meeting.
3. At a progress review meeting, reach consensus about where the organization is on target, ahead of target or behind target for each performance indicator.
4. Discuss, agree and document corrective action as required.
5. If required, adjust one or more targets.

Performance Measurement Cautions

Developing and implementing effective performance measurement is challenging. Some of the issues to be aware of with performance measurement are outlined below:

Linking performance to results — As participants realize that particular indicators will reflect positively or negatively on their individual performance, the process becomes biased as they try to slant the measures in their favor. There is typically an expectation of a reward or recognition when a target is exceeded. This reward/recognition expectation tends to encourage participants to set targets as low as possible at the outset. People respond best when rewards and recognition are structured to address individual needs and are tied directly to the results that are controllable by the individual. It is often difficult to translate organizational performance indicators directly to measures of performance for any one individual.

What to measure — What gets measured determines the performance that results. It is important that what is measured reflects the results the organization is attempting to achieve. For example, if the goal is to improve safety, is it preferable to measure the number of accidents or the number of accidents avoided? The number of accidents might not be entirely in one's control whereas accidents avoided might reflect the effectiveness of training received or it might emphasize where new training may be required.

What is most important — There are many choices of things to measure. For example, in measuring safety performance, one could measure vehicle accidents, time lost, days lost , accidents avoided, training delivered, medical aid provided, and others. Having too many measures is a sure recipe for failure. Having fewer performance indicators causes the organization to be more focused and more likely to achieve the desired results.

Keeping performance indicators simple — To be effective, performance indicators must be kept simple. The more complex the indicator, the more systems and effort required to track results. Ideal measures are simple and flexible; supported by simple, flexible systems. This can be achieved by making use of available data collection systems and information wherever possible.

Not specific enough — Some performance indicators, measuring the strategic performance of the organization, are too broad to be useful throughout the organization. In some cases it may be necessary to translate the performance indicators into more specific component indicators for use in different areas of the organization.

Engagement — The people directly involved in producing results against the performance indicators need to be given sufficient opportunity to contribute their ideas to the development of indicators and targets if they are to be committed to achieving the desired results.

Figure 11-3A, *Annual Report to the Community*, and **Figure 11-3B,** *Report to Donors,* are examples of reports to stakeholders on results achieved against the performance indicators. These figures demonstrate a combination of qualitative and quantitative descriptions of the progress made by the organization.

FIGURE 11-3A
Annual Report to
the Community

Annual Report (1999)

- **We came together with others to create collaborative action** on homelessness, child hunger, mental illness, teen pregnancy and domestic violence.
- **We invested $14.4 million in a strong network of over 190 community services** that care for the health and well being of our growing population; plus $2.8 million to individual charities at the request of our donors.
- **We inspired and broadened opportunities for involvement.** United Way's Strategic Giving Group helped corporations see how their charitable giving can impact on the community while meeting their own business goals.
- **We built skills and resources in the voluntary sector** by helping social agencies measure the effectiveness of their programs, by providing sustainable funding that allows agencies to do long-range planning, by coordinating the flow of goods and services to agencies that help them reduce operating costs, and by administering a group benefits program that enables them to attract and retain quality staff.
- **We brought people and organizations together** in Days of Caring and learning tours that helped donors understand their community and its issues, to make a valuable personal contribution of their time and talents, and to see first hand the remarkable work that is being done by our city's serving agencies.

Source: United Way of Calgary and Area, excerpts from 1999 Annual Report

FIGURE 11-3B
Report to Donors

2000 Report to Donors

Examples of the 21st century solutions we put to work this past year:

Your United Way Donations Make A Difference — Your support of United Way has made it possible for the community to address the urgent and immediate needs of people — while building sustainable solutions for the future. Here are just a few examples of the difference United Way has made in people's lives through you.

> **Domestic Violence:** 1,550 women and children found safety and shelter at the Calgary Native Women's Shelter, Calgary Women's Emergency Shelter, the YWCA's Sheriff King Home, and Discovery House.

> **Youth Violence:** 80 families participated in the Catholic Family Services FAST program (Family and Schools Together), an eight-week program involving five Calgary schools, designed to reduce the factors associated with school failure, juvenile delinquency, and substance abuse in adolescence.

> **Teen Pregnancy:** 58 teen parents received guidance and help with their parenting skills from the volunteer mentors they found through the Catholic Family Services V-TIPS program (Volunteer Teaching Important Parenting Skills).

> **Homelessness:** The Calgary Drop-in Centre provides a safe shelter to approximately 405 people a night, and serves approximately 1,500 meals a day. More than 100 permanent jobs and 7,000 temporary ones were found for clients of the job creation program.

> **Mental Illness:** Almost 8,000 teenagers and adults learned more about mental health through presentations made by Canadian Mental Health Association, and 1,000 individuals were provided with information or referrals through their Resource Line.

> **Opportunities for Children and Youth:** The Evenstart for Children's Society Home Visitor Program served 60 children from high-risk families, providing them with a centre based day program as well as two meals each day. All children showed an improvement in social skills and an increased ability at school.

Why United Way?

- For seventeen consecutive years, Calgary has exceeded its United Way campaign goal and raised a total of $193.5 million for essential services to the community during that time.
- Calgary raised $21.7 million in its 1999 United Way campaign, 12.5% more than was raised the previous year, giving Calgary the highest growth of any large United Way in Canada.
- Every year, approximately 10,000 volunteers assist United Way in the annual campaign. In addition to being a testimony to the campaign's success, it significantly reduces costs.
- United Way keeps fundraising and administration costs low, so that more than 86% of all funds raised are returned to the community.

Source: United Way of Calgary and Area, excerpts from 2000 Report to Donors

This chapter on implementation and monitoring performance concludes the description and discussion of a basic planning framework which is sufficient for many social service organizations. The remainder of this text is for those individuals and organizations prepared to move beyond the basics toward more strategic thinking and planning.

Summary

Implementation is the ultimate test of a strategic plan and a strategic planning process. If the organization stalls at this point, performance results will not be optimized and stakeholders will be disheartened and potentially put off from further planning for some time. In order to ensure the strategic plan is being effectively implemented, performance needs to be monitored and measured. Measuring completion of actions and results achieved not only ensures proper execution of the strategic plan, but also ensures a more robust strategic planning process, as the measures become part of the feedback loop which allows the organization to improve its focus, strategies and targets. From a strategic planning perspective, monitoring progress and measuring results are separate, but related activities. Monitoring progress is the process of managing and reviewing the implementation status of the action priorities. Measuring results refers to the process of measuring and communicating the performance achieved against the performance indicators. This chapter presented a system and model for measuring performance; benefits and concerns with the system, and what results should be measured.

WORKSHEET 11-1
Status Report
Template

Status Report Template Worksheet

Overall Status of Implementation:

_____

_____

_____

Reasons for Implementation Delays:

_____

_____

_____

Individual Action Priorities Status Reporting (complete for each action priority):

Objective 1:

Action Plans	Status	Action Required
1.1		
1.2		
1.3		

WORKSHEET 11-2
Measuring Results

Measuring Results Worksheet

Performance Indicator	Performance Target	Actual Result	Analysis or Evaluation	Corrective Action	Adjusted Target

Section 4

Beyond the Basics: Tools and Techniques for Advancing Strategic Thinking and Planning

Beyond the Basic: Tools and Techniques for Advancing Strategic Thinking and Planning presents a collection of advanced tools and techniques suitable for the more experienced planner. Planning frameworks are provided for developing a vision, using market research for strategic planning purposes, understanding and conducting segmentation, marketing and communications planning, fundraising planning and technology planning.

CHAPTER 12

Developing a Vision

As an organization becomes more sophisticated in its strategic planning efforts, it becomes of benefit to develop a vision statement. If significant strategic change is contemplated and the organization has choices about how their future could unfold, an assessment of alternative visions can be a valuable exercise to initiate the process of strategic redesign.

This chapter introduces the more experienced planner to the concept of a vision statement and describes a process to create and evaluate vision alternatives and select a preferred vision based on defined evaluation criteria.

Defining Vision

A vision is a statement about the future of an organization. It paints a picture of a successful future that represents real progress, achievement, and excellence for those who strive to make it happen.[1] A vision should be a stretch to achieve. It should be a source of inspiration and challenge for the organization. However, if the vision is perceived to be unattainable and unrealistic, rather than inspiring stakeholders, it will cause disillusionment.

In **Chapter 2**, *The Strategic Planning Model*, the concept of vision and mission are introduced and it is suggested that for the novice planner, it is appropriate to treat these two concepts as one. Whereas the mission is a statement of the organization's purpose, the vision is a statement of the organization's desired future. If an organization makes a significant change to its vision, that is, where and how it wants to be strategically positioned at some point in the future, this new vision may or may not imply changes to the organization's mission or purpose.

The vision statement can be used in place of a mission statement, but more often exists as an enhancement to the mission statement. The mission and vision form the apex of the planning model pyramid as illustrated in **Figure 12-1**, *Vision-led Strategic Planning Model*. Together they set the direction of the organization and provide the context and guidelines for the organization's priorities and decisions.

---

1   Nanus, Burt, 1995. *The Vision Retreat: A Participant's Workbook*, Jossey Bass Inc.

FIGURE 12-1
Vision-led Strategic
Planning Model

Vision-led Strategic Planning Model

Values
Our beliefs and principles that guide decision making

Our desired future state — **Vision**

Our distinctive identity in the social service sector — **Mission**

Where we need consistently significant results to get to our Mission — **Key Success Factors**

Ideal states to be achieved at some time in the future — **Goals**

Measurable activities and pre-determined end results to be achieved within a given period of time — **Action Priorities and Performance Targets**

Performance Indicators
Basic measures used to gauge actual results against the key success factors

A vision can be as broad ranging or as specific as is required to provide direction and inspiration to the organization given its specific circumstances. A well articulated vision:

- defines a future state but does not describe how to get there,
- focuses on a longer term desired future, usually of 5 or more years,
- is strategically rather than operationally focused,
- implies the right change, not necessarily radical change,
- is directional rather than absolute.

Successful vision development requires participants in the strategic planning process to let go of their traditional view of the organization and embrace new and innovative ideas about what the organization could be in the future. **Figure 12-2A,** *Example of a Vision,* illustrates United Way of Calgary and Area's vision for the future as they defined it in 1995. **Figure 12-2B,** *Example of a Vision,* illustrates United Way's vision as described in 1999 and helps to illustrate the progression of their strategic thinking when compared to **Figure 12-2A**.

Developing and Evaluating Vision Alternatives

Developing a vision is often an exciting and rejuvenating experience for an organization provided the effort is focused and is not allowed to drag out over an extended period of time. Developing a vision, like developing or confirming a mission, occurs after the organization has conducted an assessment of its internal and external situation as described in **Chapter 8,** *Situation Assessment.* With a common understanding about the organization's situation, strategic issues and some ideas about what the future may hold,

FIGURE 12-2A
Example of a Vision

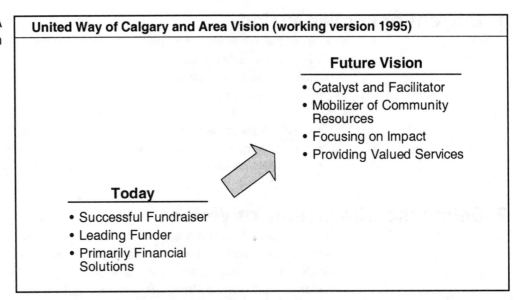

FIGURE 12-2B
Example of a Vision

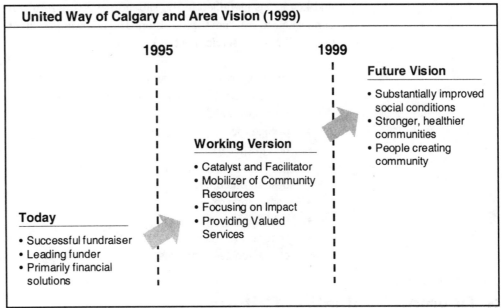

the strategic planning team is ready to follow a process to develop and evaluate various possible future visions for the organization.

There are six steps for developing and evaluating future visions:

1. Define the organization's current or implied vision,
2. Define the dimensions of vision,
3. Develop evaluation criteria,
4. Develop vision alternatives,
5. Evaluate and select the preferred vision alternative,
6. Define gaps between current state and desired future state.

The remainder of this chapter offers the details for each of these steps in the process.

1. Current or Implied Vision

Document the organization's current vision by consulting existing planning documents and key leaders. Solicit leadership views either through a group session or through individual interviews or questionnaires. Questions to ask to develop a conceptual picture of the current vision are:

- What is the mission/vision statement? What is the organization's key purpose(s)?
- Is this purpose, mission or vision understood by the various stakeholders?
- Do the organization's actions align with the mission/vision?

2. Define the Dimensions of Vision

A vision is usually described relative to a number of dimensions. These dimensions are a function of what is critical to the success of the organization and are often influenced by strategic issues and/or choices that will impact the organization's future. Therefore, consider how the existing vision was described and consider the opportunities, threats and key issues identified in the situation assessment to provide some ideas about the dimensions to consider for the vision. The following list identifies vision dimensions often used in the social service sector:

- primary driver or reason for being,
- generic strategy, for example value delivery, cost minimization, accessibility, community building,
- service focus,
- geographic focus,
- growth strategy, for example status quo, contraction, expansion, diversification,
- desired outcomes,
- community role,
- external perceptions,
- culture and values,
- competencies/key skills.

3. Develop Evaluation Criteria

In order to choose the best vision alternative for the organization, a set of criteria needs to be identified to use as the filter for evaluating all possible alternatives. The criteria reflect the critical components and aspects of the organization and its environment and the preferences of leadership. The criteria selected, and the weight placed on each, will vary by organization; however, one or more of the following criteria are often used:

- capitalizes on strengths and opportunities,
- neutralizes weaknesses and threats,
- addresses strategic issues,
- achieves desired community impact,
- appeals to clients and donors; reflects their needs,
- ease of implementation,

- organizational capability to implement the vision,
- financial implications,
- synergy with existing programs and services,
- impact on organizational flexibility,
- mobilizes resources,
- avoids duplication,
- reduces bureaucracy and costs,
- stimulates new solutions,
- risks and how to mitigate.

4. Develop Vision Alternatives

Vision alternatives are intended to define plausible, but different future states for the organization. **Figure 12-3,** *Desired Future State,* depicts the choices facing an organization when it defines and selects its desired end state or vision from a variety of possibilities.

FIGURE 12-3
Desired Future State

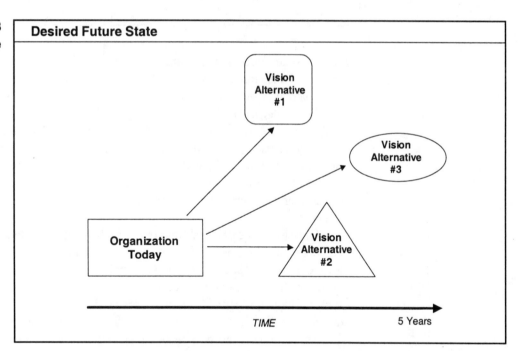

For an effective visioning exercise, at least three different alternatives should be developed and considered, including the "as is" option. Ideally, the alternatives will cover a wide range of possibilities, help the organization capitalize on its strengths and opportunities, overcome its weaknesses and threats and extend capabilities into new markets.

A visioning table is an effective tool for creating and describing alternatives, because it provides a mechanism to broaden the strategic planning team's perspective of the organization. **Figure 12-4**, *Vision Table Framework*, illustrates the layout of the visioning table. The table is usually completed in a creative session and then confirmed by individuals or small groups with expertise in specific aspects of the organization. The dimensions of

FIGURE 12-4
Vision Table
Framework

Vision Table Framework					
Vision Alternatives	**Dimension #1**	**Dimension #2**	**Dimension #3**	**Dimension #4**	**Dimension #5**
Vision Alternative #1	*(range of possibilities for each dimension)*	*(range of possibilities for each dimension)*	*(range of possibilities for each dimension)*	*(range of possibilities for each dimension)*	*(range of possibilities for each dimension)*
Vision Alternative #2					
Vision Alternative #3					
Vision Alternative #4					

vision, as described in step 2 above, are placed along the top of the table. At any time, another dimension may be added to the table; the beginning list need not be exhaustive or viewed as complete.

The strategic planning team then captures the range of possibilities for each dimension in the vertical columns under the related dimension. Here, it is often helpful to choose mutually exclusive points on the continuum of possibilities. The points should be practical or viable, but may not be within the normal range of options considered in the current organization. For example, under the dimension of donor, the range may include government(s), corporate community, funding agencies, individuals, foundations, and others.

Once the range of possibilities under each dimension is identified, the team creatively explores paths (or options) for the organization through the table. These paths take the form of horizontal lines connecting one point on one dimension's continuum to another point on the next dimension's continuum. Often it is helpful to pick a sample theme, such as "bigger," "better," "broader" or "bolder," to use in plotting a path across all the dimensions. Each path across the dimensions is a preliminary vision alternative.

These preliminary alternatives may require further development or evolution to become robust alternatives for the organization. Consider the following questions to validate or revise each alternative.

Does the alternative:

- capitalize on strengths and opportunities?
- overcome weaknesses and threats?
- create new possibilities for the organization?
- offer an alternative to the status quo?
- fit with the organization's capabilities and values?
- provide inspiration and motivation for the organization?

With the table completed, the newly minted vision alternatives are described using the points on the organization dimensions as the building blocks.

5. Evaluate and Select the Preferred Alternative

The vision alternatives can be evaluated any number of ways, but a simple and effective approach uses a qualitative and a quantitative table. Prepare a qualitative assessment of the vision alternatives by completing **Worksheet 12-1,** *Qualitative Vision Alternative Assessment,* identifying the advantages, disadvantages and roadblocks, issues and points for discussion for each alternative. Then complete a quantitative assessment by completing **Worksheet 12-2,** *Quantitative Vision Alternative Assessment*, using the criteria developed in step 3 above. Either weigh each criteria equally, in which case the alternative that satisfies the most criteria is the preferred alternative from a quantitative perspective, or apply a weighting scheme that reflects the relative importance of each criteria to the organization.

The two worksheets can be completed in draft form prior to a strategic planning team meeting and then reviewed and modified by the planning team. Alternatively, both worksheets can be developed interactively during a strategic planning team meeting. In either case, the strategic planning team must reach consensus about the preferred future vision for the organization.

6. Define Gaps Between Current State and Desired Future State

Once the preferred vision alternative has been identified, it is compared to the organization's current vision, as defined in step 1 above. This comparison of the current state and the desired end-state should help identify the gaps between where the organization is today and where it wants to be at some time in the future. These gaps, once identified, become the basis for developing goals and action priorities as described in **Chapter 9,** *Strategy Definition.*

The following chapter discusses market research and how to utilize it most effectively in a strategic planning context.

Summary

A vision and mission are similar concepts in that they provide the starting point for all planning activities. They are at the apex of the planning pyramid. A vision differs from a mission in that a mission defines the organization's purpose, while a vision defines a desired future end state for the organization. While both a mission and a vision should be a rallying point and source of motivation for the organization, a vision should definitely be inspirational for the organization's stakeholders as it defines a new and improved future for the organization. The process of developing a vision involves six straight forward steps: 1) define the organization's current or implied vision; 2) define the dimensions of vision; 3) develop evaluation criteria; 4) develop vision alternatives; 5) evaluate and select the preferred vision alternative; and 6) define gaps between current state and desired future state.

Qualitative Vision Alternative Assessment Worksheet

Alternative/ Description	Advantages	Disadvantages	Roadblocks/ Issues/ Discussion Points
Alternative #1			
Alternative #2			
Alternative #3			
Alternative #4			
Other?			

WORKSHEET 12-1
Quantitative Vision
Alternative
Assessment

Quantitative Vision Alternative Assessment Worksheet					
Criterion Weighting	Criterion #1	Criterion #2	Criterion #3	Criterion #4	Score*
Alternative #1					
Alternative #2					
Alternative #3					
Alternative #4					
* Score = Alternative Ranking x Criterion Weighting					

CHAPTER 13

Using Market Research for Strategic Planning Purposes

All Information is Interesting, but What Information is Critical?

Every organization needs information about the market in which it operates in order to position itself and its programs and services effectively relative to other organizations that offer the same, similar or compatible services. The organization also needs to be able to position itself to serve the needs of current and potential clients effectively. To do all of this the organization requires market intelligence that is usually obtained by collecting primary data, a process known as conducting primary market research.

One caution regarding primary market research is that it can be expensive and time consuming to gather. There are not many organizations that have budgets that can accommodate an ongoing comprehensive market research program. The key is to start by developing a market research plan outlining all of the data required to make decisions and that will determine how resources and energies will be directed.

Be critical of the market research that is conducted. Every market research project should start with a statement about how the data will be used and what decisions will be made on the basis of the findings. Without this, market research can degenerate into a nice to know exercise. Remember, all information is interesting, but only specific information is critical.

When to collect market research data and how often, is entirely dependent on the type of information being collected and the decisions that need to be made. This chapter describes the different types of market research that organizations typically undertake as part of their strategic planning, as well as provides some general guidelines indicating how frequently data should be collected.

Client "Listening" Programs

The most important type of market research that any organization collects is relevant data about clients. This information is invaluable in assisting the organization to develop services and determine how it should best operate to meet clients' needs. It is helpful to view this data gathering as a complete 'listening program', not as individual pieces of market research. This is important for a number of reasons:

- A client's relationship with an organization progresses along a continuum starting with needs awareness, through initial contact, use of service, to follow-up or ongoing support. At each step along the way there is valuable data surrounding client's needs, experiences and satisfaction that can assist the organization in tailoring their operations and services.
- Thinking through all the ways in which the organization is, or will, be collecting information from its clients and assembling a map of this data, will clearly show where any gaps exist in understanding clients more fully. These information gaps can then be addressed through specific research vehicles.
- Approaching client market research as an *ongoing* listening program is particularly important because the quantitative data collected is only relevant *when related to previous results*. Unless data is compared to previous and future surveys, the interpretation of the results lacks context. Is the organization improving or slipping in performance? Are clients more or less satisfied? Have changes in services produced successful results?

Results can also be compared against other organizations to determine if your group is keeping pace with others in similar lines of work. This concept is sometimes referred to as *competitive benchmarking* where an organization will compare its overall performance against another in the same or related field that consistently displays outstanding performance and is widely regarded as a superior quality organization with top marks in client satisfaction.

A Word about Market Segmentation

Market segmentation is the process of determining what separate and definable groups of clients exist in the market for a specific type of service. Market segmentation research is one of the most important types of research that any organization can conduct. For this reason, it is discussed at length in **Chapter 14,** *The Art and Science of Segmentation.*

Once completed, market segmentation research need not be repeated unless there is a major change in societal trends, the mandate of the organization, or a new competitive organization or service emerges, that would significantly affect the dynamics of how the market divides into separate and definable segments. Alternatively, if no major changes in the environment or client behavior takes place, it is wise to test the legitimacy of the segments at least every five years to ensure new elements within the segments, or new segments themselves, have not emerged.

The type of client market research that will be discussed here is based on the organization's market segmentation work and focuses on the client segments that the organization has determined it can best serve. This type of research is conducted more frequently than market segmentation research and forms the basis of any organization's ongoing market research program.

Understanding Target Clients

While market segmentation is performed on the basis of demographic and needs research, it is usually only conducted to a depth of detail that allows for the population to be divided into separate and definable groups or segments for a specific service or product. Therefore, it is advisable that once the organization has determined which client segment(s) it can best serve, that is, its target clients. Additional details should be collected on this segment(s) to understand all aspects of the members of this grouping(s) and the specific nature of their needs.

Each type of client segment that the organization has chosen to serve will have a different set of criteria and expectations regarding how their needs are to be met in order to be fully satisfied. When do clients need the service, what does 'quality service' mean, how should a service be 'packaged', what should the service include, how should the service be delivered and where, what qualifications and/or guarantees are important and what results do clients expect to achieve as a result of the organization's efforts? The answers to all of these questions can have profound effects on how the organization carries out its work in order to serve their chosen client segment(s) successfully.

Figure 13-1, *Common Issues that Define Client Needs*, list some common questions that get at specific issues surrounding client needs. There may be other relevant questions that could and should be added based on the specific nature of the organization's work.

FIGURE 13-1
Common Issues
that Define
Client Needs

Common Issues that Define Client Needs

Problem/Need Description
- What challenges are being faced?
- Describe the nature of these challenges. What caused the problem or issue? How does it manifest itself (what does the client experience, or what are they not able to do, or want to do)?
- How are the challenges affecting quality of life, happiness, success, health, future and so on?

Desired Outcomes
- In the clients words, how would they describe their ideal situation — as it relates to the problem or need?
- What specifics can be obtained to clearly define this ideal situation — for example, able to read well enough to attend school, able to walk a mile a day without pain.

Service Expectations
- What type of program or service is the client looking for?
- Describe the specific nature of this support as completely as possible. What range of services should be provided?
- Understand issues such as need for confidentiality, ongoing support, referrals to other organizations, and so on.
- How, when, and where would they like to be able to access this service?
- What services have they tried in the past? Have these services succeeded or failed? Why or why not?

Client Demographics

Demographics are very useful to provide a clear and detailed picture of the target clients in order to be able to identify, screen, contact and communicate with them. This information includes such things as age, education, geographically where they live or come from, jobs or industries where they work, income, family and marriage status.

Figure 13-2, *Commonly Used Demographic Indicators,* shows the types of demographic information that may be collected. Not all these indicators are important in every situation. Depending on the organization's work, certain information will be more important and some not necessary at all.

FIGURE 13-2
Commonly Used
Demographic
Indicators

Commonly Used Demographic Indicators*

Personal
- gender
- age
- marital status
- children/number of dependents
- disabilities
- nationality
- languages spoken
- primary language used
- religion
- own a vehicle
- take public transit or drive
- accommodations: own or rent

Contact Information
- do they have a telephone?
- own a computer?
- access the internet?

Education
- highest level of education attained
- type of educational institution attended
- journeyman papers/diploma/ degrees held
- computer literacy

Employment
- job
- title
- industry
- income level
- working/full-time homemaker/ student/retired

Geographic Location
- city, town
- province or state
- area city

* recognize that requesting some of this information can infringe upon privacy of information legislation in some jurisdictions.

When and How Often? Since serving clients is at the core of any social service organization's work, understanding their needs is critical to making even the most basic decisions about how the organization will operate, what programs and services it will offer, and how these programs and services will be distributed. For this reason, client needs research is a valuable source of information to inform program and service decision making. Client needs research is most effective if the organization has already conducted some type of market segmentation research so that only those client segments that the organization has chosen as its focus target client segments are the focus of the needs-based research effort.

If the organization is an established one, and client market research has never been conducted, or there are gaps in the data, then it is strongly recommended that plans be made and a budget allocated to perform this market research as soon as possible.

Awareness and Decision Making Behaviors

Clients experience a set of circumstances and follow a pattern of behavior that leads up to their decision to seek out a solution to their needs. Consider the thought process that a client goes through as they come to the realization that they need support because of a physical disability, versus someone who finds themselves without work and requires career counseling. The conditions and subsequent actions that result are vastly different and have significant implications for the two very different organizations serving these two very different needs.

It is therefore important for an organization to understand the series of steps, information requirements and decision-making criteria that will ultimately bring a client to their services. Once again, this data should be gathered and analyzed based upon client segments:

- How does the client describe their core need?
- What made them seek a solution for their need?
- Where did they go to look for help?
- Who did they consult for advice?
- How long did they search?
- What was the list of criteria they used for evaluating service providers?
- How did they make their ultimate decision?
- In the end, what criteria were the most important in making their selection?
- Why did they not choose to go to other organizations for help?

This type of market research can effectively be gathered through surveying new clients, or through a random sampling of existing clients. Valuable data can also be gathered through those who choose to use the services of another organization. In this case, the results should yield the perceived strengths of other competing or comparable services and the alternative ways in which these organizations communicate with and attract clients.

When and How Often? Awareness and decision making behavior is important data that can greatly assist the marketing and communication function within the organization, so it sits high on the priority list and should be done as soon as possible. This information can be collected continuously, with each new client. If continuous collection is too cumbersome, expensive or inappropriate given the organization's line of work, it can be conducted annually.

Satisfaction

Client satisfaction measures are one of the most critical measures of the organization's performance and one of the best ways in which to provide early detection of potential problems. It is important that client satisfaction questions be kept as consistent as possible so that past satisfaction scores can be compared to current results to determine if the organization is improving or failing and where problems exist.

While measures should be captured by client segment, it may also be useful to measure the satisfaction levels of new clients, existing clients and those who have discontinued using the organization's services. In each case, clients will have differing points of view. For instance, new clients are best able to comment on their experience in finding and using the organization's services for the first time. Such questions could include speed in receiving information, was the information understandable, how they viewed any processing procedures, first impressions of the service, were they informed about the organization's operating procedures or guidelines and so on.

When and How Often? Client satisfaction surveys can be conducted on an ongoing basis with each client that the organization serves. While this could prove to be onerous and expensive, random satisfaction surveys should be conducted once per year to be of value for adjusting and improving the organization's programs and services.

Designing or Improving Programs and Services

Clients must be a part of the process of developing or modifying programs and services. Testing concepts and presenting alternatives can avoid costly mistakes and greatly increase market acceptability and client satisfaction.

Information important to the new program and service design process includes:

- A complete understanding of client's core needs that the service should address.
- The outcomes the client wants and expects from receiving support.
- The elements a client wants the service to include.
- How the service should be provided and distributed.
- The follow-up services that need to be provided.
- How the service should be priced.
- The guidelines or rules that govern access to the service.

There are many creative market research tools that can be used to reduce the time and expense of gathering this information.

In some situations, dependent on the type of work the organization is involved in, it may be difficult to ask clients some of these questions directly because of language or cultural barriers, perceived power differentials, concern that services will be withdrawn if critical, or because of lack of knowledge about technical aspects of the service. In these cases, it can be helpful to develop service models for clients to use on a trial basis, and then evaluate how successfully the service meets their needs and expectations.

When and How Often? Each time the organization plans to introduce a new program or service or modify an existing one, it is an opportunity to gather client input to guide the design process and increase client acceptance and satisfaction with the end result.

Donor and Other Stakeholder Needs, Opinions and Support

For many organizations, donors and other stakeholders play a very important role in providing stability and viability. They are important sources of support in terms of time (dedication of volunteer hours), talent (supplying professional services such as accounting, marketing and communications, management and technical advising) and money (financial donations). In return for their commitment, they must receive something from the organization that meets their needs and expectations. In this way, donors and other stakeholders need to be understood in much the same way that clients need to be understood. Once again, some strategically gathered market research can be of great benefit.

Donors

Donors — *who are they, why do they support the organization and how best to attract, collect and maintain their donations?* Like clients, donors can be segmented or grouped according to differing needs and motivations for supporting certain organizations. If the organization has a separate department that focuses specifically on fundraising and donations, and if sufficient resources are available, it could consider conducting any or all of the research mentioned above.

If an extensive donor research program is not possible, the most critical types of research involve:

1. Segmentation: determining which segments (or groups) of donors are most attracted to the organization's work.

2. Needs: what types of donation opportunities and programs meet their needs for philanthropy.

3. Satisfaction: particularly if fundraising and donation programs do not meet target levels, some type of satisfaction research should be conducted to determine how the organization can improve performance.

When and How Often? Segmentation research should be undertaken as soon as possible so that the organization understands who their best prospects are for fundraising and donations of time and talent. As with client market research, donor segmentation research does not have to be repeated frequently; every five years is sufficient as a rule.

Donor satisfaction research should be conducted at the conclusion of fundraising drives and/or programs that involve donors providing support to the organization.

Other Stakeholders

Once the organization has worked through the entire strategic planning cycle at least once, and the organization has increased its capability to think and plan strategically, research related to other stakeholders (for example, funders, government, other agencies) can be added to the planning process in steps. Understanding other stakeholder needs, levels of satisfaction and segmentation are useful in determining how best these stakeholders might partner or work with the organization.

When and How Often? As with client and donor market research, research related to other stakeholders does not have to be repeated frequently; every five years is sufficient and this research may be staggered so as not to include an analysis of *all* stakeholders each year.

Understanding Peers and Competitors

All organizations need to have a good understanding of other groups within their market that provide a similar or complementary service. This knowledge is useful for a number of reasons:

- To collect information regarding best practices from other organizations. Understanding where and how others have been successful can be leveraged into your organization to great advantage. That is, discovering donor programs that have met with great success, or techniques where organizations have aligned their efforts to provide clients with new, successful services.
- To differentiate the organization's offerings from others so that unique and meaningful programs and services are available to target clients.
- To be able to communicate properly the benefits of using the organization's services without making it confusing for prospective clients who are trying to evaluate available options. For example, there needs to be clear communication about the differences in services offered by a Women's Shelter versus a Woman's Crisis Center.
- To be able to direct clients to other available options. An organization should be able to provide some basic referral information about other services in the community, province or state, or even farther afield that can provide the client with further support.

It can be helpful to collect and record data gathered on competitors and peers on a matrix that compares and contrasts services provided, typical clients, perceived strengths and weaknesses. Refer to **Worksheet 8-2**, *Competitive Assessment,* for an example of such a matrix. This type of table can become a valuable tool for management and staff to have on hand so that they can quickly refer to it to understand how their organization compares, and to identify strengths and weaknesses that should be addressed. Furthermore, it can be useful for accurately and consistently referring clients to other organizations better able to provide the specific support they require. Refer to **Figure 8-2**, *Competitor Profile Template,* for additional competitive information that is worthwhile to track.

When and How Often? Not as important as understanding clients or donors and other stakeholders, competitor/peer research should be next in the queue and should be repeated every two years in order to stay in touch with the environment in which the organization operates. In the event that a new service provider emerges, it is important to gather market intelligence as soon as possible to add to the competitor/peer service matrix.

Society-at-large: Awareness, Attitudes and Support

Understanding how widely the organization is recognized and understood by members of the public, and their attitudes about its work, is the least frequently collected research.

But it does have its place. It is most often used to get a measure of the organization's visibility and how well the public understands the organization's mandate. This is important for testing the effectiveness of communication efforts to raise awareness, and to determine the degree of support for the organization's work, or the public's impression of the organization's effectiveness in serving society.

This type of market research is often most effectively and efficiently collected via omnibus studies. Omnibus studies are most often conducted by large national research firms who, on behalf of a large number of client organizations, poll the population about a wide range of programs, services and issues at any one time. Each client organization is able to ask a small number of questions and then share proportionally in the cost.

When and How Often? While not of an extremely critical nature, an organization should have some idea of its 'popularity and acceptance' rating. Having said this, an organization should have been in operation for two or three years, with some type of visibility campaign in place, in order to expect some impressions to be formed and measurable in the public forum.

The frequency of omnibus studies or polls varies and organizations can decide to take part regularly or occasionally and can often specify the geographic region(s) where their questions will be included.

Use the Right Market Research Methodology (Tools)

There are a growing number of different types of research tools and techniques for gathering data. It is not within the scope of this text to discuss all of these, nor is it important to know or understand them in order to manage or direct the organization's research initiatives. But it is useful to have an understanding of three types of approaches to some of the broader concepts in market research.

Questionnaires

Structured, undisguised questionnaires are the most common tools used in market research. Structured refers to the fact that all of the questions are presented with exactly the same wording and in exactly the same order to respondents. The responses are also standardized, such that the respondent selects from a list of fix-alternatives; for example, yes or no, strongly agree, agree, don't know, disagree, strongly disagree. The results from structured questionnaires are always quantitative.

One drawback of the structured responses is the possibility that respondents are limited in their answers to the point that the answers don't reflect the respondent's true feelings. This can be alleviated to some extend by providing the opportunity for responses such as "no opinion" or "none apply." Additionally, some unstructured questions or opportunities for comments can be added to the questionnaire to allow for other information to surface. Of course this makes tabulation and summarization of the results more complex and quantitative measures cannot be as easily applied.

Structured, undisguised questionnaires are ideal for research that must be conducted frequently, and where consistency in questions is required, such as client and donor satisfaction surveys.

Undisguised questionnaires do not try to conceal the service or organization that is the subject of the research. In contrast, disguised questionnaires conceal the name of the organization and are used to remove any bias that could emerge because of attitudes that surround the specific service or organization. These types of questionnaires are not as commonly used for market research.

In general, questionnaires allow a great deal of flexibility in delivery from mail-out, to mall intercept (researchers hand out questionnaires to passers-by) and telephone surveying. They can be assembled and distributed quickly, distributed to a large number of respondents and tabulated easily.

One of the most important elements in questionnaire based research is the careful selection and wording of questions, and providing a range of possible responses that will, as closely as possible, reflect respondents' feelings and opinions. Conducting preliminary research via the unstructured survey techniques, such as focus groups or expert or in-depth interview, can be used to help in the design of an effective questionnaire.

Focus Groups

Focus group market research involves a small number of people, usually 5 to 12 being brought together and asked unstructured, open-ended questions by a moderator or interviewer. By the nature of the forum, discussion amongst participants is a key feature of this research to draw out opinions and details. This method is best suited for generating and exploring ideas and insights rather than quantitatively assessing the degree of support for an idea or concept. While focus groups can be relatively expensive to conduct, information can be generated quickly.

Focus groups can be extremely valuable in helping an organization understand issues through the eyes of clients, including the type of language clients use to describe their needs and opinions. This information can then be used to construct more effective questionnaires that focus in on issues of critical importance to clients and to develop a more accurate list of possible responses. In reverse, focus groups can be used as a follow-up to a questionnaire to draw out more detailed information, examples and emotions that could not be gleaned from structured questions.

The moderator is a key component of focus group research in that s/he not only asks the questions and leads subsequent discussion, but s/he must encourage and stimulate discussion amongst all members of the group, draw out the opinions of participants who are reluctant to speak, and try to control the influence of overly aggressive members of the group.

Because of the small number of participants engaged in the process, the results of focus group research are not representative of what would be found in the segment's population. It is often advisable that at least two focus group sessions are held for each client segment being studied in order to compare results and to make allowances for groups that could be thrown off track by an overly aggressive participant.

Expert Interviews

Expert or in-depth interviews are similar in approach to focus group research in that an experienced interviewer leads a respondent through a semi-structured or unstructured interview. The key difference between the two approaches is that in the expert or in-depth interview the respondents are interviewed individually, removing the effects of group-think. In this type of market research the concern is more around exploring an individual's in-depth experiences, motivations and associated opinions.

Expert interviews can be time consuming and expensive depending on the total number of respondents and the resources being applied to the project (that is, how many interviewers are used). However, the richness of the resulting data, particularly for gathering data like how a client evaluates and selects a program and service, can result in new and valuable insights that no other research method can supply.

Managing the Market Research Function

In order to manage the organization's market research function, it is not necessary to be an expert in all matters of research methodology and statistical analysis. Rather, the function involves a project management orientation. Tasks include:

- Identifying the organization's marketing information needs;
- Locating a suitable market research firm to assist with the design, implementation and analysis of survey work;
- Working to ensure that the information needed to make decisions will be collected;
- Supervising the process; and
- Disseminating and ensuring that the resulting data is included in decision making processes.

Build a Relationship with a Professional Research Firm

It is important to develop a relationship with one or two professional market research firms that can consult on research matters and assist with everything from the design, participant recruitment and implementation of the research vehicle to analysis of the data. Look for a firm that is willing and able to support a range of research projects from the very small to large, complex initiatives. If your organization is able to work over time with the same firm, the market research firm's understanding of your organization's work will increase the speed, accuracy and quality of the market research they provide.

Guidelines for Successful Surveying

The following guidelines provide some helpful advice to those who are responsible for managing the organization's market research function. Preparing a market research brief before a project commences is the only way to be sure that the information that will be gathered will result in the data required to make the decision at-hand. Too often market research produces a lot of interesting information that is worthless for making decisions because it does not provide enough clear direction for making choices. The rule of thumb is never to embark on a market research project where there is no response given when asked *"how will the answer to that question be used?"*

Additionally the market research brief is an opportunity to carefully consider other important issues such as:

- Which clients can provide this information?
- When do we need the results?

- Is qualitative or quantitative data required?
- What is the budget for this effort?
- In what format does the data need to be displayed?
- What level of analysis is required?
- Is a formal report required?

The brief then forms the basis on which the organization and research firm move forward to plan elements of the research methodology. **Worksheet 13-1**, *Market Research Briefing Template* provides an outline which should be completed by the organization for review and discussion with the market research firm who will be quoting on or conducting the market research project.

Coordinate Research Efforts

In some cases, different departments within the same organization, or peer organizations, can share data or partner in market research projects to improve the efficiency in data gathering, both in terms of cost and quality of information. It is important to share market research plans in advance with these groups to reduce duplication of effort and prevent valuable data from not being fully utilized.

Catalogue and Communicate the Results

Information gathered through market research represents a significant expenditure of time and money. Data should be shared as widely as possible throughout the organization so that it can be used in day-to day decision making and to guide strategic planning efforts. But, it should also be made clear to everyone that this information is proprietary to the organization and should be kept confidential within the organization. Refer to **Chapter 6**, *Engaging Stakeholders*, for more information about what is confidential and what is not.

Over time, market research data provides a valuable track record of the organization's efforts, successes and failures, to be used in future marketing and planning initiatives.

Once the information has been collected and analyzed, it can be put to use assisting the organization to identify distinct client segments within the market, as described in **Chapter 14**, *The Art and Science of Segmentation*.

Summary

Every organization needs information about the market in which it operates. As information gathering can become expensive, it is important to ensure that the organization is collecting the right information at the right time. Market and client information becomes valuable in identifying which client segments the organization can best serve (target client segments) and which particular programs or services specific client segments need, as well as in designing or improving services; understanding peer and competitor organizations, and the awareness, attitudes and support of the community at-large. Finally the chapter discusses a few key tools to use to effectively acquire the needed information.

WORKSHEET 13-1
Market Research
Briefing Template

Market Research Briefing Template Worksheet

TASK *Complete each question for review and discussion with the market research group who will be quoting on or conducting the market research project.*

1. **Objectives of Market Research Project**
   Describe what the market research project is expected to uncover.
2. **Decision(s) that will be made as a result of data gathered**
   What decisions will be made based on the information learned? How will information being gathered be used to make decisions?
3. **Background Information**
   Provide context for the market research including the current situation surrounding issues that will be studied (for example, environmental, political, societal, competitive).
4. **Past Market Research Conducted**
   Provide results of information gathered in the past related to the current project. This information can be used to direct the new market research initiative.
5. **Information Required**
   Describe specifically what pieces of information are required and how much detail is needed.
6. **Target Respondents**
   Describe in detail who the information should represent.
7. **How Target Respondents might be located**
   Give any details about where respondent lists can be accessed or where respondents can be found.
8. **Geographic Scope**
   Specify if there is a geographic area from where respondents would be drawn.
9. **Preferred Market Research Techniques**
   While the research group will recommend appropriate research techniques given the project's objectives and information requirements, your organization should list any preferred methods for collecting the research data along with rationale.
10. **Draft List of Questions to be Answered**
    Provide a list of questions that might be presented to respondents.
11. **Qualitative versus Quantitative Data**
    Does the data need to be qualitative or quantitative in nature for any reason? Explain.
12. **Report Format**
    What type of research reporting format is required — summary of results only, detailed findings, transcriptions, report, live presentation and so on.
13. **Findings Due Date**
    When is the information required?
14. **Budget**
    What budget is available?
15. **One-time or ongoing research project**
    Will this information be collected regularly or is this a one-time need?

CHAPTER 14

The Art and Science of Segmentation

Who Are Your Customers?

For the purpose of strategic planning, clients have the greatest impact because they define the purpose of the organization. Donors are also important because they contribute time, expertise and dollars to support and lead the organization. If both of these groups are correctly addressed in the planning process, it is safe to say that the community will be better served and that the staff, board and volunteers of the organization will be better equipped to meet the needs of clients.

Understand Client Needs

The preceding chapter outlined the types of information an organization needs in order to undertake a successful strategic planning process. A significant portion of this information-gathering focuses on enhancing an organization's understanding of client needs.

Typically, organizations feel that they have a good understanding of client needs. After all, they deal with them every day. However, some of the biggest mistakes are based upon incorrect assumptions. And, this is frustrated even more by the fact that very few clients understand or can articulate their own needs! That is why the methods used to obtain information on client needs are so important, as is the analysis of this information.

Clients have a core need or set of needs that typically correspond to the programs and services that an organization provides. These core needs should form the basis of the organization's offerings. To use an example, a women's shelter whose purpose is to assist women and children suffering from abusive relationships to transition to a better life provides a variety of programs. These programs range from residential programs and services; non-residential support groups, counseling, referrals and advocacy; to community liaison services. Through the programs and services being offered, women are assisted on a very practical level to rebuild their lives. However, the need to rebuild their lives is derived from a core set of needs for safety, security, understanding and practical guidance.

The above example underscores the importance of understanding the thought process of clients who use an organization's programs and services:

- What prompts them to seek out the programs and services?
- Do they act on their own behalf?
- What is the search process they go through in order to locate a suitable organization?
- Is there competing information that could be confusing?
- Are there a number of organizations that offer similar services?
- What information do potential clients require in order to assess if an organization can meet their needs?
- Are there any barriers to accessing an organization's programs?
- What are the mechanics of becoming a client of the organization?
- Is the process of engagement sensitive to the specific needs of clients?
- What is the client's or potential client's experience with the organization?
- Does the organization provide a full range of programs and services?
- Do clients have to obtain assistance from other organizations in addition to your organization? Does the organization assist in this search and location process?

Chapter 13, *Using Market Research for Strategic Planning Purposes*, outlines some of the key methods for obtaining information on client needs. It emphasizes how important it is to dig beneath stated needs to identify and define core needs. For example, clients will often say that they need professional or accessible service. These words actually describe service attributes (or characteristics) and will have different meanings for different clients. "Professional" may mean having certain credentials or it may refer to the way in which your organization conducts its business. Your organization must try to obtain information that will identify core needs and determine how these core needs are defined.

Understand Donor Needs

Social service organizations must also strive to meet the needs of donors who volunteer and contribute other resources. This presents a dual challenge for management and staff as they strive to ensure that their strategy is aligned with clients as well as donors. Again, the key is in understanding the needs of donors. It may seem that all donors would have the same needs, but work in this area has proven that this is not the case.

United Way of Calgary and Area embarked on a detailed process of understanding its donor needs. This was accomplished through focus groups and surveys. It was discovered that donors have a core set of needs that are often hidden under labels that have little meaning on their own.

For example, it is often assumed that all donors share a general need to give back to society by supporting causes that they feel provide good services and programs. However, this assumption is much too general to be of assistance in pinpointing underlying core needs. With further information, it may be possible to determine that the core needs attributable to an individual donor are quite different than those attributable to a corporate donor. In fact, there may be different sets of core needs within each of the individual and corporate donor segments. There are likely to be different needs between donors who only give dollars and donors who give time and expertise to your organization. It is important to understand the key differences in core needs in order to determine how best to position your social service organization within the market place for giving.

Develop Needs-based Segments

Once you have gathered information on core needs for both clients and donors, you should attempt to group clients and donors by segments. This is known as market segmentation. The objective behind market segmentation is to group together clients with similar needs and donors with similar needs. In doing this, an organization can examine the different market segments that it is currently serving:

- Which ones provide the best fit with the organization's internal capabilities?
- Which ones are unique to the organization (for example, niche markets)?
- Which ones take up the majority of the organization's resources?
- Which ones is the organization best suited to serve?

Segmentation typically follows a conventional format based on past practice. For example, clients may be segmented by disease, disability, situation, age, gender, and other demographic factors. Donors may be segmented on the basis of their giving pattern, time committed, type of volunteerism and associated demographics. Needs information enables organizations to develop segments based upon fundamental needs and motivation rather than on the characteristics that describe a segment. Needs-based segments are invaluable when defining and evolving programs and services.

For example, a social service organization whose mission is to provide social and recreational opportunities for children and youth with disabilities may have traditionally segmented its clients by type of disability and age. However, regardless of disability or age, a needs analysis would likely point to groupings or segments of clients who share common needs. Perhaps there is a segment of clients who need an intellectual socialization experience that could be provided through a variety of means, for example, book discussions and outings. There may be another segment that needs to be physically challenged through a variety of appropriate recreational activities. The key difference is not in the type of disability or the age of the clients, but rather the core need. The way that the organization would respond to each of these two types of needs segments would be very different.

Another example of needs-based segmentation from a fundraising perspective identifies that there are certain needs that underlie giving patterns, volunteer activities and corporate profiles. Some of these needs include:

- enhancing corporate image
- resolving a current public relations issue
- connecting directly to social issues
- contributing to the solution
- contributing to the betterment of society

Contrast this with a more traditional approach where segmentation is along the lines of organizational size, total dollars raised, industry sector and other demographics.

Example: McDonalds provides an example of a private sector corporation/donor that has aligned itself with a charity in order to enhance its image. Through Ronald McDonald House, McDonalds has constructed approximately 197 houses in 16 countries to provide a home away from home for families with sick children. This type of charity is a fit with the McDonalds family image and provides the company with a way to give back to society in a meaningful and visible way.

How to Conduct a Market Segmentation

The key to successful market segmentation is to view the organization's market from a needs perspective and to develop an hypothesis (a guess based on your current market knowledge) about possible needs-based segments. This is a starting point that can be evolved as the hypothesis is tested against reality.

One helpful tool for this exercise is included in **Figure 14-1**, *Needs Rating Matrix*. Once the organization has identified the core needs of its clients, the needs are listed across the top of a matrix sheet. Then, a listing of key clients or client groupings is constructed on the left side of the matrix. Participants from within the organization (preferably a cross section of program developers and program deliverers) then proceed through an exercise of rating clients against identified needs. Clients who have an identified need are marked with an X. Otherwise, the space in the matrix is left blank.

At the completion of this exercise, the visual cue provided by X's and blanks for all clients or client groupings will assist in identifying whether certain clients/client groupings cluster together around one or more needs. The organization must then analyze where there are similar needs and where there are very different or unique needs. Can these patterns be generalized to reveal needs-based segments within the organization's client population? Segments are then developed for client clusters that share the same needs and are given labels that summarize their key needs and characteristics.

This process greatly oversimplifies the sophisticated market research techniques employed by large corporations to establish market segments. However, it is a relatively easy and manageable way of approaching segmentation that should assist your organization in thinking through the eyes of your clients.

FIGURE 14-1
Needs Rating Matrix

Needs Rating Matrix				
	Needs			
	Need 1	**Need 2**	**Need 3**	**Need 4**
Client A		X	X	
Client B	X	X		
Client C	X			X
Client D		X		
Client E		X		X
Client F			X	X
Client G	X	X		X

A similar approach can also be used to segment donors.

Gathering More Information

Given the luxury of time and resources, this is the point to initiate a test of hypothesized client or donor needs-based segments. Focus groups and surveys provide an effective way of doing this. For example, focus groups allow an organization to explore specific topic areas with selected clients. This can assist in testing hypotheses and building better information about segments and their needs. Information from focus groups can be used to construct survey instruments that will then be used to canvass a much larger group of clients. Specific questions can be asked that will assist in assessing the validity of the hypothetical client segments.

If the decision is made to gather more information, the organization must recognize that it will probably require some assistance in designing and conducting focus groups, designing surveys and analyzing results. This is particularly the case if the organization intends to establish statistical verification of its client and/or donor segments. Refer to **Chapter 13**, *Using Market Research for Strategic Planning Purposes*, for more instruction on how to undertake this follow-up work.

Developing the Value Proposition

A value proposition is the key set of benefits the organization delivers to meet the specific needs of each segment. From the client or donor perspective, the value received must exceed the cost (effort) required to utilize a program and service. Consequently, each market segment requires a distinct value proposition.

To develop the value proposition, describe the key distinguishing characteristics of the client or donor segments. The list of key characteristics should include any that can be generalized to all of the clients or donors within the segment. For example, although there will always be exceptions, the organization may be able to identify common health, situation and demographic characteristics. The list should also include any knowledge about the way in which clients (or donors) utilize programs and services and the type of support that they require.

Next, the key distinguishing needs of each segment should be listed. Again, this should come from the analysis completed on core needs. This list would include needs that point to the motivation for seeking the organization's programs and services.

A value proposition for each segment can now be written. **Figure 14-2**, *Example of a Value Proposition*, provides a hypothetical example of a value proposition for a woman's shelter. The hypothetical segment is women whose primary need is to establish themselves financially.

FIGURE 14-2
Example of a Value
Proposition

Example of a Value Proposition
Inner City Woman's Shelter – Value Proposition for the Financial Stabilization segment.
The Inner City Woman's Shelter offers full financial and employment counseling services designed to assist clients who are working to establish financial stability. Services include: financial assessment, assistance in developing and implementing a household budget, review of personal skill sets and job search counseling.

Defining the Elements of the Value Proposition

The value proposition proposed for each market segment is now tested against the organization's current effort, including: the types of programs and services currently offered to meet clients' needs, the cost of providing these programs and services, the methods used to promote these programs and services, the targets of promotional efforts, as well as where programs and services are promoted and delivered.

The same process applies to donors. What are the giving programs and services that the organization has developed to meet donor needs; what are the costs associated with different types of giving (in human and financial terms); what type of promotion is being directed to the different donor segments; how is this promotion being targeted; and where are fundraising efforts being directed?

Time permitting, it is often helpful to develop a profile of the typical client and donor within each segment. The profile records key aspects of each segment for future reference.

Developing Market Forecasts by Segment

In this step, an attempt is made to size each market segment in terms of its potential demand for the organization's programs and services. The main objective is to identify which segments are currently the most significant, which are growing and which are the most susceptible to competitors.

Attempt to estimate the potential benefits and costs associated with pursuing the different market segments over a three-year period. It is important to ensure that the organization's accounting and financial expertise is involved in developing these forecasts, as it is critical to have considered not only the obvious costs associated with providing service to these segments, but also those costs that share certain fixed overheads of the organization.

On a comparative basis, the organization needs to be able to estimate the cost of providing service associated with each market segment. This information will factor into the decision regarding the focus of the organization.

Reviewing Implications of Selecting Segments

The implications of focusing on certain segments of clients and donors will be different in each case. Again, a relative assessment of implications will provide the organization with another way of thinking through its desired focus. The following list of implication questions is intended to serve as a guideline only.

Marketing Implications

- What would the optimal mix of programs and services be to meet the needs of the segment (thinking in terms of what would be possible over the next three years for new or redesigned programs and services)?
- How would these programs and services be designed?
- How would the organization reach this market — what types of promotion, outreach and networking would be necessary?
- What would the primary market emphasis be (in terms of geography)?

Organizational Implications

- Does the organization have the internal resources to meet the needs of this segment under the scenario projected for the next three years (financial, human, technical)?
- Does the organization have the internal expertise to meet the needs of this segment?

- If not, how would resources and expertise need to be modified, for example, through reassigning current staff, adding new staff, re-training existing staff?
- Would any existing functions become redundant? What would the implications of this be?
- What activities would no longer be necessary?

Key Process and Systems Implications

- What market intelligence (for example, research and data capture on clients and competitors) would be required?
- What accounting and financial support (for example, establishing systems to accurately identify program participation and costs for all programs and services) would be required?
- How will cash flow analysis (for example, to accommodate measured market growth) be conducted?
- What are the implications (for example, establishing new suppliers and methods for purchasing new programs and services) for purchasing?
- How will compensation schemes (for example, ensuring linkage between new performance measures and compensation of staff) need to change?
- What types of communications (for example, both internal and external) will be required?

Establishing Segment Selection Criteria

Now that the organization has identified the key implications of pursuing each of the potential client segments, it should think about the implications of narrowing the scope of its focus by identifying the limited number of segments the organization can best serve. This involves reviewing each segment relative to the others in terms of certain criteria that are judged to be of value to the organization. These criteria will vary, depending upon the specific situation of each organization. However, there are some criteria that seem to have a general appeal. These include:

- alignment with mission statement,
- compatibility with current organizational strengths,
- synergy between segments.

Each of the identified criteria should be defined to ensure that all those who are involved in the rating exercise have the same interpretation.

The rating of market segments relative to each other in terms of their current and future attractiveness to the organization can be turned into a very sophisticated process. However, the experience of many organizations who have gone through such an exercise supports keeping the process as simple as possible and adding complexity only if the rating does not assist in distinguishing between the relative merits of the segments. Keep in mind that since the organization is attempting to focus its efforts on a limited number of the segments, it is best to approach this task by rating each segment relative to the others. Come up with a rating scheme that will provide a way to compare the relative merit of the segments after all criteria have been considered. At this point, the organization should be able to identify those segments that are the most attractive for selective focus over the next three years.

When an organization struggles with making choices between market segments, a couple of things need to be kept in mind. The choice of segments instills a discipline within the organization. This focus means that the organization will be able to identify clearly what type of client it will focus on over the planning horizon and this in turn assists in allocating scarce human and financial resources to the tasks at hand. Focus also means that the organization can identify certain things that it can stop doing.

Two of the most common objections to choosing a focus are that the organization is unwilling to abandon past clients and is afraid of missing opportunities that arise. To respond to the first objection, focusing does not mean limiting. Selecting a segment focus does not mean that the organization will be prevented from providing service to clients who do not fit exactly within the selected segment. What the organization does mean is that the organization will focus on meeting 100% of the needs of the chosen segment(s). If the orgnaization can meet some of the needs of other client segments at the same time, this will be an added benefit. As for missed opportunities, a segment focus is a very dynamic activity. As soon as the organization selects a focus and aligns organizational processes and systems towards serving that segment, it must also begin a process of evaluation. This evaluation involves establishing a monitoring plan that will capture critical information on the success of the segment focus. In doing this, the organization will also capture information on other opportunities as they arise to see if they are a fit with the current focus. Having this screen for opportunities will act as another test for the validity of the segment selection.

The next chapter takes the reader into a discussion of further developing effective communications plans.

Summary

The most critical stakeholder group is the client group: those who benefit directly from the organization's efforts. Identifying clients' needs and understanding the implications for programs and services becomes a critical priority for the social service organization. A social service organization can be most effective by segmenting the client population according to needs, rather than by segmenting based on demographic or other factors; then designing and delivering services to those segments that can best be served by the organization.

CHAPTER 15

Marketing and Communications Planning Framework

Properly planned and executed marketing and communications initiatives can be one of the most important factors in the success of any organization. While many social service organizations may view marketing as simply a sales and advertising function, the broader role of marketing is an extremely complex one that involves aligning the organization's programs and services with clients' needs.

Marketing and communications planning is an extensive subject that could and does easily fill an entire textbook. Therefore, the purpose of this chapter is only to introduce some of the important concepts that are included in the marketing and communications function. This information will be useful for:

- Developing a straightforward marketing and communications plan that goes beyond simply producing brochures and advertisements.
- Creating awareness for the language used in marketing that is useful when working with outside marketing consultants, advertising, communications and public relations agencies.
- Evaluating proposals submitted by the external parties listed above.
- Hiring marketing and communications professionals to work in the organization.

Stages in the "Buying Process"

Without going into an extensive discussion of consumer behaviour and marketing theory, there are a few useful concepts that help to provide a context for the role that marketing plays in successfully reaching out to clients, raising public awareness of social issues, attracting donors, recruiting and retaining staff.

Before any client uses the programs or services of a social service organization, s/he goes through a basic series of steps to arrive at their ultimate decision. An effective marketing and communications plan serves to address clients' needs and provides information and support through each step in the process in order to guide clients to the organization's services.

181

While your organization may be providing counseling or support services, the phrase "buying process" is used in this case to describe how clients decide to use the services of one specific organization. The five steps in a typical buying process are awareness, need recognition, search for alternatives, decision and action.

1. Awareness

Awareness, or market awareness as it is often referred to, is clients' knowledge of the organization's existence and a basic understanding of its services *before they have used or even had need of these services*. The idea here is that the organization cannot be invisible if it expects to attract and serve clients.

Many organizations expend a great deal of time, effort and resources to instill awareness within their chosen market segments through advertising, public relations and communications efforts. For example, crisis hotlines promote their names, phone numbers and services to the public to create awareness of their existence. They also gather statistics and release these to the public via media releases to increase the markets' knowledge of the existence of social problems, like suicide, and the services available to support people in crisis.

2. Need Recognition

Either as a result of becoming aware of the programs and services provided by an organization, or for internally driven reasons, a client will decide that they have a need that requires addressing.

An organization's marketing efforts can help in fostering need recognition by clearly communicating an understanding of clients' situations that precipitate a need, and the associated benefits or solutions that the organization provides. This is why the marketing effort must incorporate client needs information into its planning and messages. Understanding when and how clients determine that they have a need for a program or service will determine where the organization should promote its services and the words or images that the organization should use to describe what they do. For example, women who are victims of domestic abuse may seek help from their doctor. Consequently, a women's shelter may choose to promote its services on the bulletin board of a doctor's waiting room.

Need recognition can come before awareness. In this case, once a potential client identifies that they have a particular need, they become much more receptive to the awareness advertising conducted by the organization. For example, a pregnant teenager will pay closer attention to transit posters talking about free prenatal care for teens than to those posters talking about mutual funds.

3. Search for Alternatives

Once a client determines that they have a need for a program or service, they will undergo some type of search process. The search and evaluation process can be extremely short and simple (opening the yellow pages and placing a call), or long and extensive (contacting, visiting and checking references). In either case, the organization's marketing program should ensure that the *right* information is available in a variety of formats and locations where potential clients typically search to ensure that the organization will be visible and the benefits of their service clearly understood.

4. Decision

Closely linked to the search for alternatives, the client ultimately makes a decision about which organization they will turn to for help. Usually the decision is based on a few key criteria. If the organization understands their clients well enough, they can make this step simpler by focusing in on key attributes of their programs and services in their communications with potential clients. Other efforts that assist clients in choosing your organization include, ensuring calls are returned promptly and inquiries are followed-up, providing references and testimonials concerning program and service quality, and clearly articulating what results can be expected from working with your organization.

5. Action

In this step the client goes out and engages the services of their chosen organization. While they have made their decision, their immediate experience in locating the service and signing-up is still being evaluated as to whether their decision was a good one or not. The potential client could still change their mind at this point and go elsewhere, or choose not to pursue help at all. In this action step, the organization needs to consider a number of factors, once again, all built upon its knowledge of its client segments' needs:

- Location of service — where do clients go to interact with the organization — is it convenient, is it the right setting and facility for conducting the organization's work, or can support be ably provided over the phone or via the internet?
- Hours of service.
- What occurs in the sign-up procedure?
- How quickly can the client receive service upon contacting the organization?
- What information is provided to new clients to develop proper expectations for service?
- What is the appropriate atmosphere: welcoming and involved; confidential and empathetic; professional and straight forward?
- What arrangements are made for second and subsequent interactions between the client and organization, for example, follow-up procedures for the client, schedule of events to attend, schedule next appointment, referrals made to other support organizations.
- What follow-up steps are taken by organization personnel? It could be valuable to contact the client to see if they have questions or comments as a result of their first contact with the organization.

Developing the Marketing and Communications Plan

Marketing and communications initiatives cannot be planned in a vacuum or in an ad hoc fashion. Rather these types of initiatives serve to support the organization's overall strategic objectives and goals and to respond to the needs of the organization's target client segments.

In order to prepare a marketing and communications plan, the following input is required:

- The organization's current strategic plan, complete with values, mission, key success factors, goals, performance indicators, and current year's action priorities.
- Market research data including: information about the target client segments that the organization will focus on serving, client needs data, demographic information, and client satisfaction measures. (Refer to **Chapter 13**, *Using Market Research for Strategic Planning Purposes*, to better understand the different types of market research organizations typically undertake as part of their strategic planning efforts.)

On the basis of these two sources of information, those responsible for marketing and communications would construct a plan consisting of a number of initiatives to support the organization in carrying out its mission and to attain its current year objectives. The following are examples of marketing and communications plans that could be developed based on the organization's goals, action priorities and client needs:

Example 1: *The organization's focus is based upon an educational program directed at children.* Marketing could develop materials suitable for children of different age groups, a mascot and special graphics established to represent the organization and its central messages, special facilities could be secured appropriate for serving children, school visitations implemented to promote the program and parent information packages prepared.

Example 2: *The organization wants to attract more single parents to their service.* Marketing initiates an advertising campaign to communicate with single parents; produces brochures dealing with this group's special needs; a childcare service is set-up so parents can attend help sessions without incurring the costs of babysitters; communications are distributed to high-schools where students who are single parents are in attendance.

Example 3: *The organization needs $1 million in funding to build a new facility.* Marketing plans and implements a major fund-raising program, including a home lottery, advertising campaign, public relations events, corporate fund-raising programs, and direct mail donation request to past donors.

Example 4: *An organization's target client segment is widely dispersed geographically.* A web site and 1-800 number are set up for clients to obtain information on programs and services. The organization establishes a presence in remote locations through a partnership program with businesses, government or regional health offices whereby office space is donated.

The Four "P's" of Marketing

There are four main areas of focus within the role of marketing. These focus areas are commonly referred to as the four "Ps" of marketing and they include promotions, place (also may be referred to as distribution), pricing and product. In the process of constructing a marketing plan, it is useful to consider the organization's needs in each of these areas. The following four sections will deal with each P in turn, describing its function and providing ideas about how they can be used to support the organization's work.

Promotions: Advertising, Communications and Public Relations

Promotion covers all of the types of initiatives that immediately come to mind as typical marketing activities. Examples of these initiatives include advertising campaigns (print, radio and television), brochures, posters, media releases, tradeshows, giveaways or promotional items (t-shirts, mugs, calendars, pens and key chains), billboards and bumper stickers.

Promotions provide a way in which the organization can communicate with its target audience and the public-at-large, creating awareness of its existence and purpose, creating interest, influencing perceptions and giving the organization a personality. Each of the tools within the broader promotions category have a specific function and should be used as required. For instance, it is not necessary or advisable that every organization should implement an media advertising campaign every year. Like all of the promotional tools, it is designed to be used in certain situations to achieve a specific purpose.

Graphic Standards and Visual Identity Elements

Every organization needs to formalize its visual identity that may comprise any or all of the following elements:

- organization's name — should be descriptive and meaningful to the target audience,
- logo and/or graphics that may accompany the organization's name,
- a theme line, also known as a tag line, that accompanies the organization's name and that succinctly and creatively describes the organization's purpose; theme lines can be used in all print communications and advertising. For example, Security House (organization's name) — Where Women Can Be Safe (theme line).
- standardized colors and typefaces (or fonts) used by the organization to create consistency and a strong visual identity,
- a standards manual that clearly defines all of the above specifications, size and placement of logo, graphic and theme lines, and shows how all elements are used in a variety of ways from full color to black and white applications.

Communications

Communications primarily refers to all of an organization's printed items that can be inventoried and distributed to clients through the mail, office locations, and through associate organizations and advisors (for example, doctors, government agencies, educational institutions). Communications materials include such items as brochures, newsletters, guides, how-to manuals, posters, and other types of literature that educate or inform clients. With the proliferation of the internet though, most of these materials can also be duplicated on-line in a website.

Communications materials such as the organization's brochures and newsletters are the most basic and important marketing tools that an organization can prepare. Before anything else, the organization must be able to articulate its mission, communications objectives, services and key benefits it delivers, so that a quick, consistent and professional response to requests for information can be provided. The key to well designed communications materials is having a clear understanding of clients needs and responding to these needs with the right information, written in terms that the clients can easily understand.

Advertising

Advertising is conducted when the organization has a specific objective to disseminate information in a time sensitive fashion to a broad audience. It can be very expensive and its effectiveness is not always easy to measure. However, in cases where the organization wants to promote a special event, kick-off a major fundraising drive, create awareness for a new service, or promote a symposium to discuss an issue of broad social concern, advertising is the appropriate method to deliver the message.

Advertising utilizes media support to get out its message. The various mediums include:

- print (newspapers, magazines, or journals),
- radio,
- television,
- outdoor (transit (buses), bus shelters, billboards).

Public Relations

Public relations acts and feels a little bit like advertising in that it presents the organization's work in the public forum, but it has a much heavier emphasis on conveying a large amount of information. Familiar public relations tools and techniques include:

- media releases,
- press conferences,
- assigned media spokespeople,
- special events (facility opening ceremonies, open-houses, symposiums),
- tradeshows.

Public relations, as the name implies, concerns itself with communicating with large numbers of people at a time, responding to requests coming from the public-at-large or the media. It can include proactive initiatives, ranging from releasing information on new discoveries emanating from research or surveys, to announcing the appointment of key personnel or board members. Public relations also include the organization's ability to respond in a reactive fashion. For example, an organization may be asked to comment on a community or world crisis and the assistance and support that they will be providing.

It is advisable for every organization to think about its potential public relations requirements and to develop formats for media releases, obtain contact lists of key media personnel, and decide who in the organization is qualified to serve as the media spokesperson.

Tradeshows are usually known well in advance due to the significant preparation required on the part of organizers, which includes the arranging of venues, booking of space for participants, invitation lists or advertising to attract attendees or delegates.

The organization too must commit to significant planning, budget, materials and personnel to support these types of marketing activities. A great deal of care should be taken to evaluate the value of attending these type of functions. Will the organization's target client audience or other key stakeholders be in attendance (for example, peers who support the organization's work such as doctors, teachers, government personnel), that would warrant being present?

Place: Where, How and When Clients Access Services

Has the impact of where, how and when clients access the organization's programs and services been considered? This element can make a big difference in terms of the organization's effectiveness, success and clients' satisfaction. It also includes other considerations regarding how access to service is facilitated through peers and alliances in the community who can provide reference and information about the organization's services to their clients.

Decisions about the appropriate methods for locating and distributing service should be based upon information known about which client segments the organization serves, how these types and groups of clients go about looking for services, client's needs and how potential clients would prefer to access service. Some of the variables include:

- Is service provisioned in person, over the telephone or via the internet?
- Where do offices need to be located geographically to be accessible to clients? Do clients have to drive or can they take public transportation?
- Are offices required or can space be shared?
- What type of facilities is appropriate? Is disabled access required? The answer to this question is almost always **yes**.
- What are the organization's hours and days of operation?
- Where can clients learn about the organization — third parties that act as agents or references?

Pricing: Guidelines Governing the Use of the Organization's Programs and Services

How an organization approaches the pricing of their programs and services must be aligned with the costs to the organization and the ability and willingness for clients to pay. And while it may not be appropriate or within the mandate of the organization to charge for its programs and services, the concept of assigning some type of guidelines, terms or rules that govern the use and cost of programs and services, are often very necessary.

The following are some issues to consider in the organization's pricing planning:
- What is appropriate given the organization's work — charging a fee for service or developing rules that control and/or encourage access to service?
- Look at the client segments served — what is appropriate given who they are, their needs and their circumstances?
- What are the organization's sources of funding? Are they adequate to support the organization's ongoing work? Does a service fee have to be applied to maintain the organization's viability?
- What creative ways can the organization "price" its service; for example, donations of money, food, used clothing and/or books?

- Can clients be sponsored through government grants, or corporate or individual sponsorship programs?
- If the organization is fully funded, what guidelines or rules should be put in place that are appropriate for the type of service provided? Should these guidelines serve to limit access (for example, clients can visit once per week), encourage progress or commitment on the part of the client (for example, the client can attend another session if they complete previous readings and homework assignments), or should these guidelines serve to control and reward clients (for example, the client is entitled to increased financial compensation from the government if they adhere to a drug rehabilitation program)?

Product: Services Designed With the Client in Mind

How a program or service is designed is not always thought of as a marketing responsibility. However, due to the need for a close linkage between what the organization delivers, the client's need for services, and the marketing initiatives to bring the two together, there are obvious advantages in taking a marketing perspective. This does not mean that programs, policies and services should be trivialized, simplified, or made glitzy. Rather it ensures that all aspects of the organization's offerings are considered in light of information known about the target client segment, including client satisfaction data.

All of the ways in which an organization can tailor its offerings to the client segment is completely dependent on what the organization offers and the clients it serves. It would be impossible to cover here all of the elements that could be considered, but the following examples illustrate how programs and services might be modified or augmented as different needs are considered.

Example 1: *The organization has children or the elderly as clients.* Printed materials should consider reading skills and abilities; support programs may be beneficial for the client's caregiver; the length of service sessions should be set to accommodate attention span, comfort and health circumstances; the amenities and location of the organization's facilities should be considered; personnel may need to be skilled in working with the dynamics presented by the specific age group of the clients.

Example 2: *The organization offers shelter services for abused women.* Should all personnel be women? Is there a doctor available on-call? Should the doctor be a woman? What support services do the clients most urgently require while being housed at the shelter — legal or financial advice, career counseling, housing locator services, psychological counseling? What follow-up services need to be provided or to whom will clients be referred? What amenities and services should be available to cater to the needs of children at the shelter?

Subsequent to identifying a service concept, a service profile can be developed by providing the following information:

- description of the service,
- client needs to be satisfied by the service,

- the benefits (or outcomes) that will be delivered by the service,
- how the service supports the direction and strategy of the organization,
- how the service will (could) be delivered,
  - what partnerships/collaborations could be utilized to deliver the service?
  - what existing processes would be required to support the service?
  - what new processes would be required to support the service?
- the conceptual revenue/cost model associated with the service,
  - would fees be charged for the service and how?
  - would the service be funded from other sources of revenue?
  - what would be the approximate costs to deliver the service?

Cultivating Marketing Alliances

Draw Upon Community Support

A tremendous amount of support is available, often free-of-charge, to organizations in the form of alliances in the community, including peer organizations, media, government (municipal, provincial/state and federal), post-secondary educational institutions, service organizations (Rotary, Lions, Shriners), and corporations. Many of these groups have specific objectives in their own marketing or strategic plans to make a contribution back to the community, which could include partnering with organizations who need support. This support can include the donation of time (volunteers), money, professional talent (marketing, editing, financial or technical advising) or even space (office or venues for special events).

It is important to select alliances based on some commonalties in terms of missions, work or values to create a compatible and successful partnership that can benefit both parties involved.

Benefits derived from partnering with peer organizations can include, sharing in the planning and costs of joint special events, increased visibility and awareness through referral programs and distributing each other's communication materials, or strengthening programs by collaborating on new services or sharing information.

In the case of media alliances, there are special services that fall outside the areas of paid advertising or news reporting available to non-profit organizations. Many television and radio stations will feature public service announcements or donate the services of their well-known personalities to speak on behalf of an organization. Their community "cruisers" and special events teams can be requested to attend the organization's events to heighten awareness and provide additional attraction to the venue.

Government offices, by virtue of their portfolio (small business, health, education) will often have a natural fit with a social service organization. Look for opportunities to be included in directories and other government listings of aid agencies and organizations, or get invited to and/or sponsored to attend symposiums and conferences.

Post-secondary educational institutions can match up undergraduate or graduate students who are working on studies in all types of research, management or specific disciplines such as medicine, management, psychology, or social work, who need practical experience or a research project to complete their course requirements. Students are a tremendous source of up-to-date and new ideas, techniques, information, data gathering, and are an additional human resource to be applied to the organization's work.

Large corporations often select causes or themes that they will support such as education, or children, working with a number of organizations who have this focus in their mandate.

Outside Professional Services

Most organizations enlist the services of companies who specialize in some form of marketing, advertising, communications or creative design work to assist with the design and implementation of marketing projects.

The following is a list of the type of firms available and the services they perform. Often the services that are offered by these firms can overlap to a great extent, depending on how they have chosen to define their business. It is worthwhile to invest some time to meet with representatives in order to understand their suite of offerings.

Marketing consultants — marketing professionals with capabilities in all or most areas of marketing. They can provide assistance in conducting market research, structuring marketing departments, designing and implementing marketing plans. Some firms will hire themselves out to serve as an organizations' marketing department.

Advertising agencies — specialize in the area of promotions. The medium and large firms typically provide full service including design, development and distribution of advertising and communications (print) materials. Advertising agencies will also manage and supervise, for a set fee or percentage of the cost, the services of other outside creative services such as photographers, copywriters, editors, designers, printers and media placement firms.

Public relations firms — Overlapping somewhat with the services provided by advertising agencies, public relations firms focus on media and shareholder relations, communicating with the public, preparing media releases, and organizing special events. Note: Some advertising agencies have public relations specialists in-house.

Media placement agencies — provide information and advise on how best to place advertisements in television, radio and outdoor mediums to reach the target audience most effectively within the budget available. They prepare media plans, then book and place the ads with the various media organizations. They can also provide news monitoring or clipping services to collect all reports on topics of interest to their clients.

Special event planners — specifically plan, arrange, manage and supervise all aspects of their clients' needs in terms of live private or public events such as open-houses, stakeholder meetings, conferences, symposiums and tradeshow appearances.

Small graphic design shops — provide a limited number of services usually focusing on production of printed materials or graphic development for use in visual identity programs (for example, logos), advertising (for example, posters, billboards) or on promotional items (for example, t-shirts and caps), layout and production work.

Speciality advertising firms — supply promotional items or giveaways like t-shirts, caps, pens, trophies, balloons and a myriad of other items customized with the organization's name, logo and special messages.

Desktop publishers — provide word processing and layout of documents and limited graphic design work.

Printers — can provide some design and layout services, but primarily focus on the printing of advertising (posters and flyers) and communications materials (brochures, leaflets, newsletters, annual reports).

Photographers — of the professional, commercial variety, may specialize in different types of photography. Choose amongst those that focus on industrial and workplace settings, still life, people and fashion, or artistic and avant-garde. Many can adapt to most requirements, but be conscious of differences in their own personal style that can greatly effect the final product.

Three Options for Managing the Relationship

Organizations can choose between one of three different options in working with outside marketing and creative services.

1. Hire an outside professional marketing firm that can act as the organization's marketing department. This type of company would not only develop the marketing plan, but handle all aspects of implementation as well, including hiring and supervising outside advertising and creative services. This approach frees up the organization to focus on its core business, but removes nearly all marketing decisions from the organization. It can be an expensive option.
2. Develop a relationship with one or two firms that offer a comprehensive list of marketing and creative services, like an advertising agency or public relations firm. In this scenario the organization has responsibility for developing the marketing plan and managing and supervising implementation of marketing initiatives, but it would draw heavily on the services of the agencies for design and implementation support. For instance the advertising agency would, on behalf of their client organization, hire, manage and supervise any ancillary services required such as photographers, copywriters, editors, specialty creative designers and/or print shops.
3. Similar to option two, but in this case the organization chooses to directly hire, coordinate, manage and supervise all marketing and creative services. To do this successfully, the organization needs marketing personnel knowledgeable and capable of working with and managing these specialty services. This option gives the organization a great deal of control and can save money, but it can also be very time consuming. The organization also assumes more risk in terms of the quality and accuracy of the finished product.

The Final Word —
You Get What You Ask For: The Marketing Brief

One final piece of advice when it comes to working with outside professional service firms is to be clear and precise about the organization's needs and expectations. Always prepare a marketing brief that fully describes the purpose of the marketing initiative. The brief should include such information as what the project needs to accomplish in specific terms (for example, number of new clients, increase in satisfaction of x%, increase in calls of x%), the target audience, relevant background information on the target audience and their needs, messages or information that must be conveyed, various creative instructions like the mood that should be created, the budget available and a contact for more information.

This document ensures that all details are covered with little chance for miscommunication or omission. It then forms the basis for one or more firms to prepare proposals and quotes to deliver on all requirements of the project.

From a review of marketing and communicating with the community, the discussion moves on in the next chapter to effective methods to mobilize support for the social service organization in the context of fundraising.

Summary

This chapter introduces the concepts that are included in the marketing and communications function of the social service organization. Not unlike consumers of commercial products and services, clients of social service organizations go through the "buying process" with its five stages. Before preparing a marketing plan it is essential to have the basic building blocks in place, including the market research and strategic plan. The four Ps of marketing are discussed, highlighting their relevance to social service organizations. Finally, a variety of approaches for drawing upon community support and outside professional services as a means of cultivating marketing alliances are described and the importance of the marketing brief is highlighted.

CHAPTER 16

Fundraising in the Social Service Agency

The capacity for a social service, non-profit agency to provide its core services often depends on its ability to supplement government funding with private sector dollars. While the degree to which this is necessary can vary, it nevertheless is a reality for most agencies and therefore for most Executive Directors and agency boards.

Resource Development Planning

It is imperative that the organization first has a written strategic plan that clearly lays out the vision, mission, goals and objectives to be achieved over the longer term, usually three years. In the absence of a strategic plan, any fundraising programs will be unfocused, poorly understood internally and externally, and largely ineffective and inefficient.

There are two critical resource development planning documents that flow directly from the strategic plan: 1) the strategic development plan — a three year plan for fund development that lays out the organization's development vision, mission, goals and objectives to be achieved; 2) and the annual development plan — which flows from this first document and defines the development operations over the next fiscal year. The annual development plan includes details about the fundraising programs, services, strategies, budgeted expenses, and projected revenues. **Figure 16-1** provides an example table of contents for a strategic development plan and **Figure 16-2** offers an example table of contents for an annual development plan.

The critically important point is that an organization cannot effectively implement an annual development program if it does not have a written plan. An annual development plan cannot be effectively implemented if a longer-term strategic development plan does not exist. And, a strategic development plan cannot be developed if the overall strategic direction of the organization is not clearly identified in an organizational strategic plan.

The development plan should also define the organization's core values. The value statement helps the organization to evaluate how choices are made about activities and guides the organization in writing policies concerning its business practices. For example, an organization that states professional development and continuous learning as one of

193

FIGURE 16-1
Example Table of
Contents for a Strategic
Devleopment Plan

3 Year Strategic Development Plan
Table of Contents

Executive Summary

Vision

Case Statement

Case for Support
> History and Role
> New Directions
> Needs and Priorities
> Key Messages

Strategic Plan for Fund Development

i	Purpose of the Campaign
ii	Role of the Fund Development Program
iii	Reasons for Donor Support
iv	Issues and Opportunities
v	Fund Development as Marketing
vi	Communication Theme
vii	Communicating with Target Groups
viii	Target Group of Donor Prospects
ix	Campaign Vehicles
x	Donor Recognition Features
xi	Staff and Volunteer Leadership
xii	Fund Development Three Year Campaign Goals
xiii	Fund Development Budget (Annual)
xiv	Critical Path
xv	Summary of Recommendations

Appendices

A	Listing of Prospective Donors (sample list)
B	Fund Development/Campaign Team Roles
C	Orientation and Training
D	Listing of contacted sources and questions
E	Sample pledge form and Benefits Matrix

Source: The Development Group, 2001

its values will ensure that staff and volunteers involved in fundraising have the opportunity to attend workshops and take courses to advance their fundraising knowledge. Where responsibility or accountability is a stated value, the organization will have stewardship policies in place to ensure donations are tracked and used according to the donor's expectations. It will also guide the organization in gift acceptance policies in areas such as gaming.

Relationship management is critical to the success of any organization and must be defined within the development plan, and ultimately within the strategies laid out for

**Annual Development Plan
Table of Contents**

Plan Overview

General Recommendations

Background

Environmental Overview

Roles of Agency

Roles and Responsibilities of Key Individuals

The Annual Giving Program
Agency Fundraising Philosophies
Annual Objectives
Strategies
Calendar
Budget

Schedules

Schedule 1 — 5-year History, Annual Donations Revenue
Schedule 2 — Revenue Projections by Fundraising Program
Schedule 3 — Agency Annual Needs for Current Year
Schedule 4 — Revenue Allocation Budget

Source: The Development Group, 2001

resource development. Central to this success is the organization's relationship with its community. How are the organization's services relevant to community issues and concerns? We have seen organizations outlive their purpose because they fail to assess the emerging needs of the community and therefore they do not adapt programs that change with the times. The relevancy of an organization also helps it to define its marketplace position and, therefore, the shaping of communications messages. The organization's primary stakeholders must also be identified and with it, strategies to develop and strengthen relationships with individuals and groups so they are ready to be asked for support and then asked to move up to higher levels of giving.

A well thought out strategic development plan involves both envisioning a desired future and developing strategies that point the way. Marketing, communications and operational plans must be linked to fund development. In the absence of such plans, the fund development process will operate on an ad hoc basis and considerably weaken the organization.

External Scanning

Strategic management within the organization extends by necessity to fund development activities. It is imperative that the fund development strategies support the agency's goals and are crafted in a manner consistent with the organization's values, mission and long-term goals. It is also important that the fund development plan and strategies be geared to the long-term, yet be flexible enough to take advantage of opportunities as they arise and to adapt to the changing local, provincial/state or national environments. This ability to respond to change, and to respond effectively, depends on an organization's commitment to monitoring its environment — in other words, to a healthy outward focus in addition to its internal commitment to service delivery.

The external environment relating to the non-profit sector and philanthropy is in a period of rapid and fundamental change. Decreased government funding, changing federal and provincial/state regulations, increased competition amongst non-profit groups and expanding needs of all organizations, all present a challenging environment even to the most sophisticated of social service organizations. Against this background, there is a shift from philanthropic support to strategic philanthropy with stakeholder emphasis. Sometimes known as "social entrepreneurs," more donors are directing funds to activities that may lead to social betterment or enable an organization to achieve greater self-sufficiency. For example, the social entrepreneur may make educational and nutritional programs available to inner city youth to reduce urban crime. The nutritional programs may be sponsored by corporate donors and delivered by a not-for-profit organization as a revenue generating activity.

It is a challenging time for any social service organization to be entering the philanthropic arena as well as for those striving to maintain and grow their public support. Trends affect a social service organization's development initiatives and should be taken into account when developing a strategic plan for resource development strategies.

Trends in Philanthropic Giving

Several key trends in philanthropic giving are evident:

- For the most part, fewer people are giving more. Giving is increasing primarily with already committed individuals.
- Major gifts, particularly from individuals and foundations are making campaigns successful. Personal solicitations have become the most predominant way to raise major gift funds.
- Corporate contributions have flattened out and unrestricted corporate giving is disappearing. Corporate donations are instead increasingly strategic, targeted and market-driven. This transaction-based giving often seeks strategic alignments through their giving philosophies and programs.
- Individuals, foundations, and corporations continue to become more selective of the causes they choose to support.
- Newer companies and the non-traditional corporate donors (for example, dot.coms and other high-tech companies) lack sophisticated community investment programs and will require considerable cultivation.
- Capital campaigns have generally become continuous major gift campaigns that build ongoing loyalty for well-established organizations that in turn make it difficult for new organizations to enter the market.
- Partnerships and strategic alliances are becoming a more significant part of development programs, and can be a great opportunity if approached wisely.
- Attracting the best, and right, volunteers is becoming more crucial and more competitive.

- Direct mail and other technological initiatives are becoming even more important for prospecting and donor acquisition.
- Pressures are increasing on staff to drive and implement fundraising programs as volunteers feel they have less time to give to implementing campaigns.
- Mutually beneficial relationships have never been more key as the single most important strength of successful fundraising.

Trends in the Non-Profit Sector

Several key trends in the non-profit sector which impact fundraising are evident:
- Government support continues to decrease on a broad scale.
- Self-sufficiency as evidenced by the accountable and transparent use of dollars and reduction of service duplication is becoming more important to potential funders.
- Charitable status is coming under greater scrutiny and will be more regulated.
- Increasing strength and professionalism of fundraising operations and fundraising professionals within many organizations heightens the competitiveness.
- The strongest non-profits will only get stronger.
- The search for new donors is becoming a competitive edge.

Six Major Principles

In order to be successful, a strong fund development plan must be flexible but should also be crafted according to six key principles that are fundamental to all successful fundraising.

1. People Give to People — to Help People

"People give to people... to help people" is the single most-quoted phrase in all fundraising materials and activities. And for good reason. Too often, organizations forget the three key parts of this phrase. Firstly, it is "people" that give, that make the decisions and who experience the motivations that underlie all charitable giving. This is true whether the giver is an individual, a corporation, a foundation or a local service group. Secondly, "people give to people." They do not give to an organization or to a program. They give "to help the people" that need help and see an organization's programs as the conduit to that help. It is a mistake to talk about the organization and how wonderful it is. Instead, speak to the issues of greatest concern to those who live and work in the community and what the organization is doing to help the people who are at the heart of those concerns. The need for a new computer, funds to pay down the organization's debt or to hire additional staff will make little headway into a potential donor's motivation. It is the individuals and the community that have needs. Not the organization. Talk about the people the organization helps, their stories, and why they need a donor's gift. This is the talk and the art of building long-lasting relationships with donors.

Finally, people also give to people on the strength of the relationship that has been established between the prospective donor and the individual who is soliciting support. Volunteer leadership, usually at the Board level, together with capable staff, has the ability to forge relationships to build sustainable fund development programs.

2. Standards of Giving

People give according to their personal means and relative to what others give. This is important to understanding how to make the best approach and to successfully cultivate the relationship. One hundred thousand dollars may be a sacrificial gift for one person but $100 or even $10 may have that same impact on another. Do not make the mistake of asking for too much. Equally important is not to make the mistake of asking for too little and robbing the donor of the opportunity to give at a meaningful level for that individual. It is also important to understand that donors tend to give relative to the gift levels of others. If the largest gift your organization has received is $5,000 by the leading corporation in town, then it makes little sense to ask other businesses for $25,000. In such cases, it would be imperative that your organization re-negotiates the lead corporate gift before approaching others.

Standards of giving are particularly important for volunteers to understand. If your goal is $100,000, and your largest previous gift on record is $5,000 then volunteers should understand that there needs to be a plan for achieving that goal and that it is based on sound analysis. For example, "we will need four gifts at $10,000, six gifts at $5,000, ten gifts at $2,500..." in order to reach the $100,000 goal. Prospective donors are then analyzed according to their ability to give level and targeted to each gift level category with the largest gifts secured first.

3. Giving Begins at Home

One of the most frequent obstacles for social service organizations is achieving buy-in to the essential principle of giving begins at home. Based on the belief that if the organization's mission is valid, and the project is needed, then those closest to the organization should lead the way in giving generously before any external fundraising is contemplated. Common objections include "I give my time" or "I have already purchased tickets to annual events." Consider the message this sends to individuals and corporations and then consider the position of the volunteer who can make that request with the knowledge that 100% of the Board and staff have given a significant (relative to their individual means) gift.

4. Successful Fundraising

"Successful fundraising is the right person asking the right prospect for the right amount for the right project at the right time in the right way." Six "rights" that are all key and that reflect the essential ingredient of all fundraising — that of building relationships. The "right person," usually a volunteer with a peer relationship, to ask the "right prospect," one with an interest in the organization or issue, for the "right amount," an amount that is reasonable and researched for that individual, for the "right project," one with a known or demonstrated interest in the project or similar projects, at the "right time," when you have nurtured a positive relationship, in the "right way," with respect and recognition that you are offering an opportunity for the prospect to fulfill their philanthropic objectives.

5. The 90/10 or 80/20 Rule

This maxim — that 10% of donors will provide 90% of fundraising revenues — holds true time after time. The shift from 80/20 to 90/10 reflects the narrowing trend of the last decade and underscores the growing importance of cultivating strong individual relationships. It also helps us to see that broad, shotgun, or "tin-cup," fundraising approaches are an ineffective use of available resources. Focusing on relationship building has more potential for long-term success for an organization.

6. Achieving Balance Through an Integrated Development Strategy

If you remember that donors are individuals (regardless of whether they are corporations or foundations), one will see the need to have a variety of fundraising methods, programs and approaches in order to achieve that all important broad base of support. Focusing on one type of giving will exclude many potential donors from giving to the organization. It is both wise and effective to develop a comprehensive set of giving opportunities through development programs that are integrated with each other.

Overview of a Traditional Fund Development Program

Fund development (refer to Appendix 16-A at the end of this chapter for an extensive glossary of fundraising terms) is characterized as being a highly future-oriented process, that is, it is continuous and ongoing; that defines the organization's development goals, and then seeks to accomplish them through a balanced and integrated set of diverse activities that produce the support required — whether it is money, relationships, volunteer effort or other. Successful fundraising is relationship building and, it is people not programs that build relationships and raise money. However, successful donor relationships are built over a long period of time and within a well-planned and structured development program that is an integral part of an organization's structural framework. Successful fundraising is conditional upon all of these activities being initiated and working together in concert.

As indicated in **Figure 16-3**, *An Integrated Development Plan Model*, there are three basic elements common to the balanced and integrated development process:

- annual giving programs,
- capital and/or major gift giving,
- planned giving.

Within each of these elements there is a wide variety of methods available to encourage institutional support while at the same time elevating the exchange process between the recipient and the donor from transactional to relationship based.

The relationship between the three key elements is more clearly defined in **Figure 16-4,** *The Donor Giving Pyramid,* a diagrammatic description of the hierarchy of donors by size of gifts. The diagram reflects that: as the size of donations increases, the number of donations decreases; as the number of years a donor is asked to renew increases, the number of donors decreases; as a campaign sophistication progresses

FIGURE 16-3
An Integrated
Development
Plan Model

An Integrated Development Plan Model		
Annual Gifts	**Major Gifts**	**Planned Gifts**
Gifts are made regularly (monthly/annually)	Gifts are a "stretch" and are made periodically.	Are generally gifts made in the present but redeemed in the future.
Usually asked for by telephone or mail	Always asked for face-to-face.	Generally asked for face-to-face unless provisions are made in will without consultation.
The Ask/Negotiation/Close sequence is usually done simultaneously.	The Ask/Negotiation/Close sequence may take several months or years to complete.	The Ask/Negotiation/Close sequence may take several months or years to complete.
Gifts are usually given in cash from current income	Gifts are usually given from appreciated assets (e.g. real estate, stocks, bonds)	Gifts are usually given from capital rather than income, and relate to the donor's estate plan.
Gifts are usually solicited on a cyclical basis with the organization's need in mind.	Gifts are solicited with the prospect's financial circumstances in mind.	Gifts are solicited with the prospect's financial circumstances in mind.
Gifts are usually secured by staff working alone.	Gifts are usually secured through a team effort using volunteers and staff in the process of contacting, cultivating, and soliciting prospects.	Gifts are usually secured through a team effort using a great deal of research and consultation between staff, donor, and financial and legal advisors.

Source: The Development Group, 2001

from annual to planned giving, the number of donors decreases; as donor involvement increases, the size of the donor's contribution increases and the response to campaign sophistication increases.

Each of the three elements has its own distinctive goals, objectives, audience and underlying necessities for success.

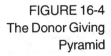
FIGURE 16-4
The Donor Giving
Pyramid

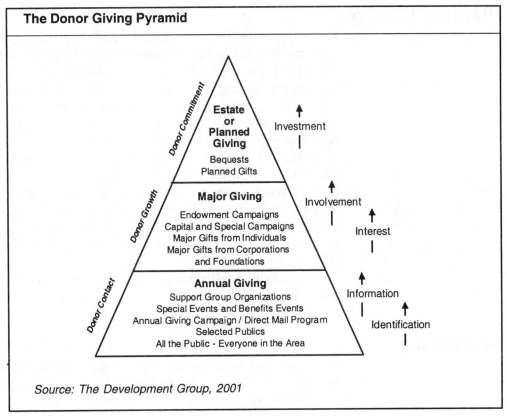

Source: The Development Group, 2001

Annual Giving

In terms of vehicles usually associated with annual giving, these include direct mail fundraising, special event fundraising, project specific fundraising, special and annual appeals (for example, Christmas, Easter) door-to-door campaigns, annual renewals and unsolicited and general gifts. Annual giving represents the broadest base of the overall development program and should eventually provide a certain amount of core operating or program funding that can be relied upon (but not guaranteed) on an annual basis. One of its most important contributions is the provision of a prospect pool that can be developed into relationships with potential for future major or deferred gifts.

Capital and/or Major Gift Giving

Capital programs and special campaigns include ongoing capital giving, naming opportunities, and special campaigns for specific capital or building funds. The trend is currently away from capital campaigns to special major gift appeals that are not necessarily bricks and mortar driven. The distinctive feature of capital campaigns is that they are one time, deadline driven, intensive campaigns, involving significant volunteer time and input. For this reason, they are planned separately and treated differently than an ongoing annual giving program. Major gift programs, however, represent the upper level of gift giving and provide fertile and qualified prospects for building long-term, mutually beneficial relationships. These ongoing programs form the foundation of most institutional programs and require a significant commitment of time and resources to nurture and grow these relationships.

Planned Giving

Planned giving includes memorials, charitable bequests, annuities, charitable remainder trusts, and other tax related methods of giving. One of the fastest growing estate planning options is the gifting of corporate shares in order to qualify for a capital gains exemption claim on personal income tax that would otherwise have to be paid. The gifts can be either current or deferred in nature and typically represent a deep relational commitment to the organization probably begun through the individual being introduced to the development process by an annual giving program.

Community foundations are a great resource for smaller social service organizations that lack the expertise in developing and promoting planned giving opportunities. Foundation staff can be helpful in setting up a framework for planned giving and even suggest phrasing for use on fundraising brochures. It may also be able to set up an account within the foundation for the handling of donor designated gifts and to create a vehicle for donors who have an interest in the cause represented by the social service organization.

The final chapter of this text explores basic steps and methods to follow for determining how technology can be used to enhance strategic planning.

Summary

There is a natural process attached to successful fundraising. While some elements may be inappropriate or just deferred at any given time, *the reality is that long-term development sustainability and success is conditional upon the execution of the fundamentals on an ongoing basis.* To be effective, this execution requires community, Board and senior management leadership. It also requires the necessary commitment of professional, staff and technical resources.

Glossary of Fundraising Terms

Accountability — the responsibility of a recipient organization to keep a donor informed about the use of the donor's gift.

Acquisition — the process or act of acquiring new donors.

Annual Fund — total gifts made on a yearly basis to support (in full or in part) yearly budgets or general operations.

Annual Gift — a donation given annually, usually without any restriction.

Annual Giving — a fundraising program that generates gift support on an annual basis.

Association of Fundraising Professionals — a professional society that fosters development and growth of fundraising professionals, works to advance philanthropy and volunteerism and promotes high ethical standards in the fundraising profession.

Audit — an evaluation and examination of an organization's fundraising practices, policies, and results, usually performed by an outside consultant, who issues a report on the effectiveness of the organization's fundraising program.

Average Gift — the total dollars received divided by the total number of gifts received.

Campaign — an organized effort to raise a specified amount of money for a particular purpose in a specified period of time.

Canada Customs and Revenue Agency (CCRA) (formerly Revenue Canada) the department of the Canadian government responsible for assessing and collecting revenue from taxes on income, excisable goods, and so on. CCRA is the only governing authority on the charitable sector in Canada at this time.

Capital Campaign — an intensive fundraising effort to meet a specific financial goal within a specified period of time for one or more major projects that are out of the ordinary, such as the construction of a facility, the purchase of equipment or the acquisition of endowment.

Capital Gift — gift of a capital asset.

Charitable Gift — a gift made outright (with no conditions) to a charitable organization and which is eligible for a tax receipt.

Charitable Organization — an organization that is eligible to receive charitable donations and is tax-exempt under federal tax law. 501(C),3, the section of the U.S. Internal Revenue Service Code designation that exempts certain types of organizations (such as charitable, religious, scientific, literary and educational) from taxation and permits these organizations to receive tax-deductible donations.

Charitable Registration Number — an identification number assigned by Revenue Canada to every charity that qualifies under tax law.

Constituency — people who have a reason to relate to or care about an organization. These people typically fall into customary groupings, such as faculty, alumni, medical staff, users, parents, donors, and so on.

Corporate Foundation — a private foundation, funded by a profit-making corporation, whose primary purpose is the distribution of grants according to established guidelines.

Corporate Giving Program — a grant-awarding program established and controlled by a profit-making corporation.

Corporate Sponsorship — financial support of a project by a corporation in exchange for public recognition and other benefits.

Cultivate — to engage and maintain the interest and involvement of (a donor, prospective donor or volunteer) with an organization's people, programs and plans.

Deferred Gift — a gift (such as a bequest, life insurance policy, charitable remainder trust, gift annuity) that is committed to a charitable organization but is not available for use until some future time, usually the death of the donor.

Designated Gift — a gift, the use of which is designated by the donor.

Development — the total process by which an organization increases public understanding of its mission and acquires financial support for its programs.

Development Plan — a written summary of fundraising goals and objectives and the means by which an organization will achieve them within a given period of time.

Direct Mail — mass mail sent by a non-profit organization directly to prospects for the purpose of soliciting donations, product sales or subscription sales.

Disbursement Quota — the amount (80%) of receipted donations received in the preceding year that, with certain exceptions, a registered Canadian charity must spend each year on certain activities or donate to qualified recipients in order to meet the requirements for continued registration.

Donor Acquisition — the process of identifying and acquiring new donors.

Donor Bill of Rights — the rights provided a donor to assure confidence in the cause for which support is requested.

Donor Pyramid — a diagrammatic description of the hierarchy of donors by size of gifts. The diagram reflects that: as the size of donations increases, the number of donations decreases; as the number of years a donor is asked to renew increases, the number of donors decreases; as a campaign sophistication progresses from annual to planned giving, the number of donors decreases; as donor involvement increases, the size of the donor's contribution increases and the response to campaign sophistication increases.

Donor Recognition — the policy and practice of providing recognition to a donor, by a personal letter, a public expression of appreciation, a published list of donors, or in another appropriate way.

Endowment — a permanently restricted net asset, the principal of which is protected and the income from which may be spent and is controlled by either the donor's restrictions or the organization's governing board.

Face-to-face Solicitation — the soliciting in person of a prospective donor.

Federated Campaign — a unified fundraising program administered by a not-for-profit organization that distributes funds to similar agencies. The United Way is an example.

Foundation — an organization created from designated funds from which the income is distributed as grants to not-for-profit organizations. In Canada, foundations are either private (financed from private funds and make grants to other charitable organizations) or public (financed through general public fundraising in support of a specific charitable organization).

Fund Development — the planning and implementing of programs that are meant to increase contributed financial support for an organization.

Fundraising Cycle — the practice of fundraising that progresses in logical sequence from planning to preparation, execution, evaluation and back to planning.

Fundraising Tripod — the three components of a fundraising program: the case, leadership and sources of support.

Gift Range Table — a projection of the number of gifts by size (in descending order: leadership, major and general gift) so as to achieve a particular fundraising goal.

Giving Formula — a system, based on past performance or other criterion, for determining the level at which a person, a group of people, or a business firm might be expected to contribute to a campaign.

Internal Revenue Service, U.S. — the department of the federal government responsible for assessing and collecting revenue from taxes on domestic goods and incomes, Abbr. IRS.

Internal Revenue Service Code, U.S. — the compilation of federal laws regarding the taxation of a person, trust, corporation, or tax-exempt organization. Criteria are included for determining the tax-exempt status of orgnaizations and the regulations governing donations.

L-A-I (linkage, ability, interest) - the three factors, when considered together, that are indicators of the likelihood of success when soliciting a major gift. Linkage is the association with an organization or constituency; ability is the capacity for giving; interest is the concern about the cause, need or project.

Matching Gift — a gift contributed on the condition that it be matched, often within a certain period of time, in accordance with a specified formula. A gift by a corporation matching a gift contributed by one or more of its employees.

Not-for-profit Organization — an organization that pertains to or provides services of benefit to the public without financial incentive but does not qualify to issue charitable receipts. In the U.S. a not-for-profit organization is qualified by the Internal Revenue Services as a tax exempt (501) organization. In Canada, a not-for-profit can be qualified by Canada Customs and Revenue Agency as a tax exempt organization.

Philanthropy — love of humankind, usually expressed by an effort to enhance the well being of humanity through personal acts of practical kindness or by financial support of a cause or causes, such as a charity.

Prospect — any potential donor whose linkages, giving ability and interests have been confirmed.

Prospect Profile — a research report detailing the pertinent facts about a prospective donor, including basic demographic information, financial resources, past giving, linkages, interests, potential future giving and such.

Sight Raising — a planned effort to induce a previous donor to elevate a previous level of giving. Also, upgrade.

Social Contract — an agreement among people forming an organized society or between a government and those governed, to define and limit the rights and duties of each.

Solicitor — a person, paid or volunteer, who asks for donations on behalf of an organization or cause.

Stewardship — a process whereby an organization seeks to be worthy of continued philanthropic support, including the acknowledgment of gifts, donor recognition, the honoring of donor intent, prudent investment of gifts, and the effective and efficient use of funds to further the mission of the organization.

Source: The NSFRE Fundraising Dictionary and The Development Group, 2001

CHAPTER 17

Technology Planning Framework

This chapter describes the steps to take and methods to use in evaluating how technology can enhance strategic planning in a social service organization. It is not intended as an organizational technology plan, but rather as a springboard to allow the members of your organization to interact with technology solution providers.

Does the Organization Need Technology?

In the broadest sense, the answer to the question is *yes*. Most social service organizations will benefit from the use of technology for delivering services, enhancing productivity, performing specialized tasks or simplifying manual work processes.

Technology and Clients, Staff and Donors

When looking at a social service organization and its technology needs, it is important to consider technology in relation to:

- current and potential clients,
- staff,
- donors, including volunteers, board members and funders.

With these three key stakeholders in mind, the organization must then consider the information related activities of the organization on a day-to-day basis; what information is needed, which people in the organization need access to that information and what processes and record keeping are involved with each. Understanding these information related activities will provide valuable insight into the technology solutions that might be useful.

1. Client — How does a client initially contact the organization? How is client information processed? Are the processes manual? Could they be more efficient using automated processes?

2. Staff — How are staff kept up to date on the operations of the organization? How often does the communication occur? How is program and service delivery information managed? Could technology improve the amount or frequency of communication?

3. Donor — How does a donor initially contact the organization? How is donor information processed? How are volunteers matched with tasks and responsibilities? How are donor funds processed and tracked? How is donor communication kept up? Could any of these tasks be simplified using automated processes?

Worksheet 17-1, *Operation Procedures,* will help an organization to think about the day-to-day activities as they relate to clients, staff and donors.

Technology in Daily Organizational Activities

After information has been gathered about the flow of information within the organization, consider how technology might be used to improve information flow. Technology can generally be used to deliver services, enhance productivity, perform a specialized task or simplify a manual work process. Activities such as communication, document preparation, accounting, research and information gathering, delivering a program or service, tracking contact information and document filing can all be simplified and made more efficient with technology.

Consider the following activities as they relate to your organization and the three stakeholders groups listed above:

1. Communication: Is communication conducted primarily by paper mail, electronic mail, fax or phone? Technology could make these communication activities simpler, faster or cheaper through the use of electronic mail, automated fax sending, or web page posting. For example, volunteer schedules could be posted on the Internet, so all volunteers would have a central location to find the necessary information, eliminating the need for a person to telephone volunteers. Board members could be kept up to date with meeting schedules, itineraries, and meeting minutes via email or web pages. Staff could be kept up-to-date on activities and meetings via intranet. Electronic tax receipts could be issued, greatly reducing mailing costs to donors. If the organization serves clients that have access to computers, telephones and fax machines, these clients might be better served with more frequent or less costly communication. The use of technology in communication can often broaden the number of people reached at a reduced cost.

2. Document preparation: What kinds of documents does the organization currently prepare and how is it done? Consider the organization's use of annual reports, funding proposals, position papers, presentations, brochures and other documents. The desktop publishing software available today is easy and inexpensive to use and if the organization has the services of someone who is experienced in using this software, the cost of producing documents can be greatly reduced by publishing them within the organization.

3. Accounting: How is the accounting function currently performed for the organization? Accounting system software reduces the amount of time needed for bookkeeping tasks and therefore reduces costs. The use of software also enables the accounting functions to be outsourced more easily.

4. Research and data collection: Depending on the types of research and data gathering the organization does, this is one of the most cost effective uses of technology. If the organization must keep abreast of the latest research in a particular field, the internet is usually more up-to-date than printed material. Searching for information is much quicker with the use of a computer than manually, and tracking the information once found is also more efficient with the computer.

5. Promoting programs and services: How does the organization currently reach out to potential clients? Does your organization do any advertising? Electronic mailings and faxes can be very cost-effective methods of broadcasting information to target audiences.

6. Managing information: How and where is client information stored and who has and needs access to it? The amount of information that can be maintained on clients increases ten fold when undertaken with database technology. The information can be sorted, tracked, processed, and used in many automated tasks when it is stored electronically. Paper storage is one of the most costly and least efficient methods of storage. Electronic is one of the least costly, and can increase access and simplify searching.

A cost benefit analysis is helpful when making a decision about whether or not the organization can benefit from the use of technology. In order to conduct a cost benefit analysis, you must understand the nature of the problem and the approximate cost of the solution.

What Technology Does the Organization Have Now?

After looking at the operations of the organization and where technology can simplify manual processes or provide faster services to wider audiences, the next step is to look at the technology the organization currently uses. Understanding the operations of the organization and what technology is currently in place will enable the organization to make sound technology decisions for the future.

A technology audit is a useful first step in understanding the organization's current technology. **Worksheet 17-2,** *Technology Audit,* is a helpful tool to follow when conducting and recording the results of a technology audit.

The second step is to document the information passing through the various levels and locations of the organization. **Worksheet 17-3,** *Information Flow,* is a helpful tool to record the results of this assessment.

What Technology Will Meet the Organization's Needs?

General Issues to Consider

To determine the types of technology that will benefit the organization, some general issues must be considered.

1. Software must be adaptable to your existing technology systems if you plan on continuing to use them. For example, if you use a proprietary software package to organize client information, any further software you add to your system must integrate with that package or you need to reconsider the client information system. Often, off-the-shelf products such as accounting systems, do not integrate well with the custom built solution. This problem can also be found if current computers run with one operating system and new computers use another. Often the software packages used will not be able to run on both computer types.

2. The technology should be flexible so that it can be changed to accommodate slight modifications in the organization or its structure. For example, if clients are currently tracked by location, but it then becomes necessary to track them by specific need, can the software system be easily changed to manage the new tracking systems?

3. Is the hardware and software scalable? What would happen if the organization's client base grows significantly? Can more computers be added to the network without having to purchase new networking technology? Can the database software be grown to the upper limits of what the organization could ever expect to be? At the same time, most software will be obsolete within three to five years, so avoid buying the most expensive software to fit the upper limit of expected need if this upper limit is not reasonably expected to be reached within that time frame.

4. The software and hardware solutions must be inexpensive. However, the cost of technology does not arise in purchase price alone. The cost to maintain the technology, train the staff, and deploy and implement the solution must also be taken into account. Usually, the more custom the solution, the higher the maintenance costs will be.

Categories of Software

After considering these general issues, several broad categories of software need to be considered as possible solutions to the organization's technology needs. These categories are:

1. Document preparation software: This category includes desktop publishing software as well as word processing software. In this category, ease of use is an important consideration, as a typical organization will use a small fraction of the features available in the software.

2. Database software: This category of software will generally meet the client and donor information management needs of the organization. One of the most important characteristics of a good database solution is flexibility. For example, good database software will allow the easy addition and deletion of fields, allowing the organization to adjust what client attributes to track.

3. Accounting software: This software will perform the bookkeeping functions of the organization. The most important characteristic of this software is likely portability. Typically, a social service organization will use the services of an accounting firm to perform year-end accounting functions, and therefore, using the same software as the accounting firm will be the most important consideration. If the software used is different, the accounting firm may not be able to use the organizations electronic bookkeeping records. The cost to convert to their system may be substantial.

4. Communication software: This software performs tasks such as electronic mail, automatic faxing, message boards and similar internal communication functions. The characteristics of this software will depend on the organizational structure. If your organization is locally operated only and does not need remote access, the solution can be quite simple. If the organization operates in multiple sites or is a province/state-wide, national or international organization, then the solution may be quite complex. There are many companies that provide communication solutions, including e-mail and web hosting, message boards, and other services, at a fraction of the cost of implementing an in-house solution. These companies are able to suggest, implement and maintain the optimum solution. Local internet service providers are a good place to start in looking for one of these companies.

5. Hardware: The organization's hardware needs will be dictated by the software being used, which in turn is a function of the size and complexity of the organization's client and donor base. If the organization must keep information on 100 clients or donors, the hardware needs will be simple. If information must be kept for 10,000 clients, the hardware needed to run the necessary software will be more complex. Most hardware manufacturers have developed a network of authorized resellers that are trained to sell the manufacturer's products.

The Internet and the Social Service Sector

Use of the internet is becoming more and more a part of everyday life. The social service sector will benefit from using the internet to improve access to clients, staff and donors, make more information available on-line and deliver some elements of service on-line. Below are some examples of how an organization might benefit from using the internet.

Example 1: Donors are using the internet more and more in researching worthy organizations for their funds or their time and expertise. Setting up an on-line donation capability, where-by a donor can use a credit card to make an electronic donation should be considered. An alternative is to register with a charity portal that establishes an internet presence for charitable organizations, accepting on-line donations and issuing on-line receipts on behalf of the organization.

If a website is used to accept donations, it is important to register with internet search engines so that donors searching for information on areas served by the organization will be able to locate the website. The organization's website URL should be sent to each search engine for inclusion, alternatively, the organization can enlist the services of an announcement site that will send the required information to all of the search engines.

> **Example:** Some client services may be suitable for offering or delivery via the internet. For example, information on the services offered by the organization could be posted on the organization's website and advertised via other websites so that clients have easy access to it. Client screening or follow-up services could also be offered via the website. Organizations delivering services adaptable to the internet, such as counseling, may be able to offer these via the web.

> **Example:** Another potential on-line activity to consider is advertising. It may be possible to increase donations by advertising on sites with similar interests. It may also be possible to increase funds by accepting outside advertising on the organization's site. There are many link exchange programs to consider participating in which would increase the organization's exposure at very little cost.

Because of the dynamic nature of the internet and relative instability of websites, this chapter does not contain references to specific internet addresses and websites.

Hiring a Technology Consultant

In a typical social service organization, technology expertise and solutions is not a core competency. Because technology solutions have the potential to increase productivity, increase the number of clients served and increase donor funding, they are an important consideration for the organization. Therefore, the best advice is to find a good technology consultant and have them recommend and implement the optimum technology solution. When considering hiring a consultant, it is important to consider referrals. Contact other social service organizations and inquire about their technology consultants. If they have had good experiences, ask for a referral to their consultant.

If referrals are unsuccessful, consider the following:

Experience: A consultant should be able to offer referrals demonstrating their level of experience. Alternatively, they may have implemented solutions within their own organizations and should be able to demonstrate competency this way.

Authorized Training: Technology consultants may be able to show accreditation from software or hardware companies, which demonstrates proficiency in the company's products. Usually accreditation involves passing of exams and upholding ethical selling practices.

Manufacturer Product Certifications: A consultant may also be certified to deploy a certain product (as opposed to being authorized to sell the product). Product certification involves studying material, working with the product and passing an exam. An individual with product certification on the software your organization is using will be well qualified.

Consultants may be known by one of several names, including — value added provider (VAP), technology integrator, solution provider or technology consultant.

Funding

Funding for technology is often hard to justify. The cost-benefit analysis mentioned earlier in this chapter will go a long way towards justifying the funding required. There are also government programs available to help with technology funding. One place to start is searching the Government of Canada web site for *funding* or *not-for-profit funding*. This site can be reached at *www.gc.ca*.

Summary

Most social service organizations will benefit from the use of technology for delivering services, enhancing productivity, performing specialized tasks or simplifying manual work processes. This chapter describes basic steps to take and methods to use in evaluating how technology can enhance strategic planning in an organization, and will assist members of a social service organization to interact with technology solution providers.

Operation Procedures Worksheet

Client Flow

1. How does the client contact the organization?

_____

_____

_____

_____

_____

2. How is the client's contact information tracked and stored (e.g., Rolodex, database, notebook, back of a napkin)? Who performs the task?

_____

_____

_____

_____

_____

3. Who needs access to client information? At what stage of client contact do these people need to access the information? What location do these people need to access the information from (e.g., home, out-of-town, off-site)?

_____

_____

_____

_____

_____

4. How is initial client follow up performed (e.g., phone, fax, letter, personal visit)? How is that contact arranged and scheduled? Who does the follow up?

_____

_____

_____

_____

_____

5. Once the client begins receiving the programs or services of the organization, how are these clients tracked?

_____

_____

_____

_____

_____

6. If the client leaves the organization, how is that tracked? Who needs access to that information? What, if any, follow-up is conducted later?

_____

_____

_____

_____

_____

Staff Flow

1. What information is kept on staff and how is it tracked and stored (e.g., rolodex, database, notebook)? Who performs the task?

_____

_____

_____

_____

_____

2. What information does staff receive on a regular basis? Where is that information stored? How do they receive it (e.g., phone, fax, e-mail, web page, printed document)?

_____

_____

_____

_____

_____

3. What information and systems do staff need access to? Where are they accessing that information from (e.g., local, national, international, home, office)?

_____

_____

_____

_____

Donor Flow

1. How does a donor initially contact the organization?

_____

_____

_____

_____

2. What information is kept on donors and how is it tracked and stored (e.g., rolodex, database, notebook, back of a napkin)? Who performs the task?

_____

_____

_____

_____

3. Who needs access to donor information? At what stage of donor contact do these people need to access the information? What location do these people need to access the information from (e.g., home, out-of-town, off-site)?

_____

_____

_____

_____

4. How is initial donor follow up performed (e.g., phone, fax, letter, personal visit)? How is that contact arranged and scheduled? Who does the follow up?

_____

_____

_____

_____

WORKSHEET 17-2
Technology Audit

Technology Audit Worksheet

Computer Assets

Computer Number	Serial Model	Hard Disk Number	Capacity	Monitor RAM Total	Type	Location

Peripherals

	Model	Manufacturer	Serial Number	Location
Printer				
Modem				
Scanner				
Fax Machine				

Software

Software Product	Version	License Information	Serial Number	Number of Installs	Disk or CD Location

Communication

Device	Manufacturer	Maintenance Phone	Contract
Phone			
Fax			
Modem			
Internet Access			

WORKSHEET 17-3
Information Flow

Information Flow Worksheet

Organizational Structure

Staff Name	Title	Function	Reports To	Location

Office / Service Centre Location

Center	Street Address	Mailing Address	Phone	Fax

Glossary of Planning Terms

Accountable — Individual that ultimately makes the decision (designated as an "A"); holds the "yes" or "no" authority over the action or decision and has veto power. Only one "A" can be assigned to a task.

Action Priorities — The specific steps, or tasks, needed to implement goals.

Budget — The month-by-month targets that have to be achieved to maintain an effective operating plan. The quantification of plans as revenues and expenses for control purposes.

Clear Imperative — A clear driver or issue that demands organizational attention.

Clients — The recipients of the service provided by the social service organization.

Communication - Is a function that encompasses what we say, how we behave and how we reinforce our words and actions through the use of policies, infrastructure and support systems.

Communications - Are the tools or the operational aspects of communicating; for example, the medium used, timing, sequencing.

Competencies — The key skills, knowledge, processes and technology of an organization.

Consensus — A state of affairs where a clear alternative appears with the support of most members, and the others feel that they have been listened to, had a fair chance to influence the decision outcome, and support the final decision.

Consulted — Individuals that must be consulted before a final decision or action is taken (designated as a "C"). They usually provide input to and support for the activities being performed, but have no role in the approval process.

Donors — The source of time, money and talent provided directly or indirectly to the organization.

Focus Group — A market research tool that involves a small number of people, usually 5 to 12 being brought together and asked unstructured, open-ended questions by a moderator or interviewer.

Goals — The longer term areas targeted by the organization for emphasis. They provide direction for fundamental change and their time horizon typically extends beyond the annual budget cycle.

Informed — Individuals who need to be informed once a decision has been made or action has been taken (designated as an "I"). They cannot influence the decision or action.

Initiative — A non-routine activity that requires an expenditure of a pre-defined amount of money and human resources with a defined start and end date. It is not an ongoing activity.

Issue — A trend, event or factor, either internal or external, that will likely result in change within the time frame of the plan.

Key Success Factors — Characteristics, conditions or variables that when properly sustained, maintained or managed can have a significant impact on success.

Leadership Support — A willingness to champion the planning process and fight for the resources (both financial and human) necessary to see it through.

Market Segmentation — The process of determining what separate and definable groups of clients/donors exist in the market for a specific type of service or fundraising effort.

Mission — Communicates the distinctive identity, or purpose, which the organization seeks within the social service sector.

Organizational Readiness Assessment — A self-evaluation focused on the culture and attitude of the staff and volunteers.

Parking Lot — A meeting tool where digressive issues are noted to be addressed at a later time.

Performance Indicators — The measures used to gauge actual results against the key success factors.

Performance Measurement System — The system of performance indicators and targets used by an organization to monitor success.

Performance Targets — A desired end-result to be achieved for each performance indicator within a specified period of time.

Responsible — Individual or individuals who actually complete tasks (designated as an "R"). These individuals are responsible for implementation; consequently, responsibility can be shared amongst several individuals. The degree of responsibility is determined by the individual with the "A" (i.e., accountability).

Situation Assessment — An evaluation of current issues, trends, and future developments for the social service sector, and SWOT analysis.

Stakeholder — Anyone internal or external to an organization who has an interest or stake in the organization and its future, including those responsible for creation, approval, communication, and implementation of the strategic direction.

Strategic Audit — An evaluation (usually a questionnaire) of what planning has been performed within the organization identifying where the gaps lie within the organization's planning framework and prioritizing what needs to be accomplished through the anticipated planning effort.

Strategic Plan — The document summarizing the results from strategic planning.

Strategic Planning — An iterative activity focused on discussion and consensus building that clarifies and builds commitment to the organization's future direction and priorities, within a changing environment.

Straw Model — An initial draft of any document or presentation for discussion purposes.

SWOT Analysis — Assessment of an organization's internal strengths and weaknesses, and external opportunities and threats. The analysis assists in the identification and prioritization of action priorities.

Temperature Check — A simple evaluation tool used to gauge ongoing staff and volunteer reaction to broad or specific issues relevant to the strategic planning effort.

Value Proposition — The key set of benefits the organization delivers to meet the specific needs of each market segment.

Values — Fundamental principles and beliefs that serve as implicit criteria guiding all actions and decision making.

Vision — A picture of the future the organization seeks to create, typically described in the present tense as if it were happening today.

Bibliography

Allison, Michael, Jude Kaye, *Strategic Planning for Nonprofit Organizations: a Practical Guide and Workbook*, New York: John Wiley and Sons Inc., 1997.

Finley, Donna and John Galloway, *What's All This Mission, Vision Stuff?* Calgary: Framework Partners in Planning Inc., 1994.

McConkey, Dale M., *How to Manage by Results*, New York: AMACOM, 1983.

McFarlane, Susan and Robert Roach, "Great Expectations: The Ideal Characteristics of Non-Profits", *Alternative Service Delivery Project Research Bulletin*, Canada West Foundation, Number 3, June 1999.

Migliore, R. Henry, Robert E. Stevens, David L. Loudon, Stan Williamson, *Strategic Planning for Not-for-Profit Organizations*, Bimghamton: The Haworth Press Inc., 1995.

Nanus, Burt, *The Vision Retreat: a Participant's Workbook*, San Francisco: Jossey Bass Inc., 1995.

Rowley, Daniel James, Herman D. Lujan, and Michael G. Dolence, *Strategic Change in Colleges and Universities*, San Francisco: Jossey Bass Inc., 1997.

Tiffany, Paul, Steven D. Peterson, *Business Plans for Dummies*, Foster City: IDG Books Worldwide Inc., 1997.

United Way of America, *United Ways' Marketing Workbook: A Step-By-Step Guide to Developing Strategic, Realistic and Practical Marketing Efforts In United Ways Today*, 1994.

United Way of Calgary and Area, *Leaders of the Way: Honour Roll 1998*, Calgary: 1998.

United Way of Calgary and Area, *United Way of Calgary and Area Strategic Plan (1994-98)*, Calgary: 1994.

Index

AGMV Marquis

MEMBER OF THE SCABRINI GROUP

Quebec, Canada
2001